POSTCARD HISTORY SERIES

Around Oxford

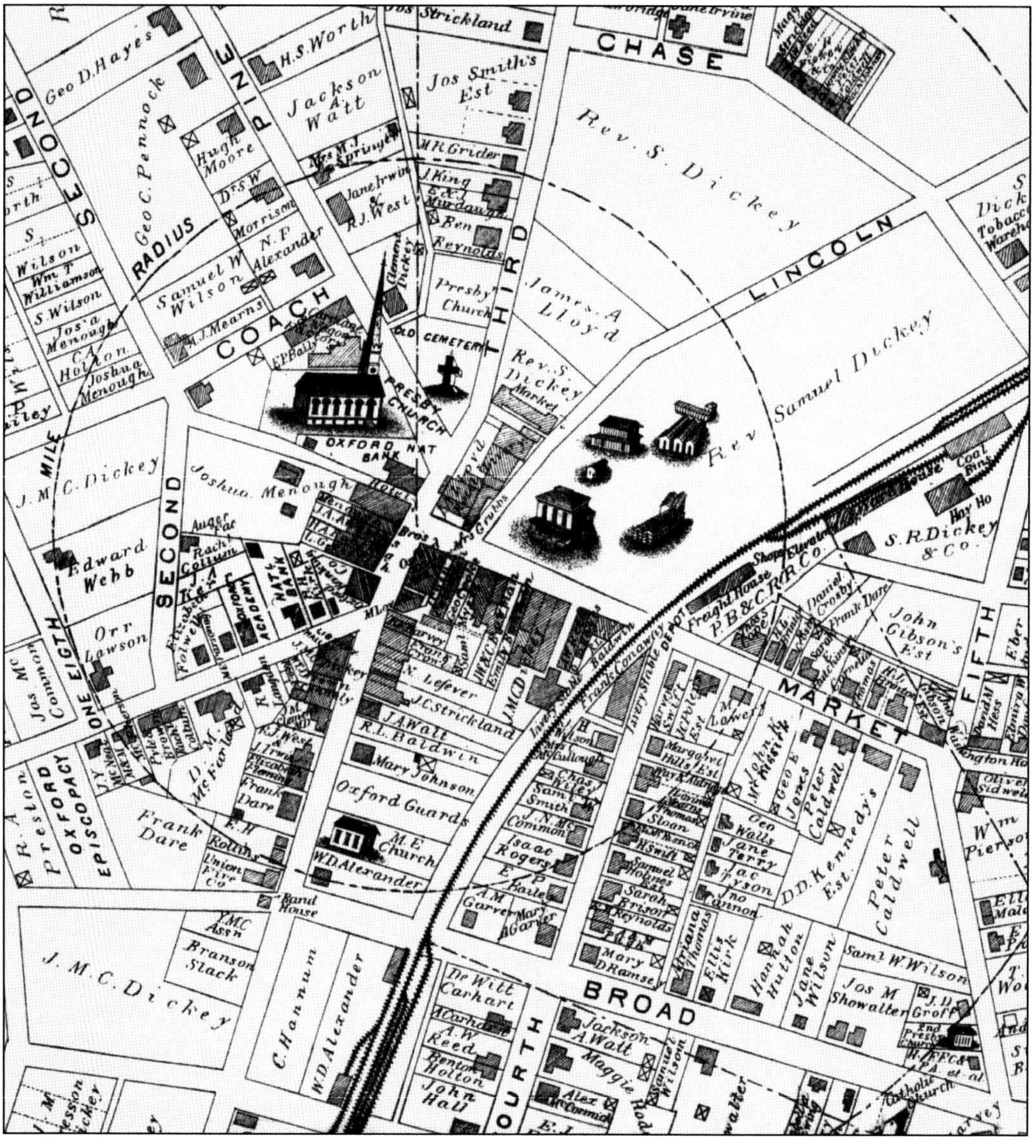

This map is of the business section in Oxford from Breou's *Official Series of Farm Maps: Chester County, Pennsylvania*, published in Philadelphia in 1883 from W. H. Kirk. (Courtesy of the Bayard Taylor Memorial Library.)

On the front cover: This is a 1907 view of Market Street looking west in Oxford. (Authors' collection.)

On the back cover: The firemen's carnival was held in Oxford on August 13–21, 1927. (Authors' collection.)

POSTCARD HISTORY SERIES

Around Oxford

Joseph A. Lordi and Dolores I. Rowe

ARCADIA
PUBLISHING

ISBN 978-0-7385-7210-9

Published by Arcadia Publishing
Charleston SC, Chicago IL, Portsmouth NH, San Francisco CA

Printed in the United States of America

Library of Congress Control Number: 2009927789

For all general information contact Arcadia Publishing at:
Telephone 843-853-2070
Fax 843-853-0044
E-mail sales@arcadiapublishing.com
For customer service and orders:
Toll-Free 1-888-313-2665

Visit us on the Internet at www.arcadiapublishing.com

Contents

Acknowledgments

We would like to thank the following individuals for making this publication possible: John T. Bradley, Oxford High School; Ralph Denlinger; Dr. Faye Doyle, Oxford Historic Commission; Michael Hoffmeier, Robert Treate Hogg Cabinetmaker Shop; Frances Jackson; Lou Mandich; Esther Maule; Prof. Susan G. Pevar, special collections librarian, Langston Hughes Memorial Library, Lincoln University; Ken Pienkos, director, Laurie Slauch, and Linda Teel, staff, at the Oxford Public Library; Pamela C. Powell, Diane P. Rofini, and Margaret M. Baillie, Chester County Historical Society, West Chester, Pennsylvania; Robert Prettyman, Union Fire Company No. 1; Vernon Ringler; Howard Steinberg; Patricia E. Vail; Mrs. Esten Gay Willis and Philip S. Willis; the staff of the microfilm department, Morris Library, University of Delaware, Newark; the many individuals who spoke to us while we were wandering around Oxford photographing and gathering information; and lastly, to Michael R. Cooney and Leon E. Rowe Jr. for kindly critiquing and editing the final manuscript. Again, to all of you—thank you. Unless otherwise noted, all images are from the authors' collection.

INTRODUCTION

Originally settled by mostly Irish Presbyterian immigrants, the southeastern Pennsylvania town of Oxford is in a unique location that sets it apart from the rest of Chester County. It is only six miles north of the Mason-Dixon Line and nearly equidistant from West Chester, Pennsylvania; Bel Air, Maryland; Wilmington, Delaware; and Lancaster. It is also about halfway between Philadelphia and Baltimore. Three arterial highways meet at Oxford. One of these, locally known as Limestone Road (the Octoraro Trail or Nanticoke Trail), follows an original Native American trail along the ridge of the watersheds of the Susquehanna and Delaware Rivers to the Chesapeake Bay.

One of the first buildings in what would become the town of Oxford was John Hayes's tavern. Although the date is uncertain as to when the tavern was built, we know that he is listed on the county tax rolls for 1735 and that the building was in place by 1753. In 1754, Walter Hood, who married Hayes's daughter, took over the operations of the tavern, and the settlement around it became known as Hood's Tavern. During the Revolutionary War, George Washington used the tavern as a depository for food, grain, ammunition, and other provisions. The name was changed to Oxford (after Oxford, England) when the post office was established in 1805 with David Dickey the first postmaster. The Oxford House, or Oxford Hotel as it is now known, still sits on the site of the original two-story log tavern. The village of Oxford was incorporated as a borough on April 8, 1833, and included land from Lower Oxford Township and East Nottingham Township. Five years later, on April 16, 1838, a supplement to the original act of incorporation was enacted, and on May 11, 1838, the citizens of Oxford gathered in William Rutherford's tavern (the Oxford Hotel) and elected the first borough council. Thomas Alexander was appointed the first burgess. The council's first ordinance prohibited pigs and hogs from roaming within the borough limits.

The Dickey family is the most well known of Oxford's original founders. Samuel Dickey (who died in 1778) came to America from Ulster with his wife and infant son about 1730. Members of this impressive family became ministers, doctors, community leaders, inventors, advocates of universal education (including women and blacks), manufacturers, politicians, bankers, and innovators in the fields of agriculture and transportation. Samuel Dickey Jr. (1730–1794) was instrumental in organizing one of the first libraries in Pennsylvania and took part in the Revolutionary War. His son, Samuel Dickey III (1769–1835), patented a stove that fit into the kitchen fireplace and was responsible for a thriving factory where cotton was spun into thread and woven into cloth at the nearby village of Hopewell. Rev. John Miller Dickey (1806–1878) established the Oxford Female Seminary and, later, the Ashmun Institute. Each succeeding generation continued to enrich the community of Oxford in various ways. John Miller Cresson Dickey (1848–1908) was a lawyer, creamery owner, chief burgess of Oxford, member of the borough council, vice president of Oxford's agricultural society, and could be credited with many other accomplishments. In 1908, at his death, he was hailed as "Oxford's most prominent citizen."

Oxford was one of the most fertile areas for all sorts of agricultural activity, so it became well known for its dairy farms; creameries; cattle and sheep raising; the production of hay, grain, and produce; a chicken hatchery; a duck farm; and, later on, the growing of mushrooms. Within a few miles were also found chrome and iron mines, limestone and magnesium, kaolin clay for brick and pottery making, and quarries for serpentine and other building stone. Limestone Road was so named because of the portage of limestone down its length.

Two railroads helped the town expand its business, industry and tourism: the Philadelphia and Baltimore Central Railroad and a narrow-gauge railroad—the Lancaster, Oxford and Southern Railroad, affectionately known by locals as "the Little, Old and Slow." City folk traveled to the area in the warm months for the cooling breezes and open space that helped in the establishment of many camps such as Tweedale, Saginaw, and Horseshoe (in nearby Cecil County, Maryland) that are still in existence today. There were many facilities that catered to travelers, including the Center Restaurant and bus terminal, the Oxford and Octoraro Hotels (both in Oxford), the Post House Restaurant and Greyhound Bus Terminal at the edge of town, and Ferguson's Villa, a tourist home in the nearby village of Cream. Besides agriculture, Oxford and the surrounding vicinity became the home of many specialty businesses, including a hardwood-flooring mill, cabinetmakers (such as Robert Treate Hogg Jr.), several carriage works, a brick maker, a marble and granite works, a nail factory, bottling works, machine and foundry shops, a cotton weaving factory, and potteries such as Wilmer Cope and Brothers. Many mills sprung up along the Octoraro Creek and its branches, including paper mills, sawmills, gristmills, cotton mills, and flouring mills. Candy making has a long history in Oxford. Nathan Patterson Alexander made a full line of candies at 10 and 12 Market Street, including high-end confections and "new designs in penny goods." The Oxford Caramel Factory was the only one of its kind in the world in 1894 that was built especially for caramels. The Oxford Confectionery Company advertised "Uncle Van Rip, Right-o-Way Rolls, and Nutty Ruffles." Today Neuchatel Chocolates continues the tradition, making the finest Belgian chocolate truffles and other confections. The nationally known Herr Foods, Inc., makes its headquarters in this area and runs free factory tours that include samples of its potato chips and other snack products.

Oxford is a vibrant town that, over the years, has had three movie theaters; performances of opera, plays, minstrel shows, and other stage productions; chautauqua meetings; fairgrounds (with a horse racing track and exhibit buildings); a park (the site of band concerts, ice-skating, and a merry-go-round); and a circus that wintered in town and traveled up and down the East Coast. Three U.S. presidents or presidential candidates have visited Oxford—William Taft, William Jennings Bryan, and Warren Harding. Beginning in 1909, the Union Fire Company No. 1 had carnivals every year (until recently). They were one of the most highly anticipated entertainments in town and the surrounding communities.

The first African American college, Lincoln University (originally Ashmun Institute), is right outside Oxford and claims as its alumni Supreme Court Justice Thurgood Marshall, musician Cab Calloway, and famous poet Langston Hughes, among others. Southwestern Chester County is also home to the 651-acre Nottingham County Park. The park sits atop an outcropping of green serpentine stone, one of the largest serpentine barrens in the eastern United States.

Between 1906 and 1908, various trolley lines were proposed to connect Oxford to other communities, including West Chester (via the Oxford, West Grove and Avondale Street Railway), Parkesburg, Elkton, Maryland, and Strasburg, Lancaster County. Unfortunately, none of these plans ever materialized. When a paved road was built from Parkesburg to Oxford in 1925, the program published for the festivities called Oxford "The Biggest Little Town in the Commonwealth." With an expanding population and many new businesses, Oxford might reclaim that title today.

One

The Business Section

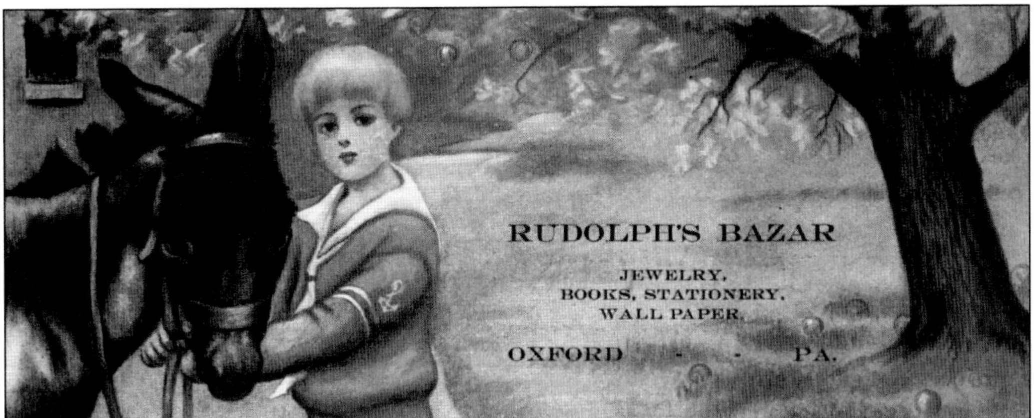

J. Warren Bowman's Bazar opened on September 20, 1875, in a building at 314 Market Street. It was a true department store as it offered such varied items as art, china, clocks, cut glass, silverware, novelties, books, jewelry, wallpaper, blinds, stationery, picture framing, music, and pocket books. In 1886, a new building was built around the original. George M. Rudolph took over the business when Bowman retired in 1890.

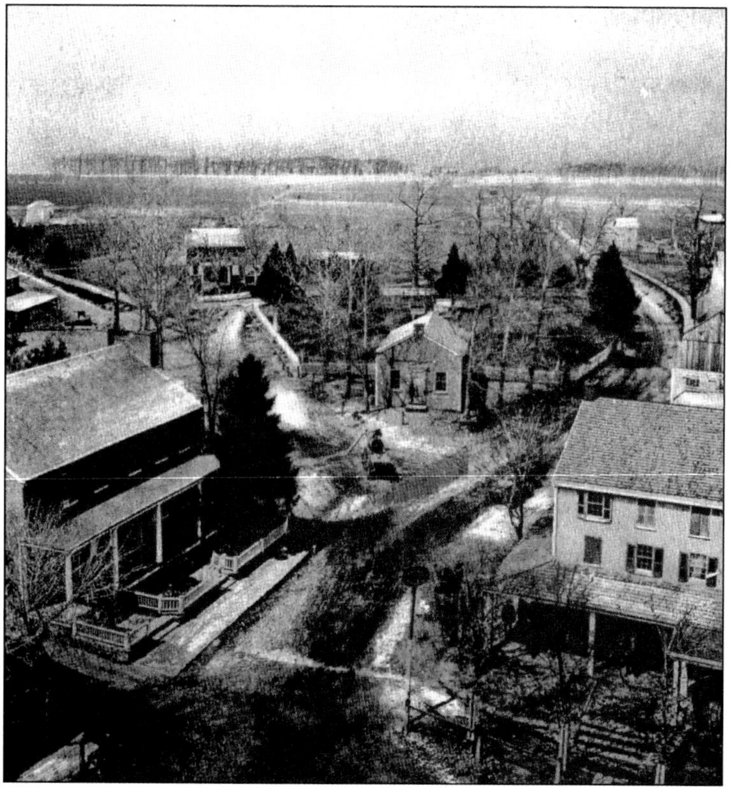

In the center of this 1866 lantern slide image by early photographer Alexander McCormick is the Presbyterian Sessions House; to the right is the Oxford Hotel; and on the left is a country store, now a landscaped commons for the First Presbyterian Church.

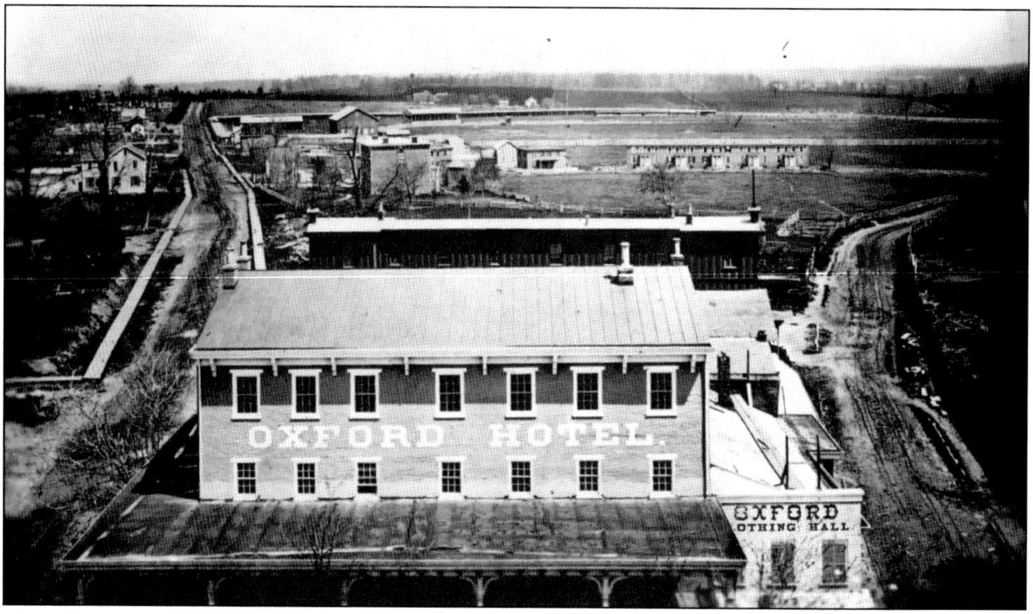

This photograph dates from between 1874 and 1894 and shows the Oxford Hotel in the foreground and the Oxford Fairgrounds in the distance. The old farmers' market is clearly visible behind the hotel. In the background is "Chase Row," a row of homes built in 1873 and located at 407–419 Chase Street. North Third Street is on the left.

The Oxford Hotel was originally a two-story log structure with four rooms on each floor and was known as Walter Hood's Tavern. By the time of this 1866 lantern slide photograph postcard, it had added a story and been enlarged. To the right of the hotel is H. H. Grubb's Clothing Emporium (where the hotel dining room was later located).

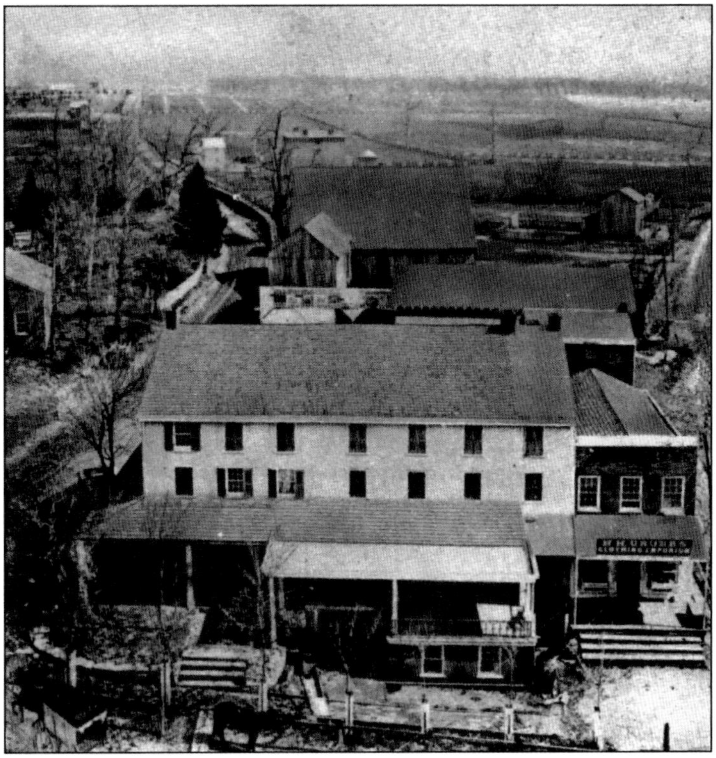

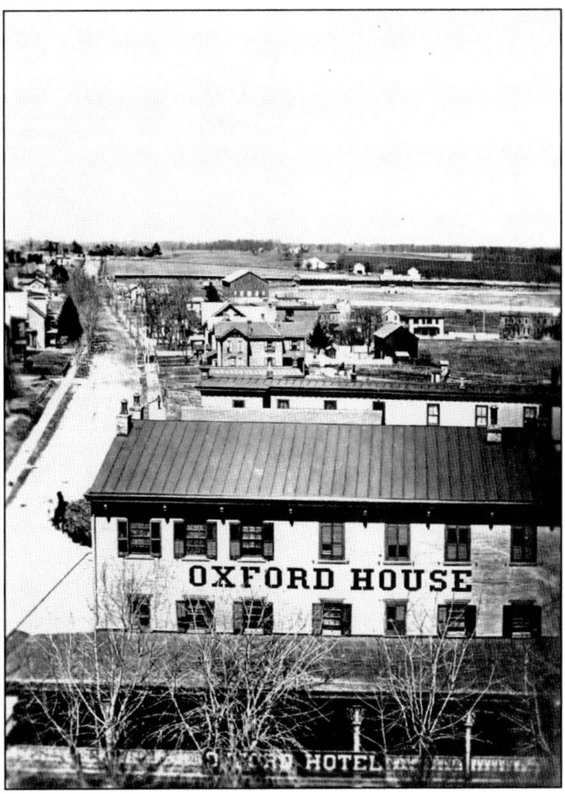

Dating from a period between 1874 and 1894, this early photograph shows the Oxford House (later Oxford Hotel). Directly behind the hotel is the two-story wooden-frame farmers' market. Samuel Dickey had the market constructed in July 1869. In 1895, it was torn down by his wife, Jennie Rutherford Dickey, and replaced with the Masonic building. In the background, the Oxford Fairgrounds can clearly be seen.

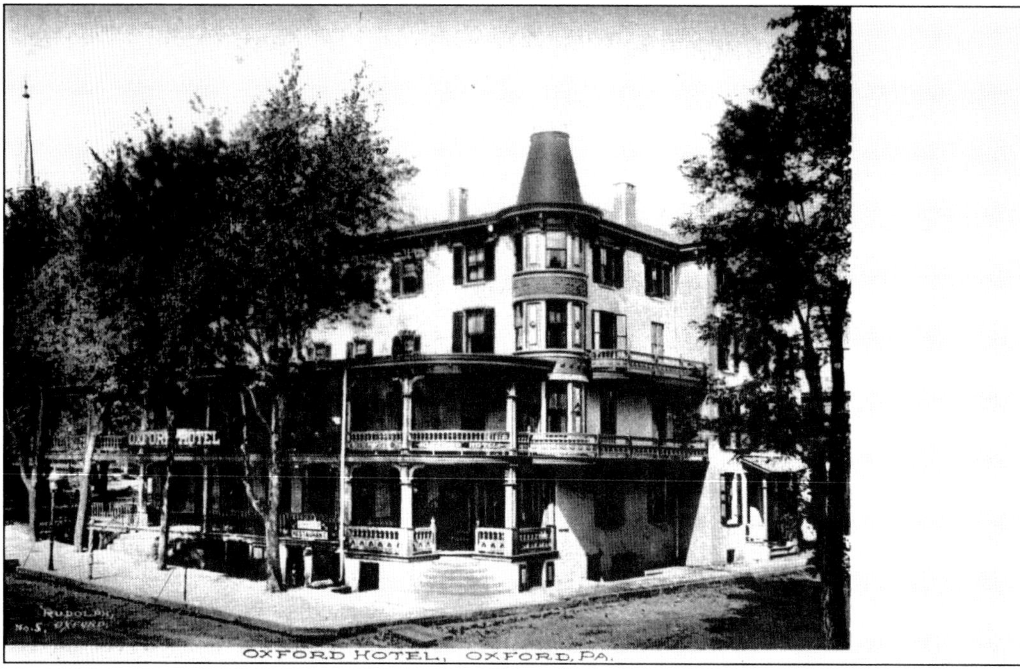

When Oxford elected its first borough council in May 1838, William Rutherford was the proprietor of the hotel. Rutherford was known to always eat with his hat on. When the railroad arrived in Oxford in 1859, W. T. Marchbank and T. H. Richey were the hotel's proprietors. In 1869, the hotel was renovated and the double porch added. In 1875, the log structure was renovated using imported English bricks; and in 1876, it was known as Lloyd's Hotel after the owner, James A. Lloyd. In 1906, Elwood E. Smith sold the hotel to Walter D. Biddison for $65,000.

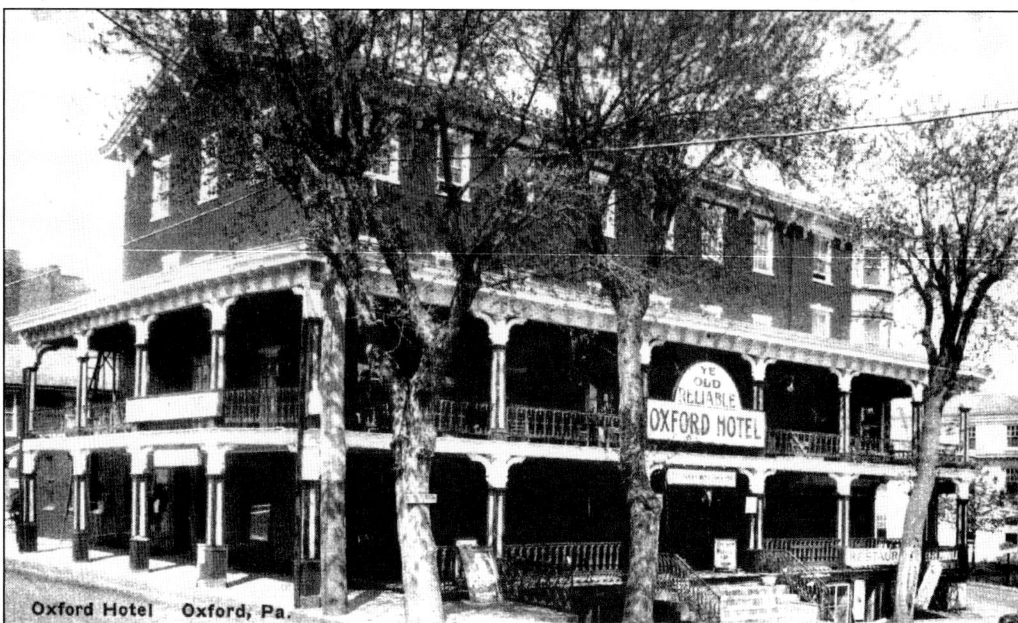

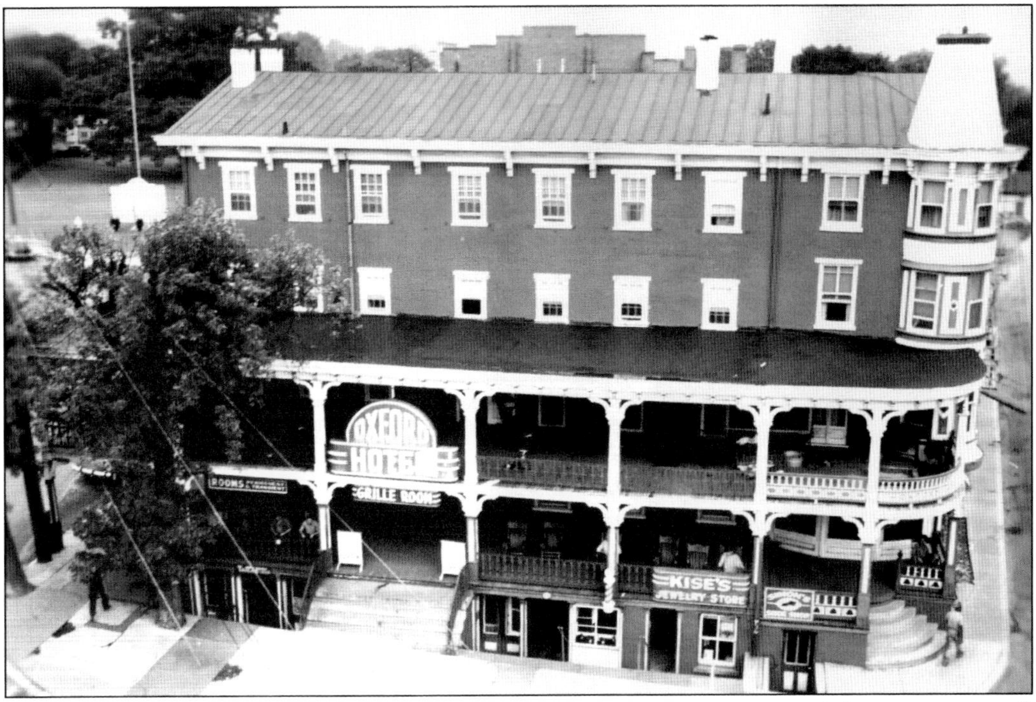

By 1926, the hotel was enlarged to include a larger kitchen, dining room, and sleeping rooms, all with private baths. In 1943, Chris and Mary Vergos became the new owners, and on November 18, 1949, they had a grand reopening. At that time, the hotel boasted the John Hayes cocktail lounge (named for the first owner), the Robin Hood lounge (named for Walter Hood, a previous owner), the Londonderry Ball Room "where ladies may dance an occasional reel," the Mason Dixon dining room, a coffee shop, and a new kitchen. Note the sign for Paul R. Kise's jewelry store, which was located at this location from 1940 until 1948. Below is a linen postcard dating from the early 1950s.

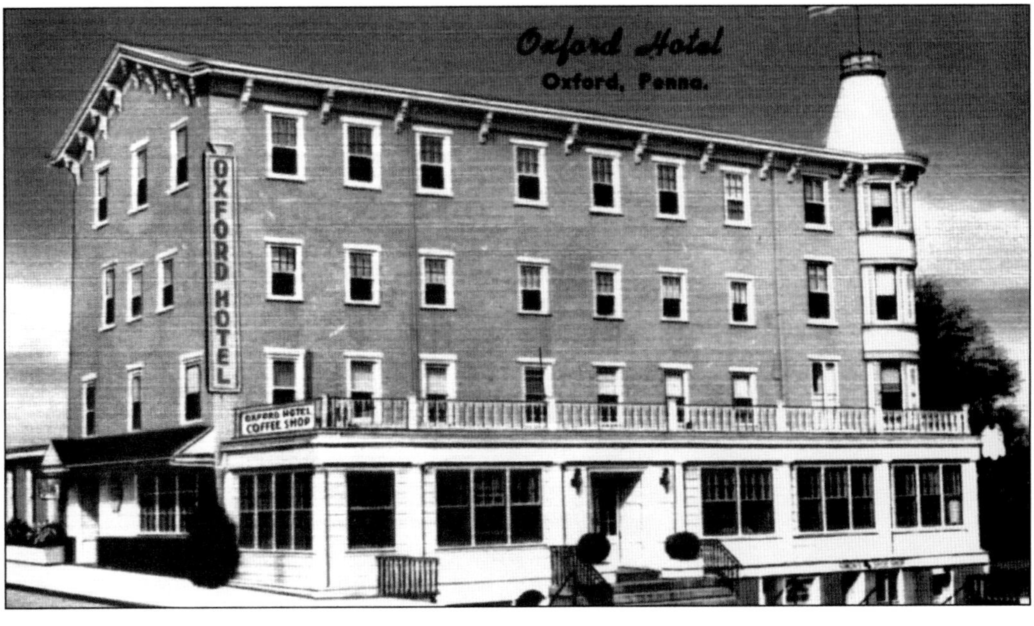

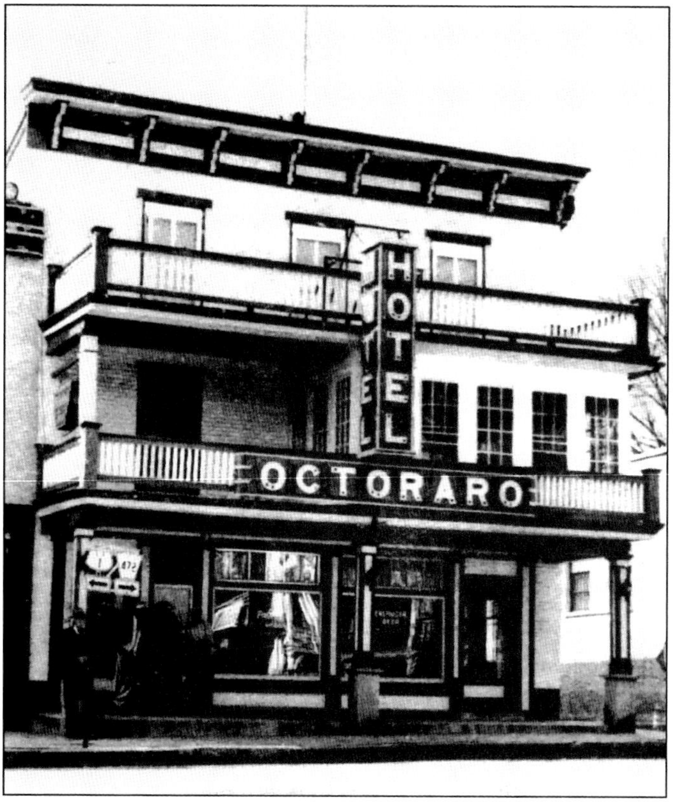

Previous to the Octoraro Hotel, Rev. John Wright and Amos Biles kept a store on the site. In 1860, part of the Oxford Female Seminary property formerly belonging to John and Samuel Dickey was sold for $6,000 for the purpose of establishing the hotel. Timothy Kirk was the first proprietor of the hotel/tavern. By 1883, the hotel was owned by Joshua Menough. Menough was born in New London Township in 1829 and came to Oxford in 1865. He was also an auctioneer and is said to have been one of the best "criers" of his day. Behind the hotel was a stockyard where regular auctions were held. By the 1920s, Jeremiah Knight was associated with the hotel's ownership. The top porch of the hotel was added in 1912.

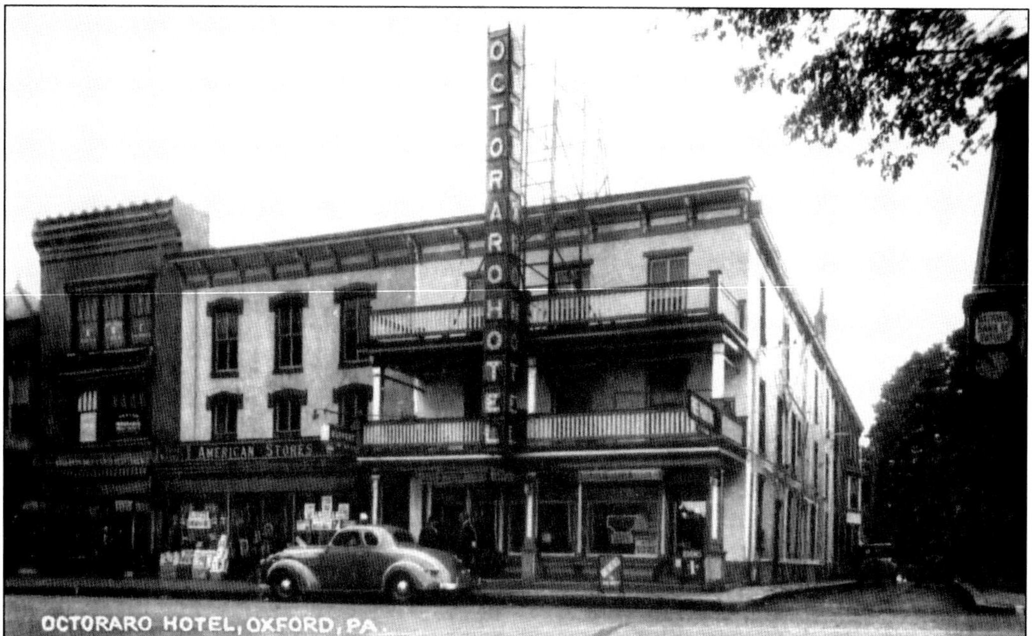

This postcard dates from the late 1930s and shows, on the left, Walter Winchester's Men's Store, with the second-floor window sign for Wilson's Insurance and Real Estate; next, the American Stores in the middle; and to the right, the Octoraro Hotel.

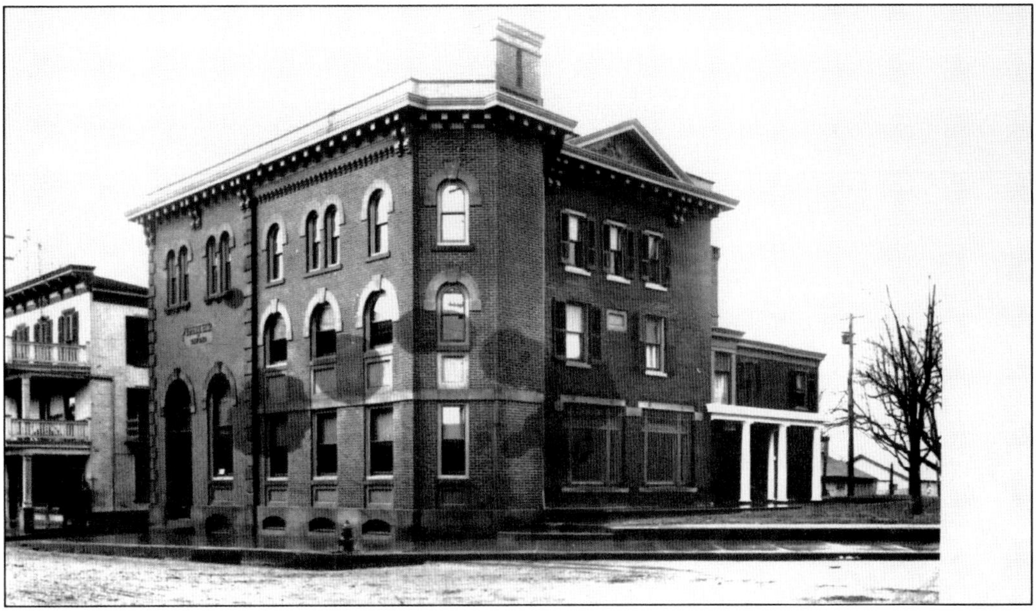

The National Bank of Oxford was chartered in 1865, successor to the Octoraro Bank, which itself was chartered in 1857 under the direction of Ebenezer V. Dickey (1821–1858). In 1859, the bank purchased the domestic-style building as seen on page 10, and at a later date constructed the building shown in this early real-photo postcard. The bank later merged with J. A. Watt and Company, a private bank founded in 1881. In 1934, the building was sold to the American Stores Company and then razed.

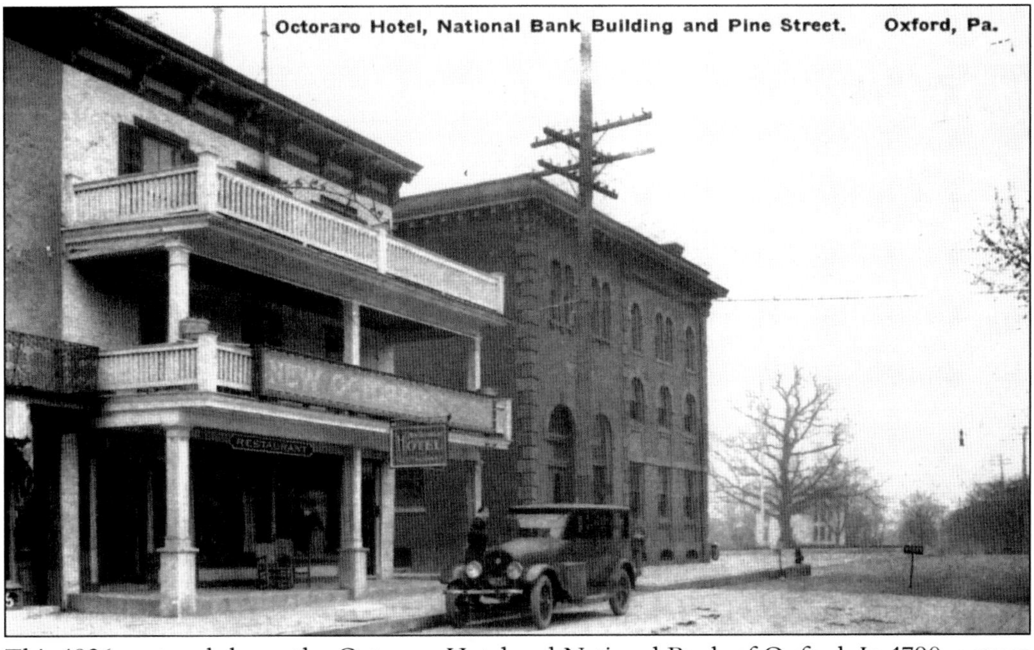

This 1926 postcard shows the Octoraro Hotel and National Bank of Oxford. In 1790, a stone schoolhouse stood on the site of the bank; it was followed by McCormick's Hat factory, then a tavern known as the Sign of George Washington; then the home of bachelor William Rutherford, proprietor of the Oxford Hotel; and lastly, a country store.

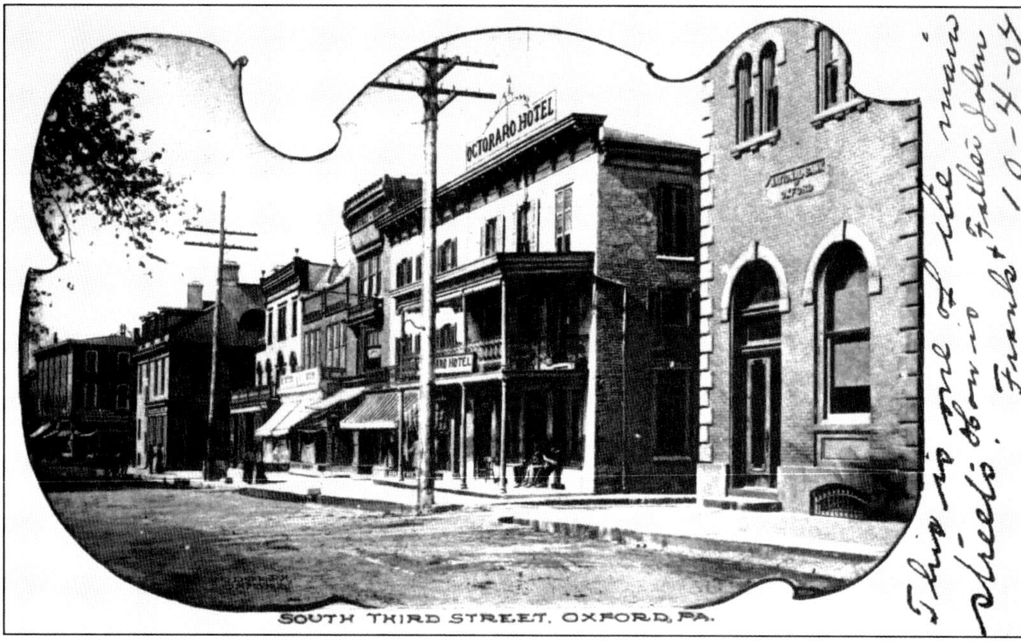

The top postcard shows the west side of South Third Street looking south in 1904. At the far left is the J. M. Cresson Dickey Building, which became the People's Bank of Oxford (now the National Penn Bank) and at the far right, the National Bank of Oxford. The postcard below shows the same side of South Third Street looking north around 1906. Two banks, the Farmers National Bank and the National Bank of Oxford, span the block with several shops and the Octoraro Hotel in between. The Oxford Female Seminary, established by Rev. John Miller Dickey in 1837, was situated on this block.

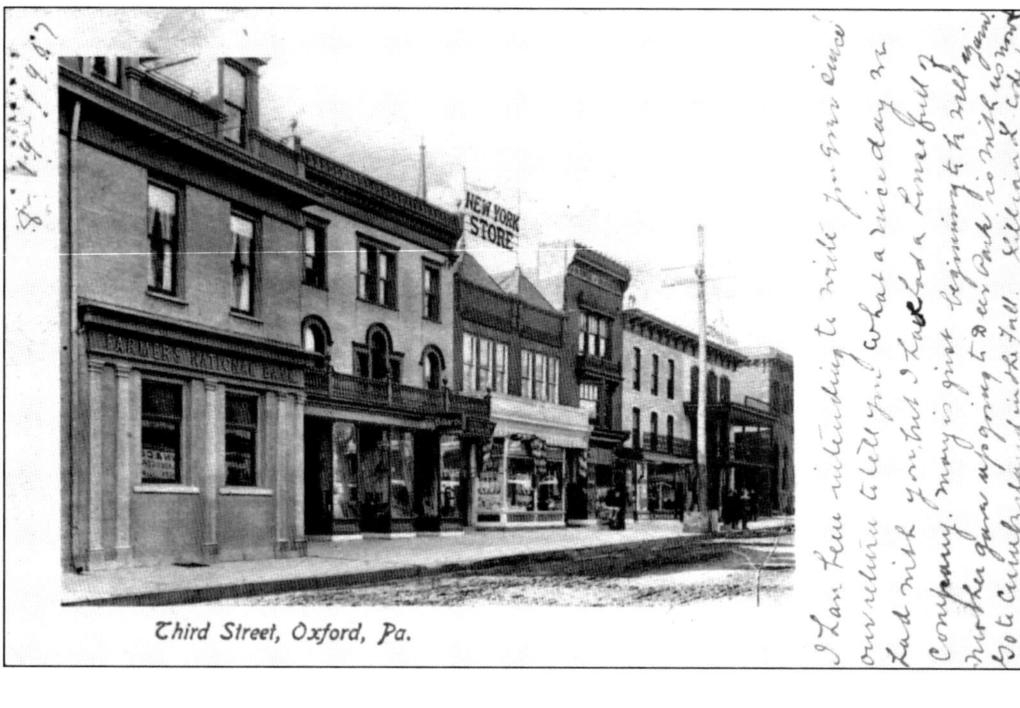

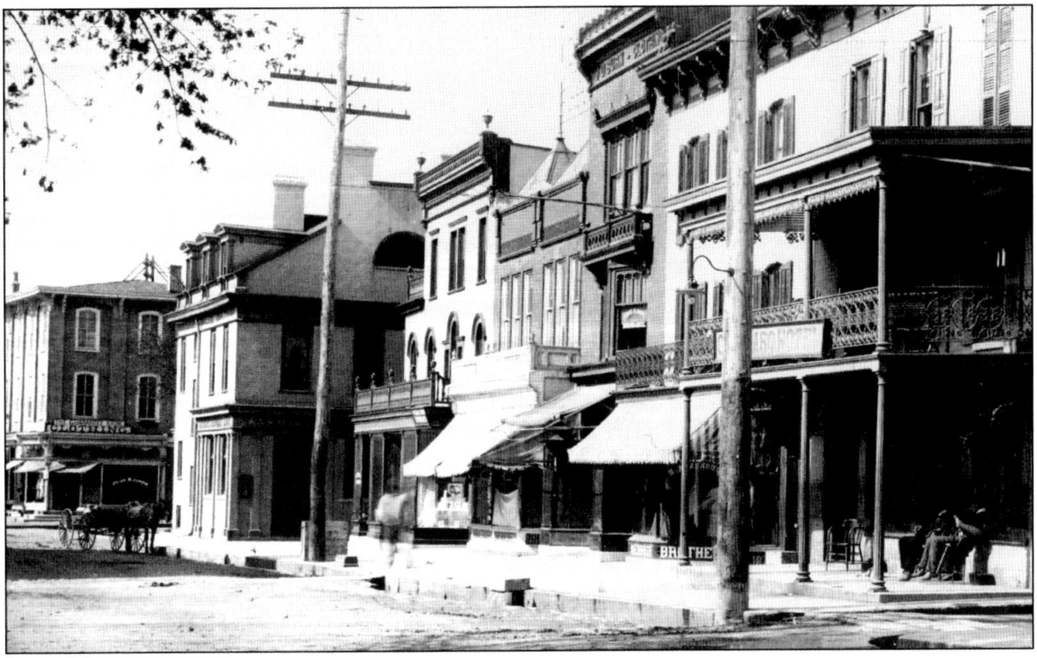

Starting from the left, this 1908 real-photo postcard shows the west side of South Third Street and the following establishments: Julius Bechman's Guarantee Store—Clothing (in the Dickey Building), Locust Street, the Farmers National Bank (once the store of Thomas Sloan), the George T. Press Jewelry Store, the photography Studio of C. Ward and Dora E. Thomas, James R. Garvin's New York Store, James D. Burn's Gentlemen's Store, the dry goods store of Harry A. Menough, and the Octoraro Hotel.

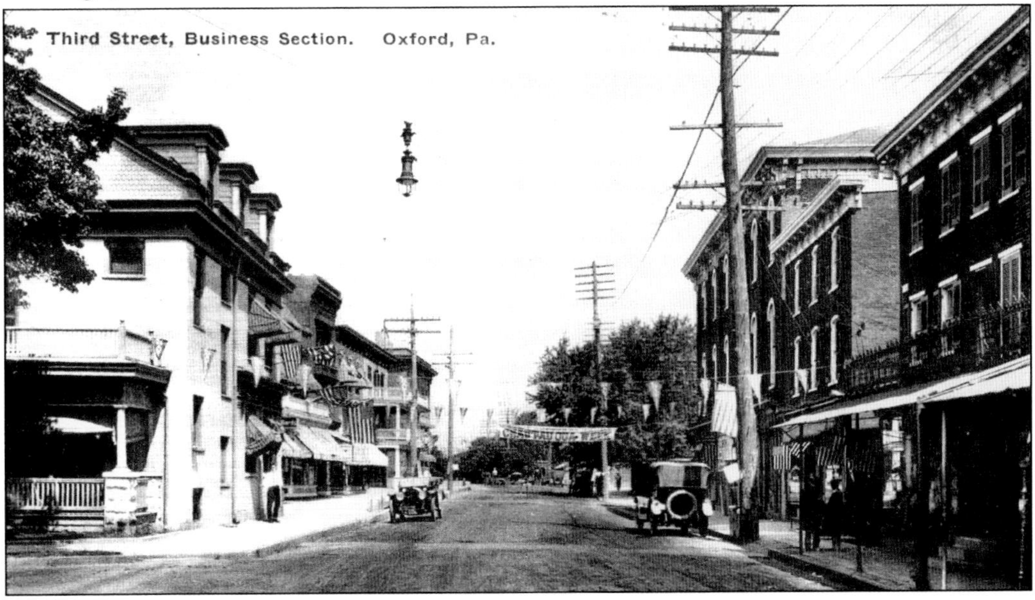

Looking north on South Third Street from Locust Street, the banner is advertising chautauqua week sometime between 1908 and 1912. Chautauqua was an adult educational and cultural movement that began in upstate New York in 1874. The circuit, or tent, chautauqua began in 1904, and peaked in the mid-1920s.

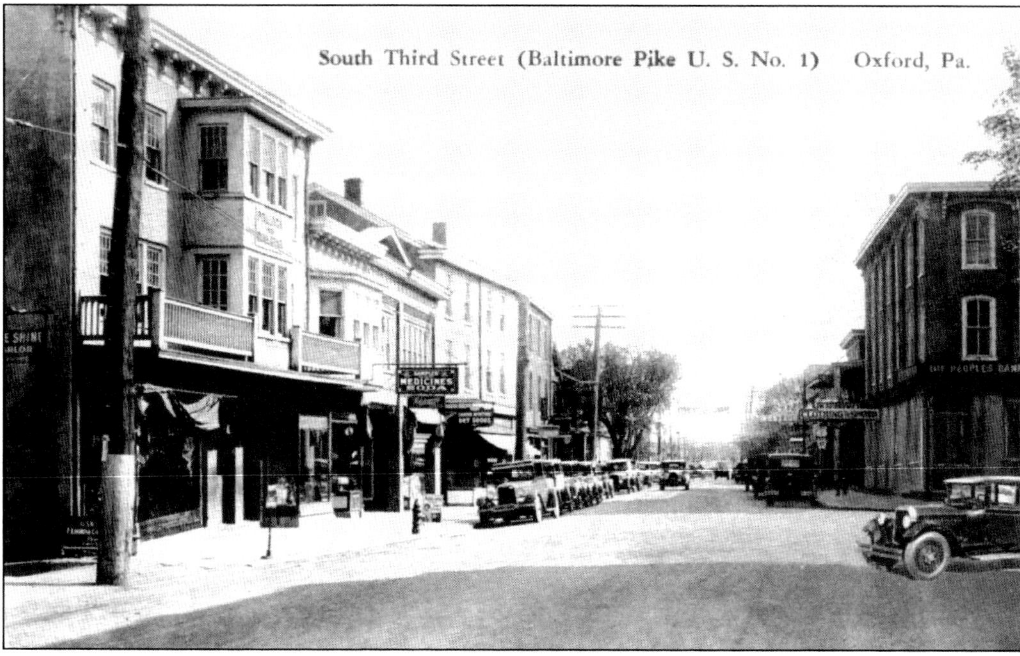

This view looks south on Third Street in the early 1930s. On the left can be seen the sign for Samples' Drugstore advertising medicines and sodas with a smaller sign for Whitman's Chocolates. Farther down the street is a sign for Carson McIntire, dry goods. On the right is the Farmers Bank building and a sign for M. Berkowich, dry goods.

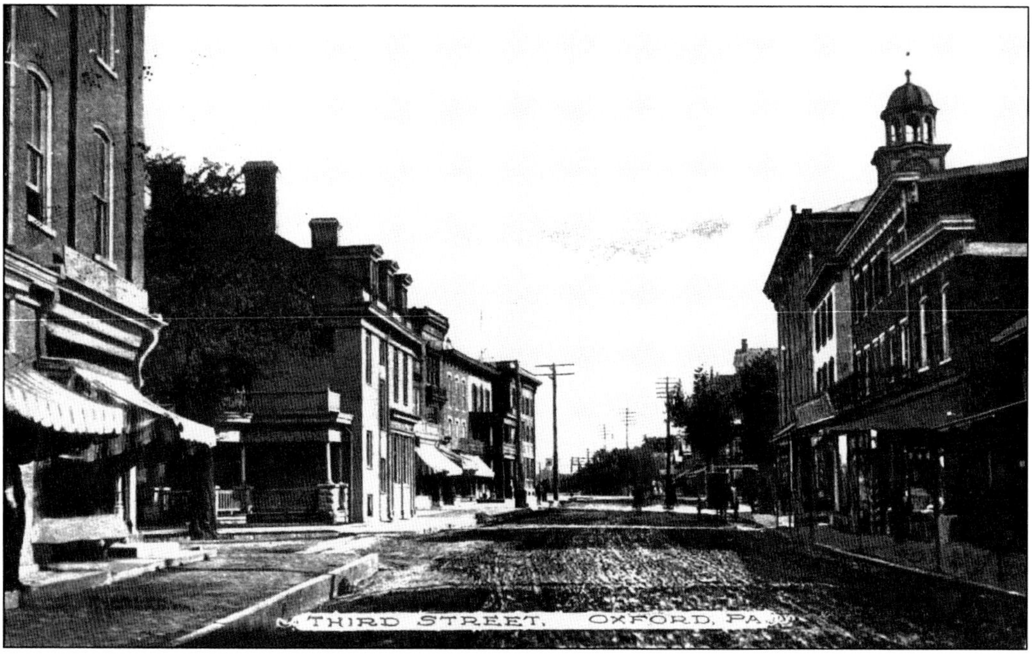

Looking north on Third Street from below Locust Street, on the far left is the Dickey building (site of the 1914 People's Bank and now the National Penn Bank), the Farmers Bank across the street, and the various shops leading up to the National Bank. On the right is Oxford Hall. This Albertype postcard is dated September 1909.

Located at Locust and Third Streets, the Farmers National Bank was established in 1868 as a private bank by Kirk, MacVeagh and Company of West Chester. In 1870, it became a state-chartered bank known as the Oxford Banking Company, and in 1883, it was chartered as a national bank. An earlier bank building (as seen in several postcards) was replaced by this neoclassical building on land that once belonged to Timothy Kirk, proprietor of the Octoraro Hotel. The new bank opened for business on May 1, 1926. The Fulton Bank now occupies the building.

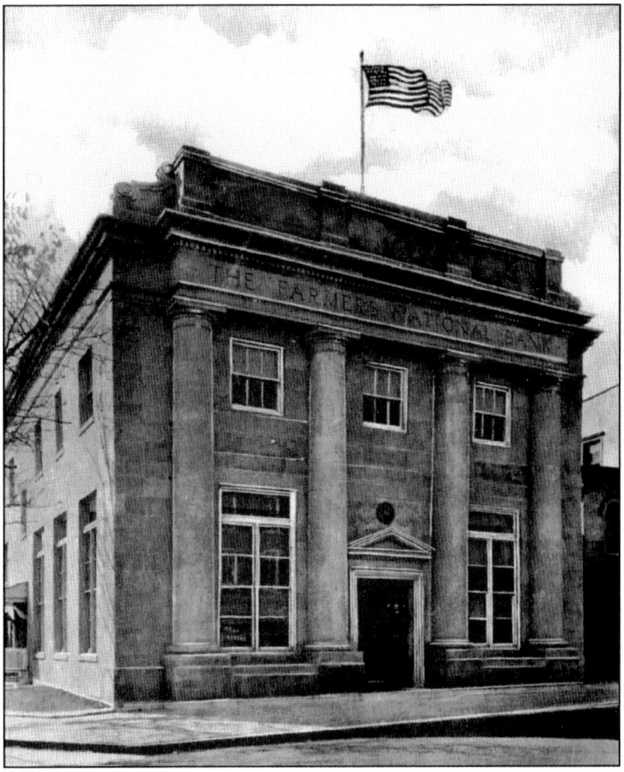

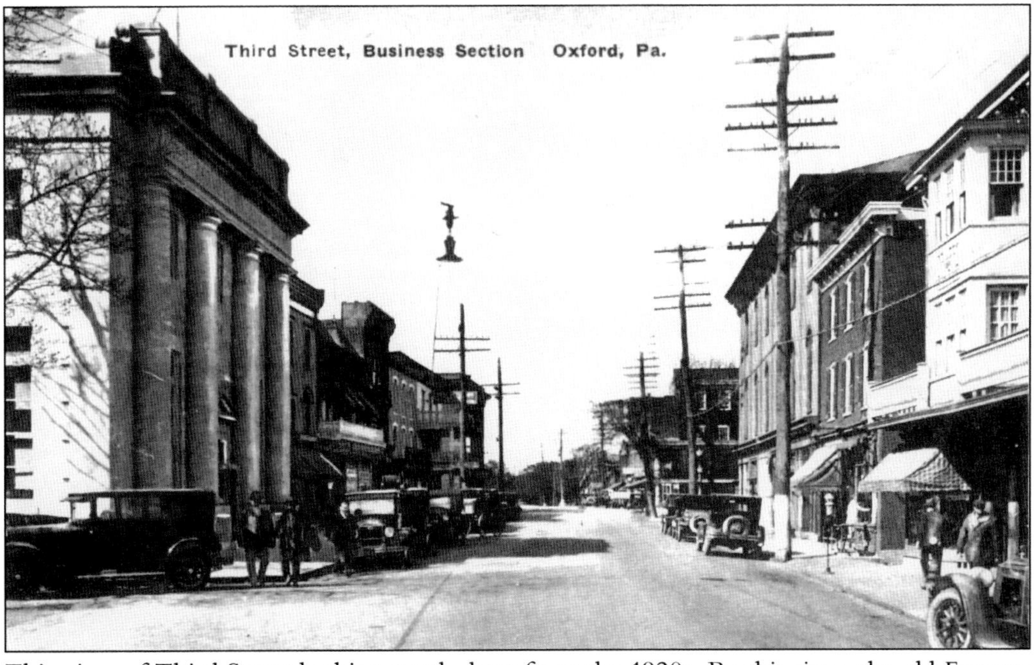

This view of Third Street looking north dates from the 1920s. By this time, the old Farmers Bank had been replaced with a new neoclassical building. The Pollock Building, with its added second-floor balconies, is at the lower right. In June 1937, some of the stores on the right included a drugstore, a grocery store, and an ice-cream shop.

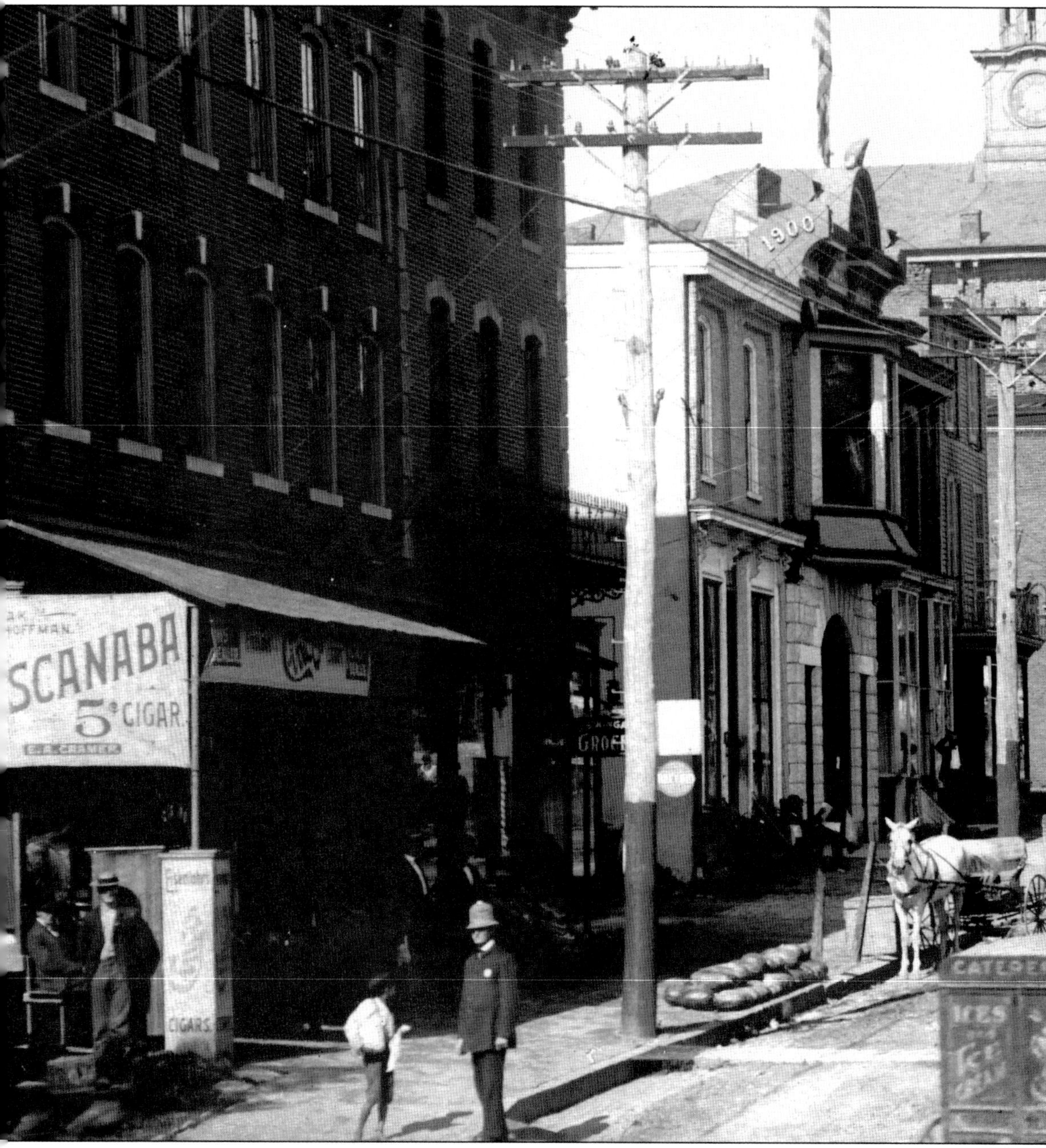

Dora E. Thomas produced this real-photo postcard in the summer of 1907 (note the row of watermelons) showing the south side of Market Street looking west. The F. E. Brown building with its beautiful clock tower and cupola is seen at the top of the hill. It was also known as Oxford Hall and served the community for many years as a meeting place for borough council and various social groups. The tower and cupola were removed in 1915 to save on repairs. The Union Fire Company building can be seen in the center, and the grocery store of Joseph S. Wingate is just left of the telephone pole. Note the sign for Escanaba 5¢ cigars. The buildings on the left were built in the early to mid-1870s. The first regularly appointed policeman appeared in 1870. Moving up Market Street toward Third Street, there were several businesses in 1908–1909.

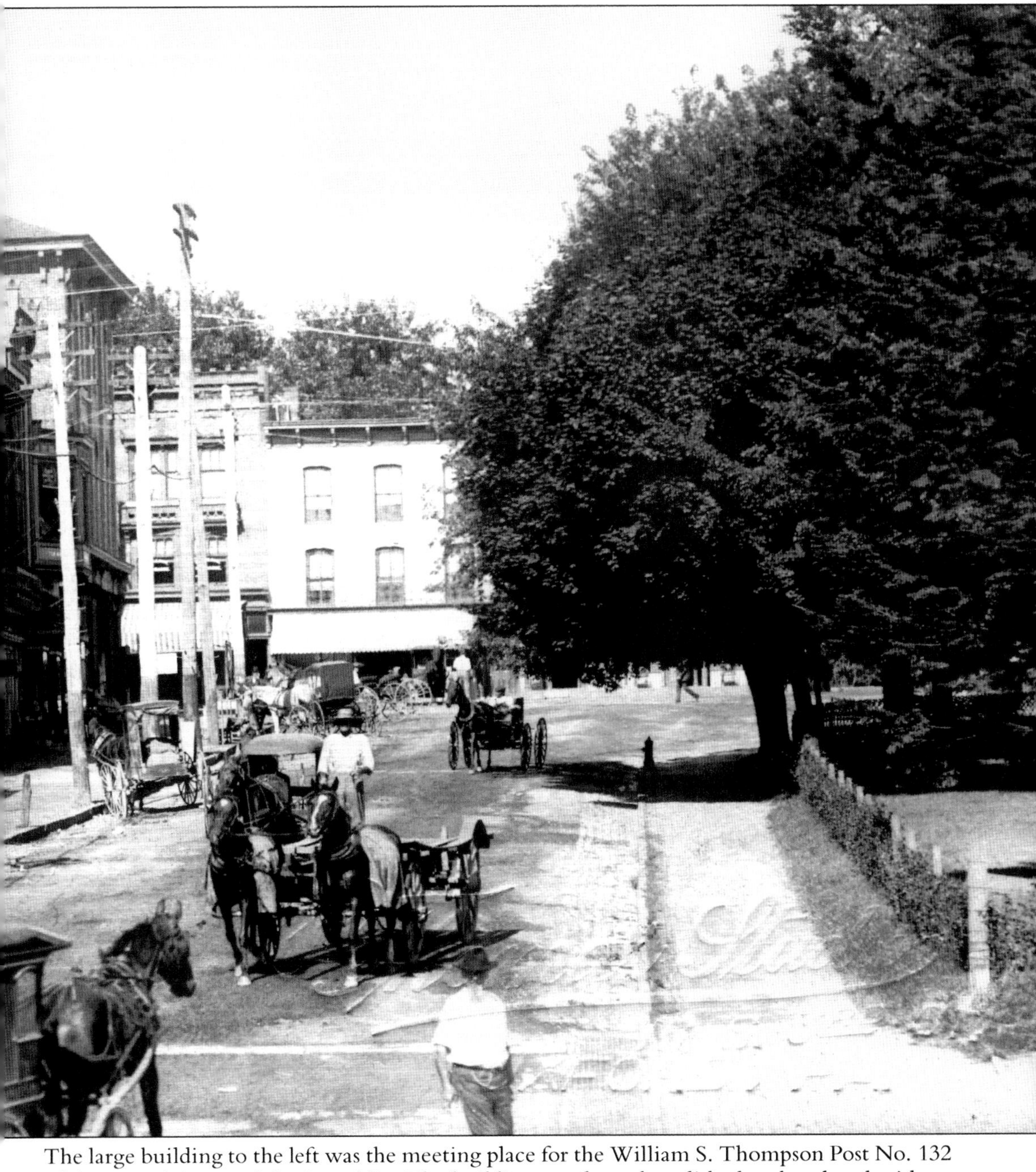

The large building to the left was the meeting place for the William S. Thompson Post No. 132 of the Grand Army of the Republic. The building was later demolished and replaced with an apartment house. On the corner is Edward Cramer's cigar shop, and moving up the street are Thomas J. Manyoun's tin shop, Guss Bleckman's men's store, Joseph S. Wingate's grocery (note his sign) with Daniel A. Stubbs (a notary) atop, McCommon and Smith (hardware), the Union Fire Company No. 1, John T. Fox's bakery, the home of J. Frederick Engler, George Rudolph's stationery store, the bakery of Engler and Murdaugh, Coates Caldwell (druggist), William Burling (hardware), and the Oxford Hall restaurant.

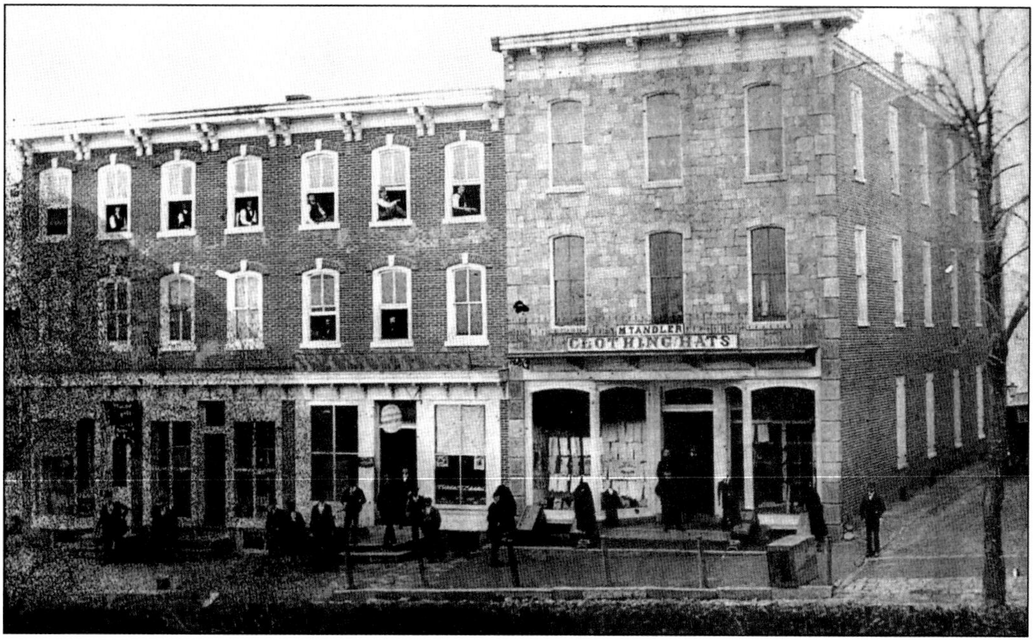

This photograph dates from 1877 to 1880, when M. Tandler had his clothing store in the serpentine stone building at 330 Market Street. During this period, Tandler had stores at several locations, including this one. When Tandler moved to Anthony, Kansas, in 1880, Klein and Sommer of Philadelphia purchased his stock. Note the pre-1907 change of facade from serpentine stone to brick as seen in the picture below. (Courtesy of Pat Vail.)

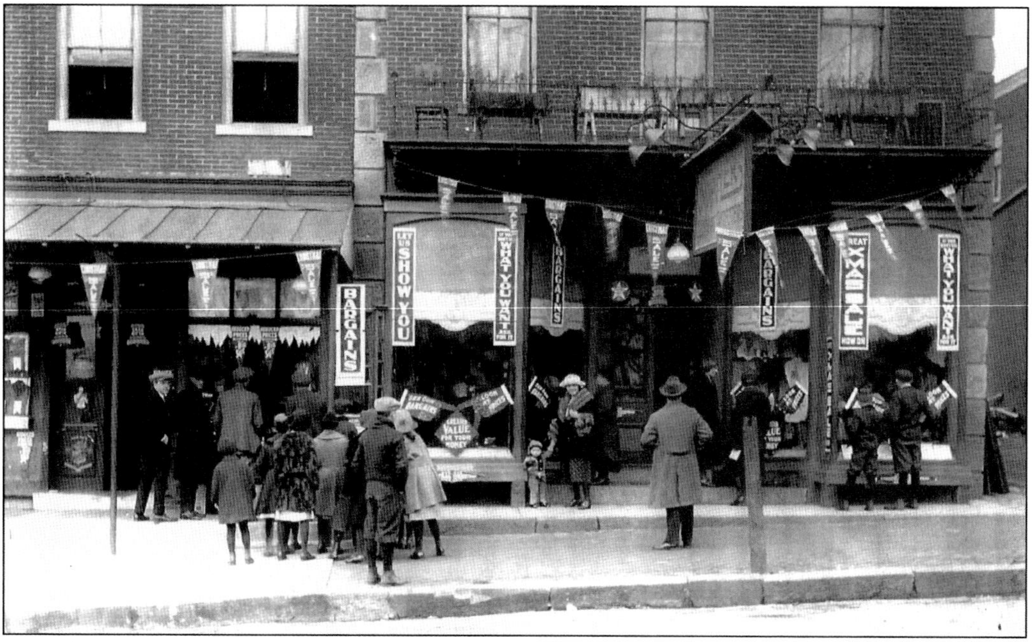

On July 15, 1917, George Sopher moved to Oxford and bought out Guss Bleckman's store at 330–332 Market Street. Sopher ran the business from this location until 1942, when he and his wife, Esther, moved to the 11 South Third Street location formerly owned by Mattie Pollock. The photograph dates from 1923. (Courtesy of Pat Vail.)

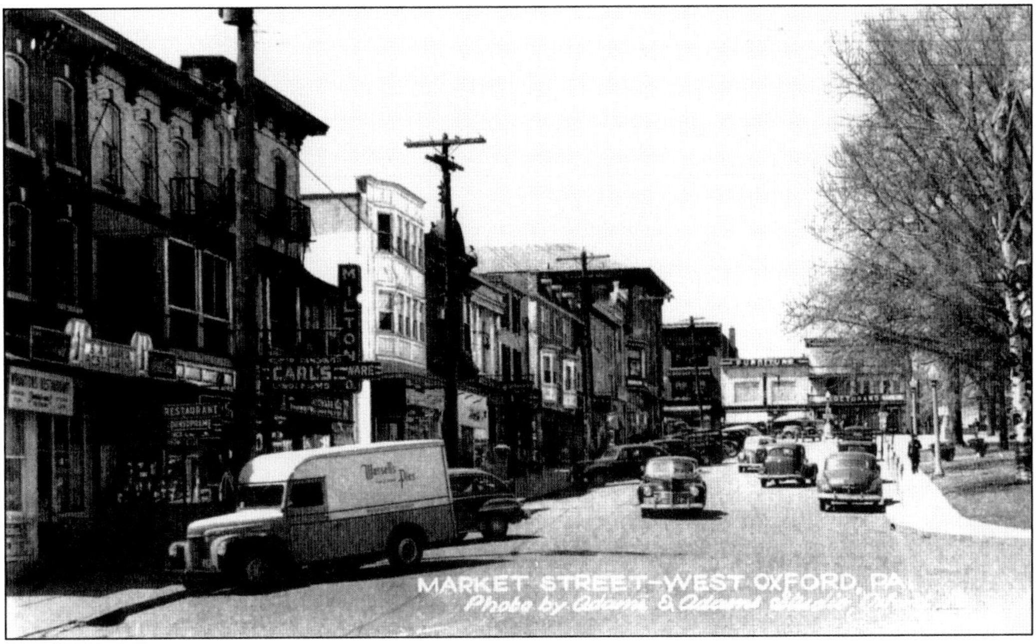

This *c.* 1940 postcard shows the same row of businesses as seen in the postcard on page 20. Moving west up the street, Samuel A. Cooper's restaurant advertising Penn Supreme ice cream, Carl's furniture store, Milton's hardware store, and a sign for Schmidts beer can be seen. The old firehouse is behind the middle telephone pole.

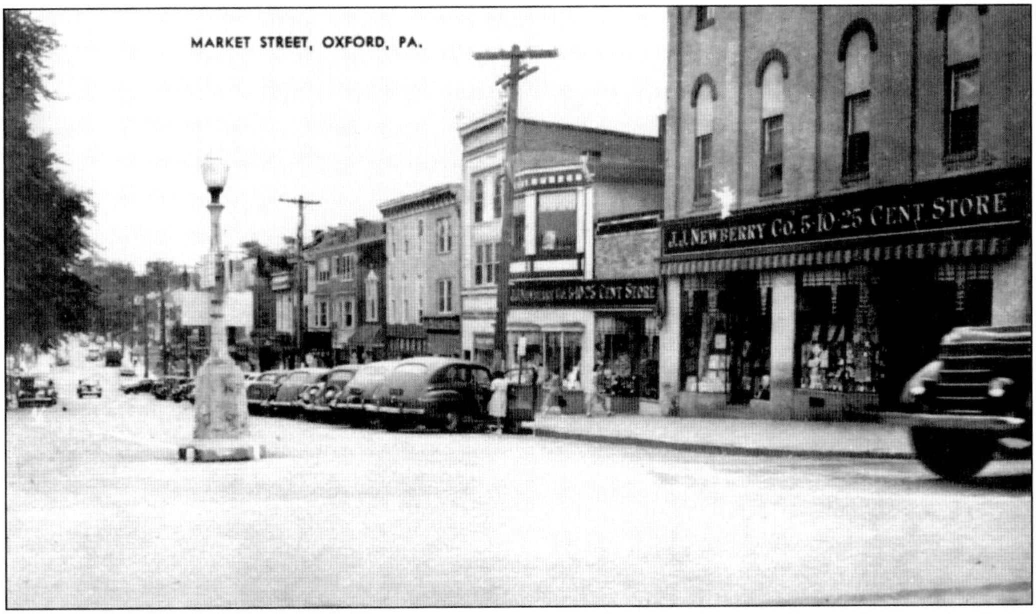

The J. J. Newberry store opened on August 4, 1944. It had another grand opening on April 14, 1949, after the store was enlarged to include two buildings to the east. The three-story building to the left was once the drugstore of Charles C. Baer. He died at his Market Street store on October 21, 1944, after 30 years in Oxford. He belonged to many social organizations, including the public library, of which he was once president. George Cooke and Coates Caldwell also had their drugstores at this location.

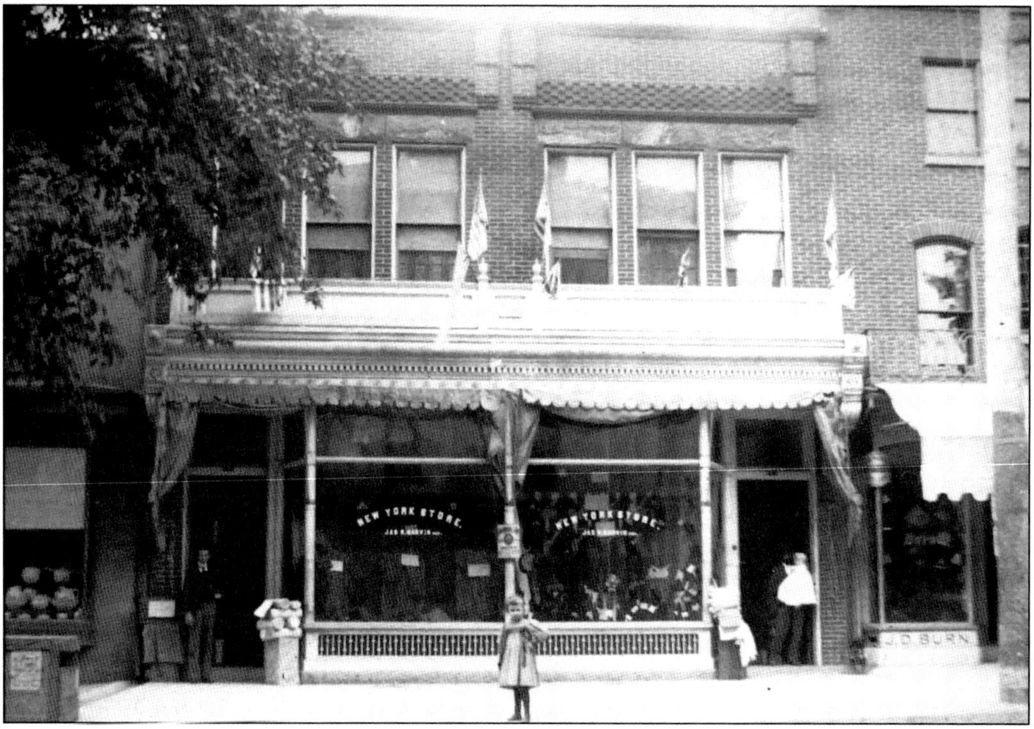

At the time of this photograph, James R. Garvin was the proprietor of the dry goods store known as the New York Store, located at 12 South Third Street. On the right, at No. 10, is part of the clothing store of James D. Burn. Burn was in partnership with K. E. Dare in the mid-1880s, and both stores flourished during the late 1890s and early 1900s.

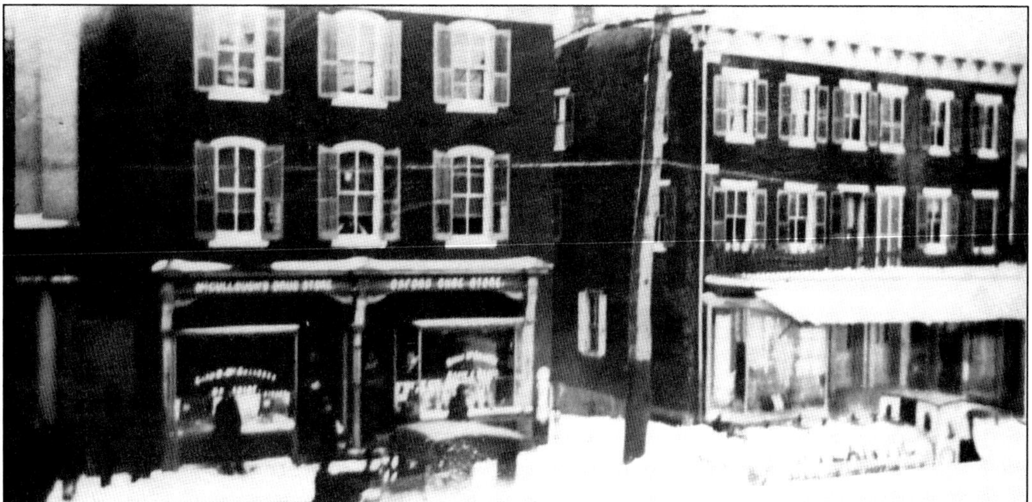

During a severe February snowstorm in the early 1900s, two trucks (one for Atlantic Oil), are trapped in front of the drugstore of Clement B. McCullough at 7 South Third Street and at No. 9, the Oxford Shoe Store of Howard B. Gibson. Gibson was located at 11 North Third Street in the late 1890s. The drugstore was in business into the 1940s, when it was in the hands of M. L. McCullough. In the next building, at No. 13, was the notions and dry goods store of Martha M. Pollock (fl. 1886–1909).

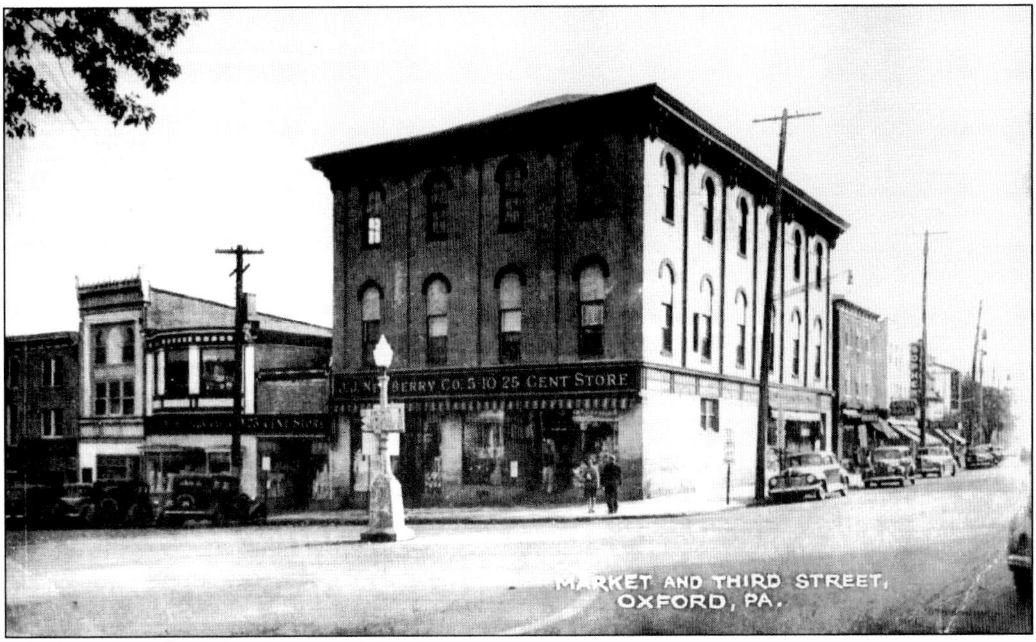

Originally on the corner property of Thomas Boland, Oxford Hall was constructed in 1864 after a meeting of several local citizens. It has served many purposes, including as a town hall and general merchandise store. F. E. Brown took over full ownership of the building in 1897. By 1905, he expanded his department store, eliminating the public meeting spaces. Baer's Drug Store was the three-story building to the left. Charles C. Baer, who was previously located at 16 South Third Street, purchased the store from Coates Caldwell in 1921. At the time of the 1940s postcard above, the J. J. Newberry Company occupied the ground floor. The photograph below shows the same scene at a later date.

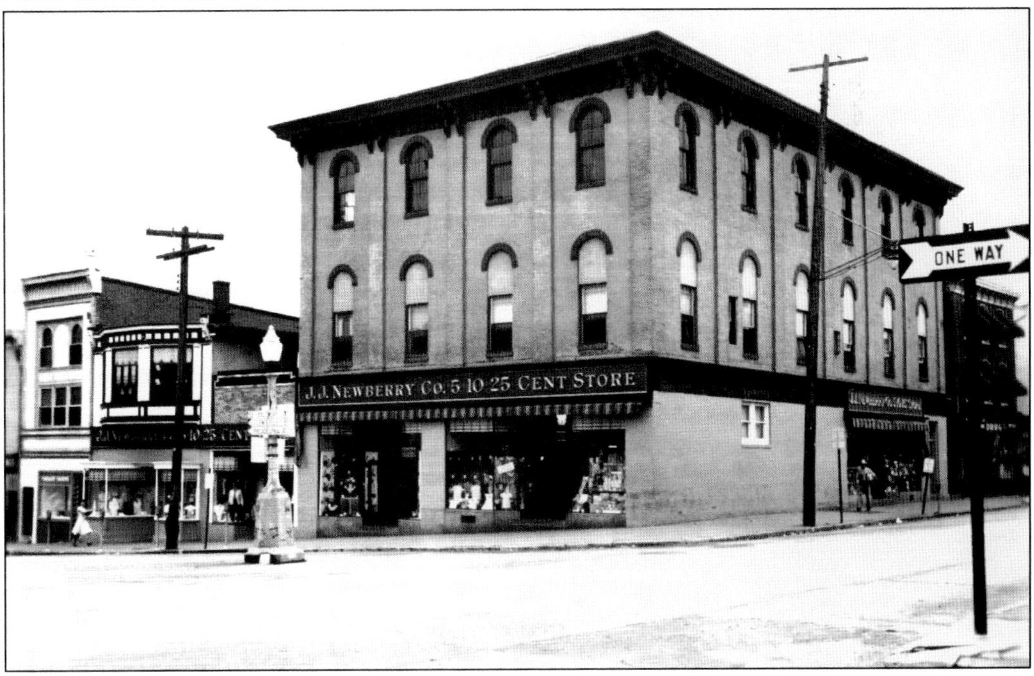

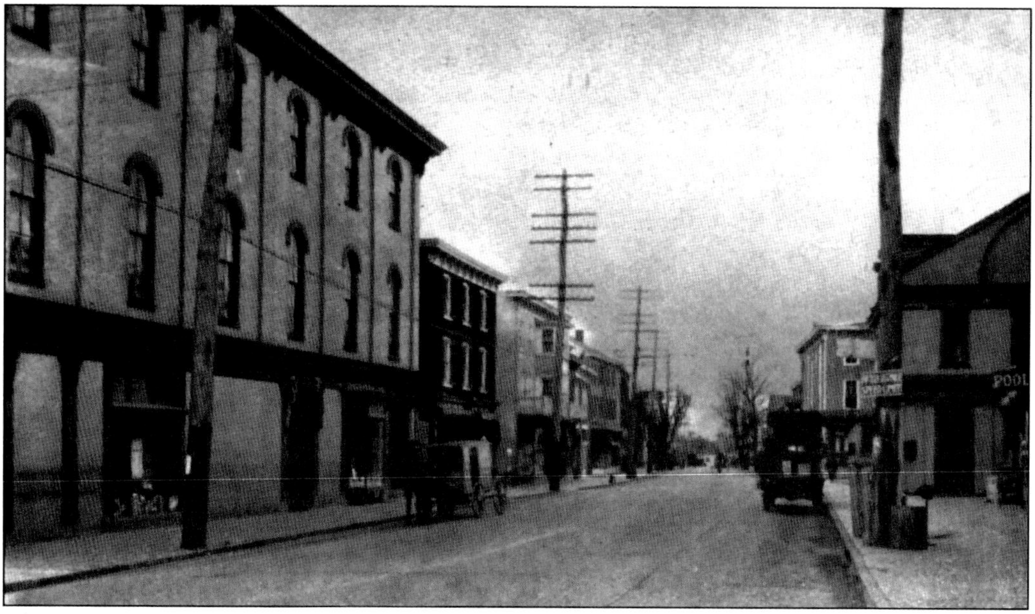

This postcard, published by C. Alfred Winchester, shows the same view of South Third Street as the later postcard seen below. Winchester had a cigar shop at 25 South Third Street and produced many Oxford postcards in the 1920s. This view shows the Pollock Building before major changes. Note the pool sign on the right at 18 South Third Street.

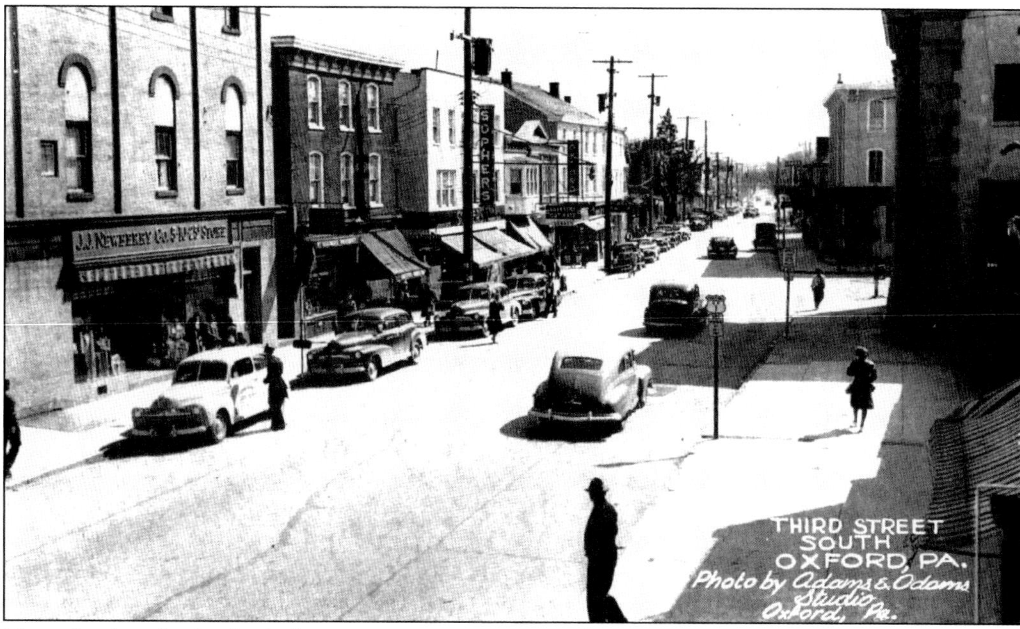

Note the sign for Sopher's department store at 13 South Third Street, formerly Mattie Pollock's store. Sopher's was "The Town's Leading Outfitters for the Family." George and Esther retired in 1965 and sold the store to Horace and Celeste Sopher Goldstein, who expanded the store in 1968. Farther down the street is a sign for Gillespie's Cut Rate at No. 17, and the Oxford Theater at No. 21. The postcard dates from the late 1940s.

George M. Rudolph's Bazaar at 314 Market Street continued the tradition of J. Warren Bowman. When George M. Rudolph retired in January 1913, his clerk, Lewis W. Collins, took over the business. The building itself was very historic, having had the first electric light generated in the basement and being the first building in Oxford to be wired for electricity. In 1919, a new three-story building was erected on the site. The blotter on the right is an advertising piece for Ticonderoga pencils distributed by Collins. The building is still in place, but the facade has been altered.

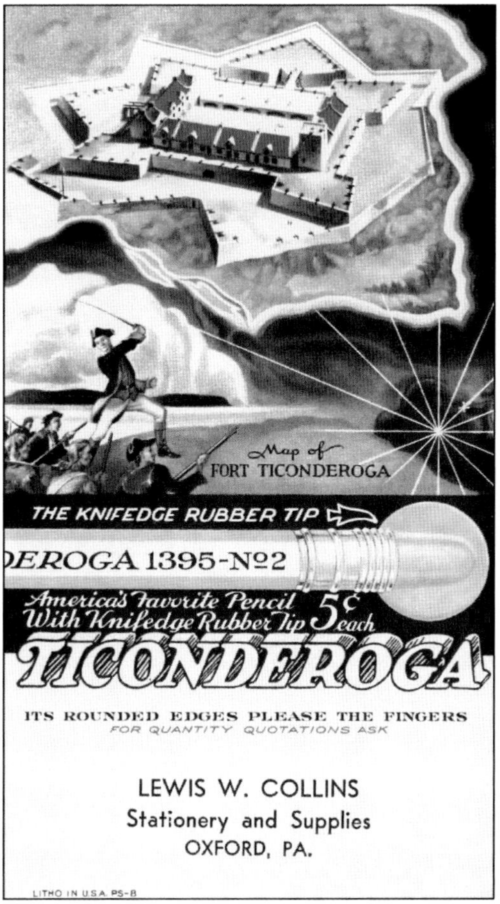

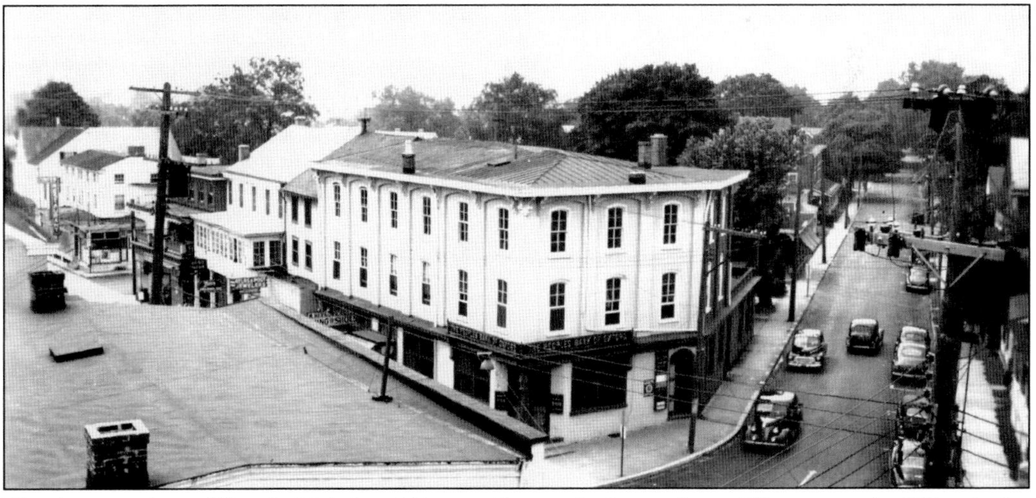

The intersection of South Third and Locust Streets is shown here. The corner building is the 1868 J. M. C. Dickey building; at the time of this photograph, it was the home of the Farmers National Bank. Many businesses and social and fraternal organizations have been associated with this building, including the Oxford Public Library. The Center Restaurant is located farther down Third Street to the left of the telephone pole.

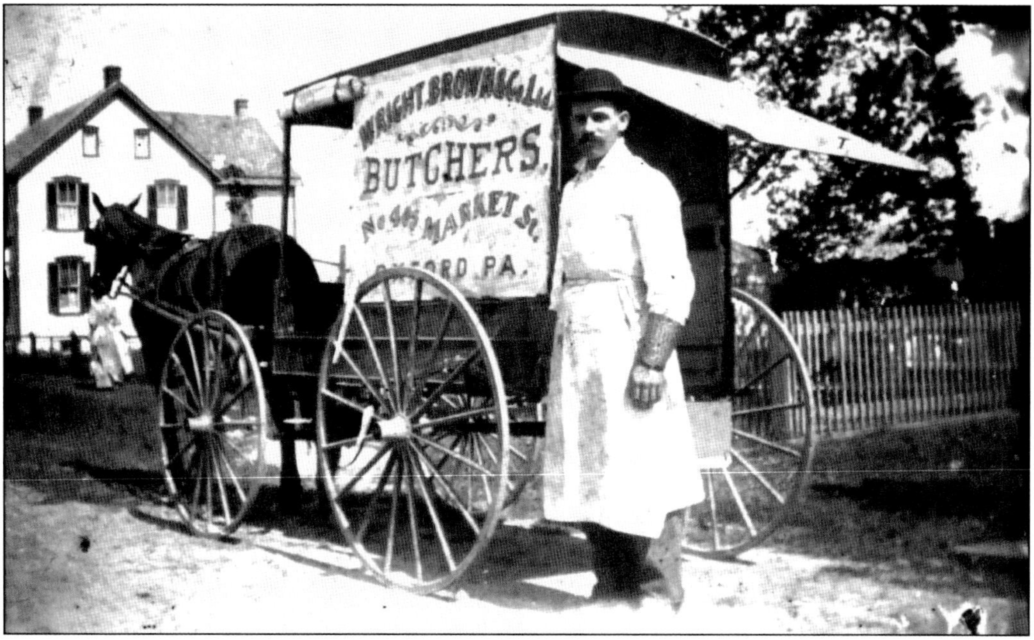

This 1890s photograph shows the Wright Brown and Company, Ltd., butcher's wagon. The store was located at 330 Market Street by 1893 and later at 405 Market Street. Alonzo Brown and John S. Wright were in business with David A. Caldwell. A. M. Wright made deliveries on Tuesday, Thursday, and Saturday. By 1904, the business consisted of only Brown and Caldwell.

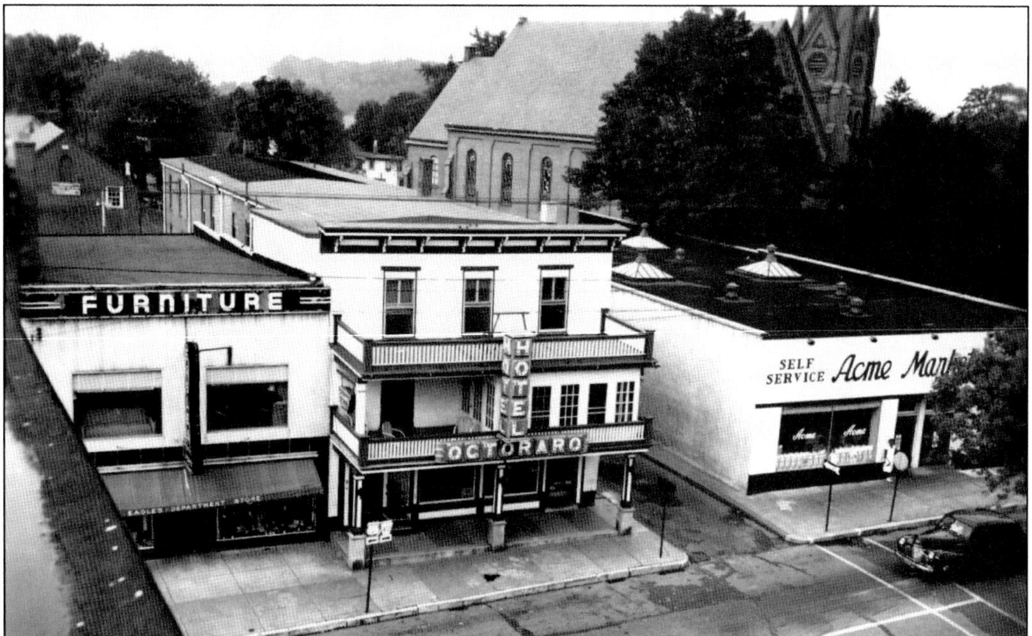

Moving from 8 South Third Street, a new Acme Market was built on the site of the old National Bank of Oxford in 1940, with Howard W. Dickinson as manager. After the move, the building on the left became the Eagles department and furniture store. In 1956, the market was sold for $50,000, and a larger facility was constructed south of town.

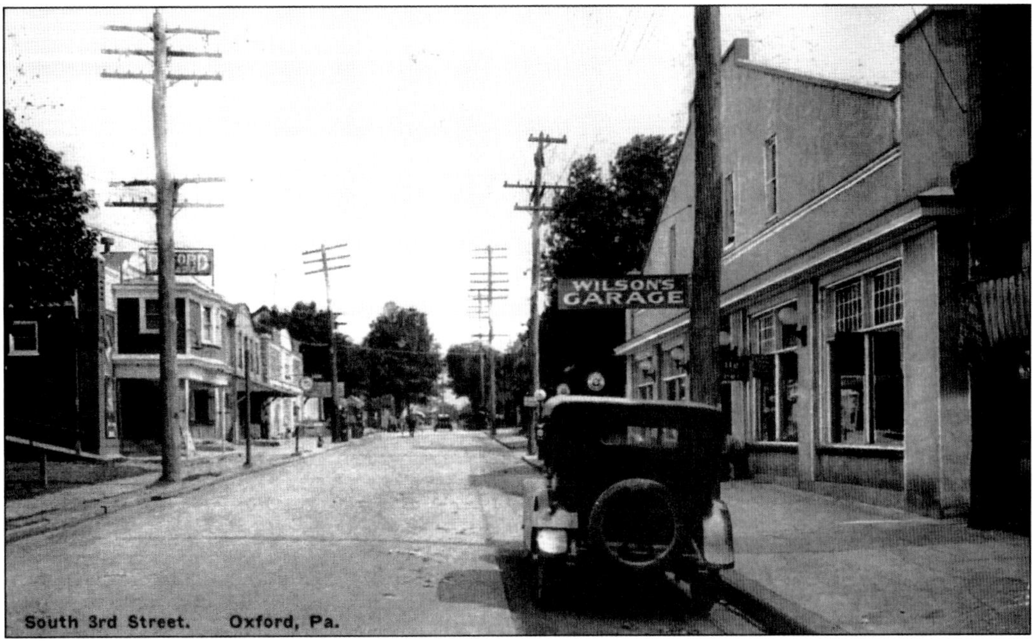

Wilson's Garage, built in 1920, was located on the southeast corner of South Third and Broad Streets. It was one of several garages owned by Frank G. Wilson. Thomas L. Buker managed the garage in the 1930s, selling Studebakers, Plymouths, and DeSotos. He sold the business back to the original owner, F. G. Wilson, in 1939. The building is now used by Oxford Auto Parts. Note the sign for the Oxford Theater on the opposite side of the street.

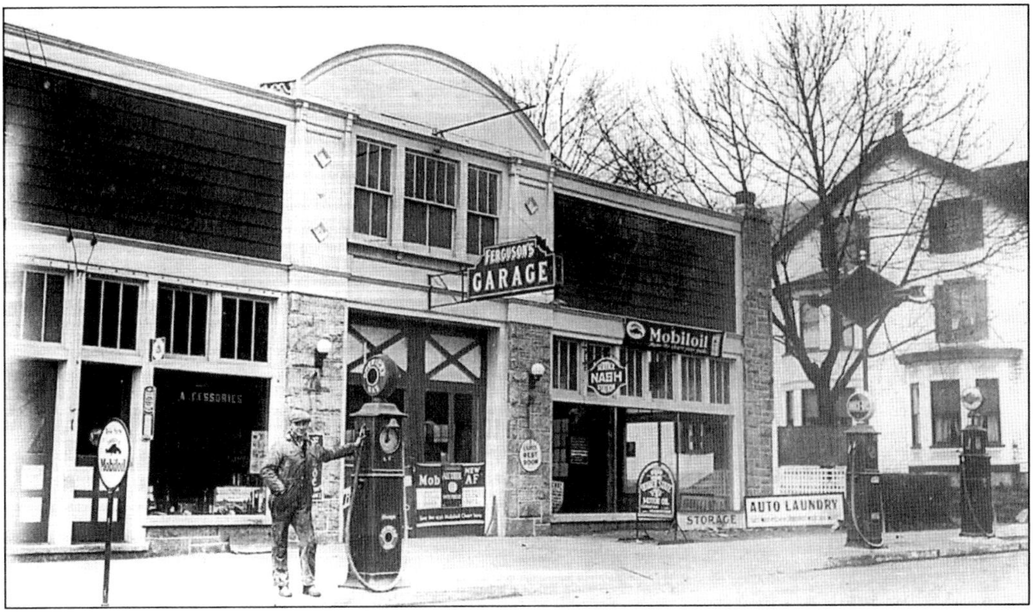

A. Allen Kirk (1853–1930) built this garage at 56 South Third Street some time before March 1921. The tile building measured 60 by 125 feet and had a capacity for 50 cars. Kirk sold Buick cars and had previously been in the carriage and hardware business. Although known as Kirk's Garage until the 1940s, the garage passed into the hands of several others, including Parke R. Rhodewalt. (Courtesy of Frances Jackson.)

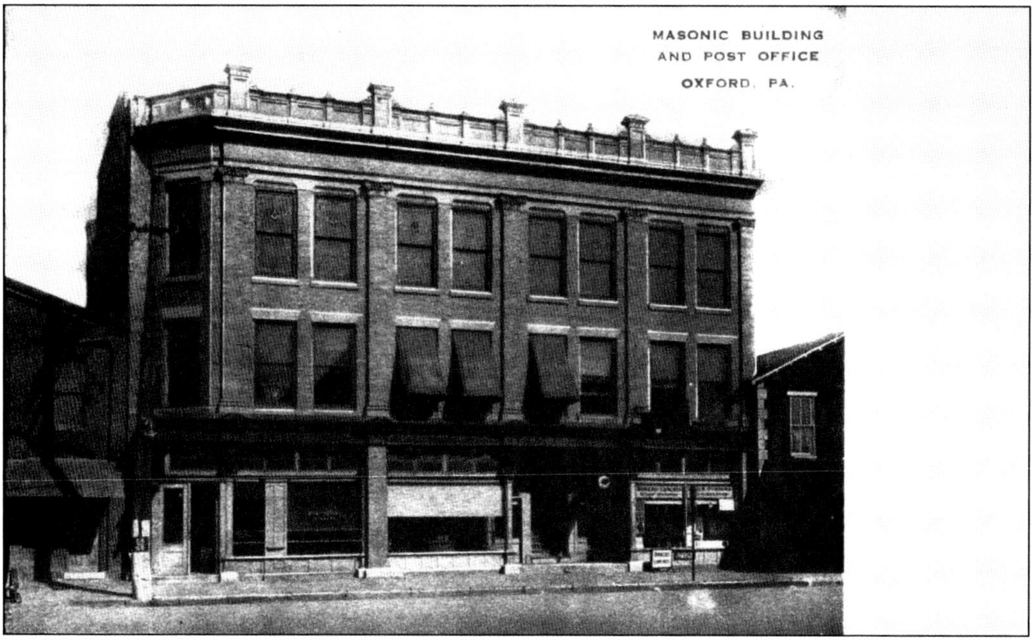

The Masonic building at 11–15 North Third Street was built in 1895. The post office moved into the building on April 14, 1904, and remained at this location until January 31, 1961, when it moved to new quarters on Locust Street. The Oxford Masonic Lodge No. 353, founded in 1864, also met there. S. Jefferson McIntire had an oyster bar, restaurant, and ice-cream parlor in the building from 1896 until 1914, when he moved to South Third Street.

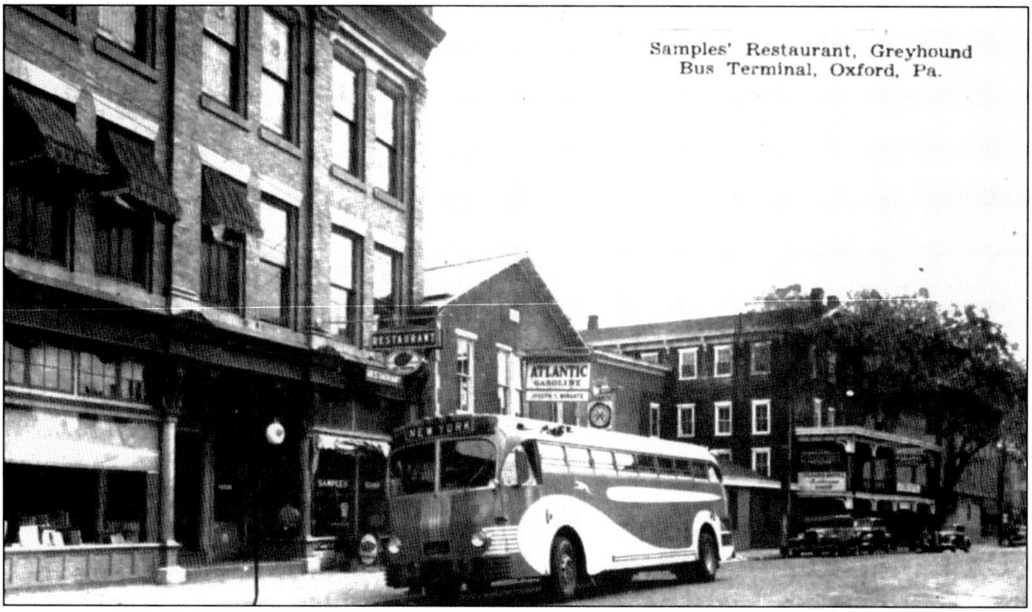

John H. Kimball had a grocery store in the Masonic building from 1896 to 1898, at which time he sold it to Dewitt C. Carhart. At the time of this 1930s postcard, Samples Restaurant was located in the Masonic building. The restaurant also served as a bus stopover for the Greyhound Bus Company. The two-story brick building behind the bus was built in 1887 and served as a livery stable for the hotel.

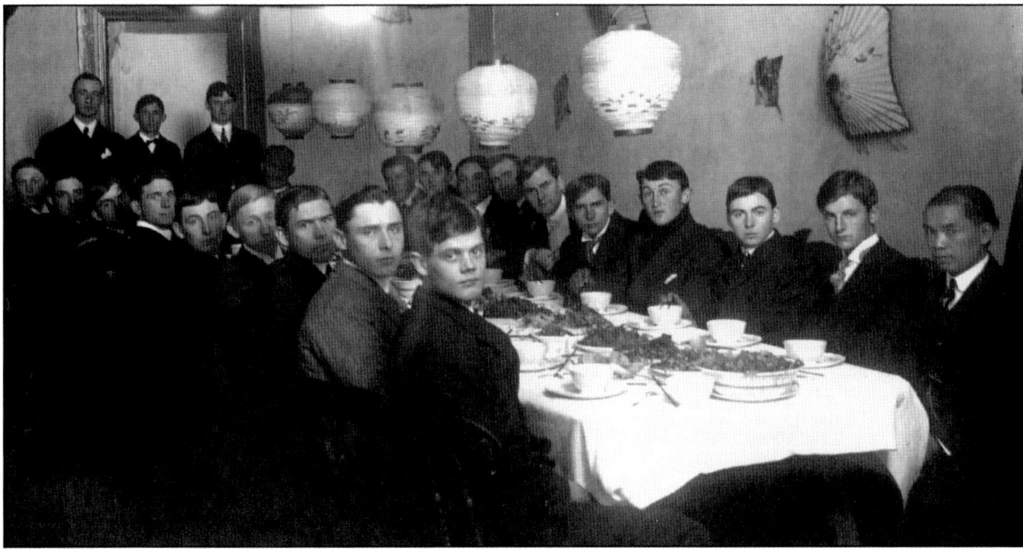

In 1894, Toy Fook Laon, the first Chinese person to open a business in Oxford, operated a laundry at Fourth and Market Streets, and later at 30 South Third Street. Previous to coming to Oxford, Laon operated laundries in Wilmington, Delaware, and Havre de Grace, Maryland. The young men of town welcomed him with a treat of American food. Laon was very pleased and, in return, treated them to a full-course Chinese meal. He is seated at the front right with the young men of Oxford at that dinner. In October 1909, Laon returned to China via Vancouver, British Columbia. He left the business in the hands of his friend and partner Mock Wing.

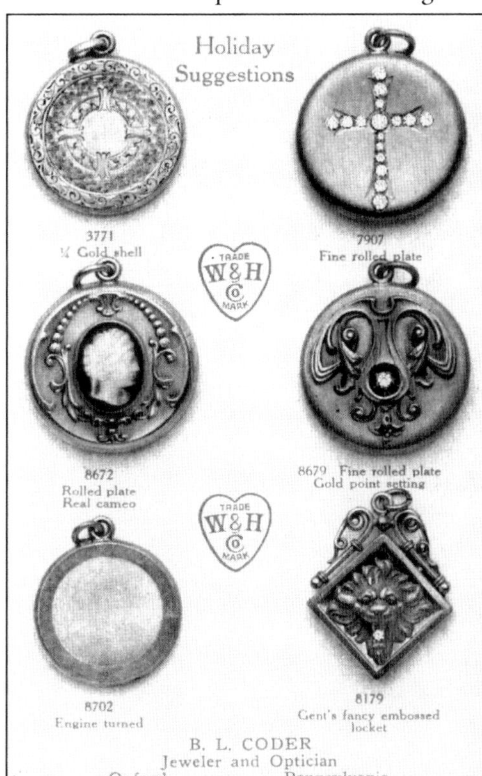

Bernard L. Coder, jeweler and optician, is listed in the 1908–1909 Boyd's West Chester directory as having a store at 29 South Third Street. Various pieces of jewelry produced by the W and H Company are suggested for purchase in this holiday advertising card dating from the 1908–1915 period.

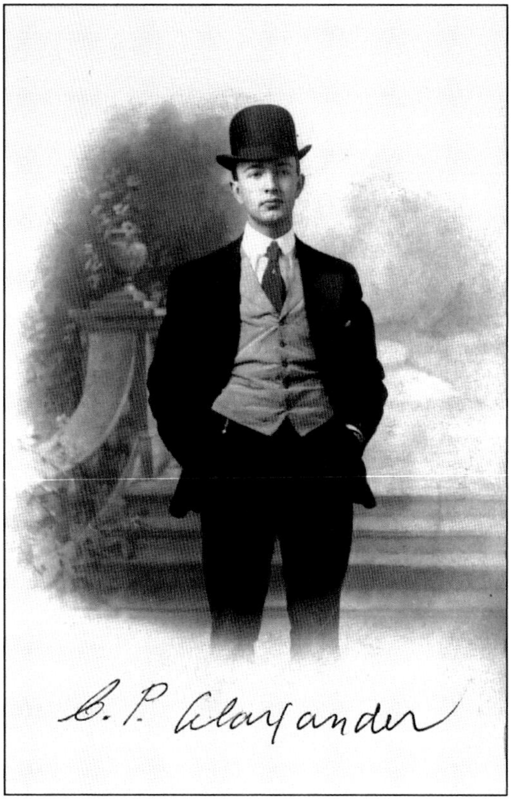

Taken at Steeple Chase Pier in Atlantic City, this photograph is a portrait of Clyde P. Alexander. Alexander was a prominent Oxford merchant known for his scrapple and sausage. He owned and managed Alexander's Meat Market on South Third Street for over 55 years. Alexander, who died in 1966, was a generous man who left the Oxford Public Library $250,000 to build a Colonial-style library in memory of his wife, Katherine B. Bicking Alexander, who died in 1954.

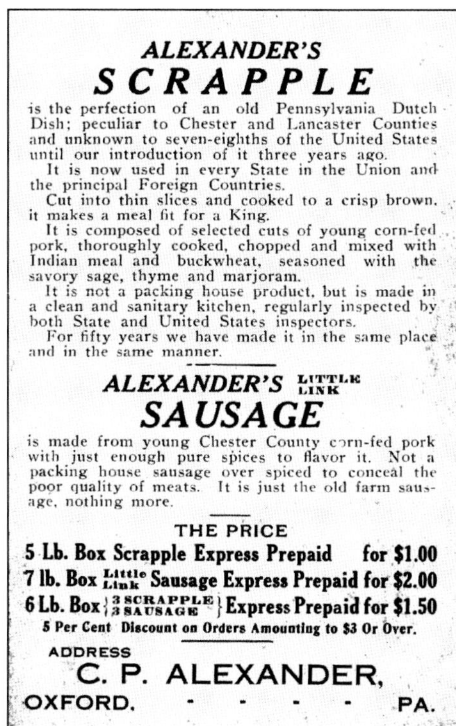

This advertisement card states that the scrapple is "composed of selected cuts of young corn-fed pork, Indian meal, buckwheat and seasonings and is . . . fit for a king." A humorous quote from a 1907 town tour states, "He made a fortune by persuading some suckers in the west and south that it was stylish to eat the remnant part of a hog for breakfast food. He is not the richest man in town, but will be soon."

Two

Transportation and Industry

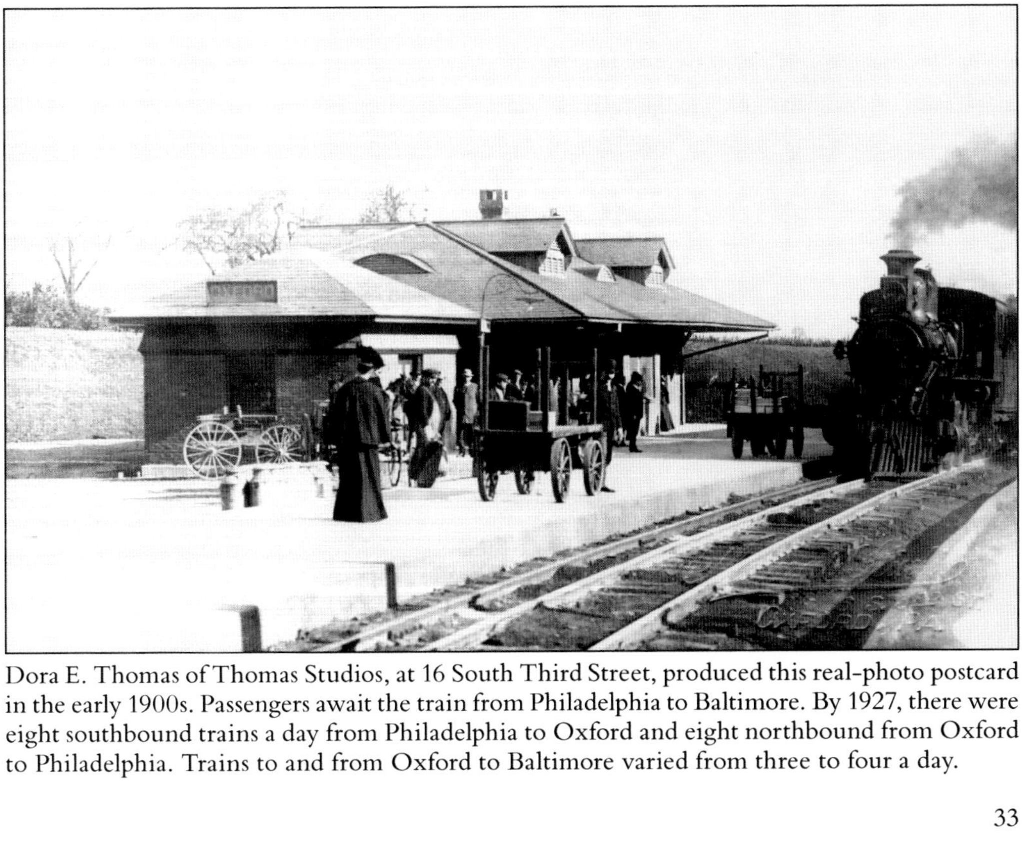

Dora E. Thomas of Thomas Studios, at 16 South Third Street, produced this real-photo postcard in the early 1900s. Passengers await the train from Philadelphia to Baltimore. By 1927, there were eight southbound trains a day from Philadelphia to Oxford and eight northbound from Oxford to Philadelphia. Trains to and from Oxford to Baltimore varied from three to four a day.

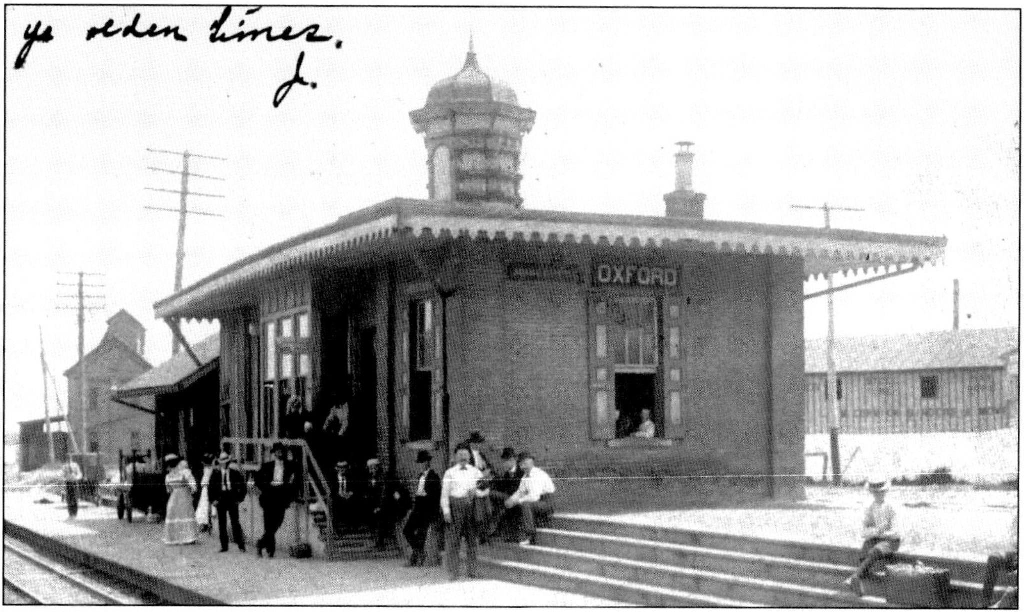

The first depot was built in 1860 in anticipation of the arrival of the engine *Rockdale* on December 22, 1860. The brick station was 20 by 40 feet and located on the south side of the tracks. Oxford was one of the principal towns on the Octoraro branch of the Philadelphia and Baltimore Central Railroad. The railroad had its shops in Oxford with a turntable and water tank as well as a three-stall engine house. In 1891, a freight station was constructed. Dora E. Thomas took the photograph below in the early 1900s, while the above real-photo postcard dates from 1903–1904. Note the hay, feed, and grain warehouse of S. Ralston Dickey and Company in the background.

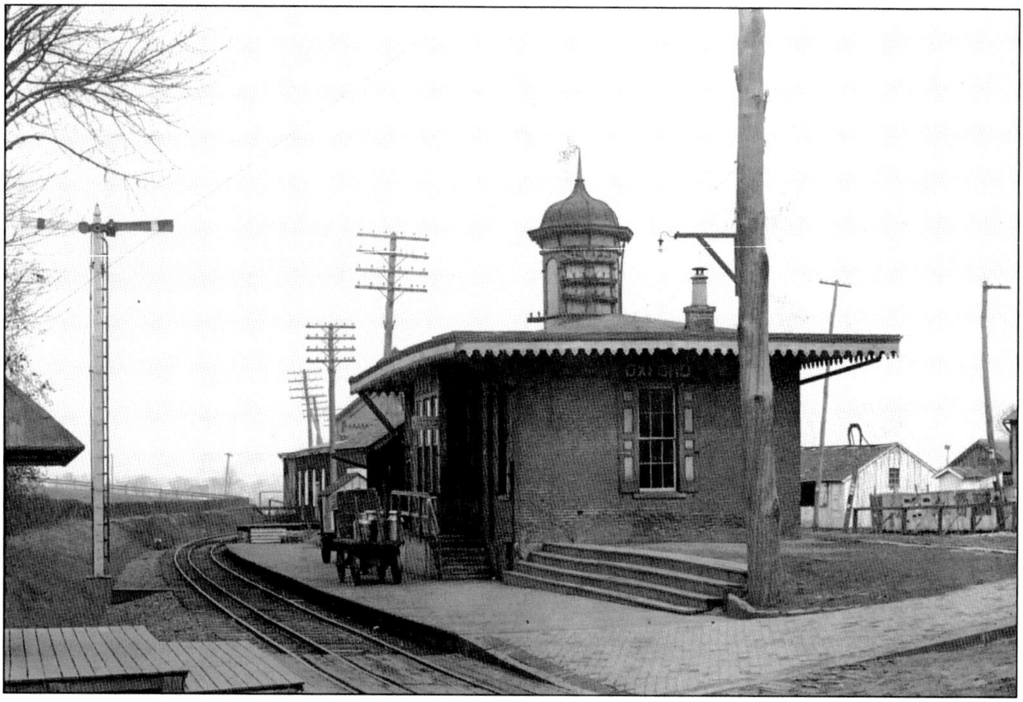

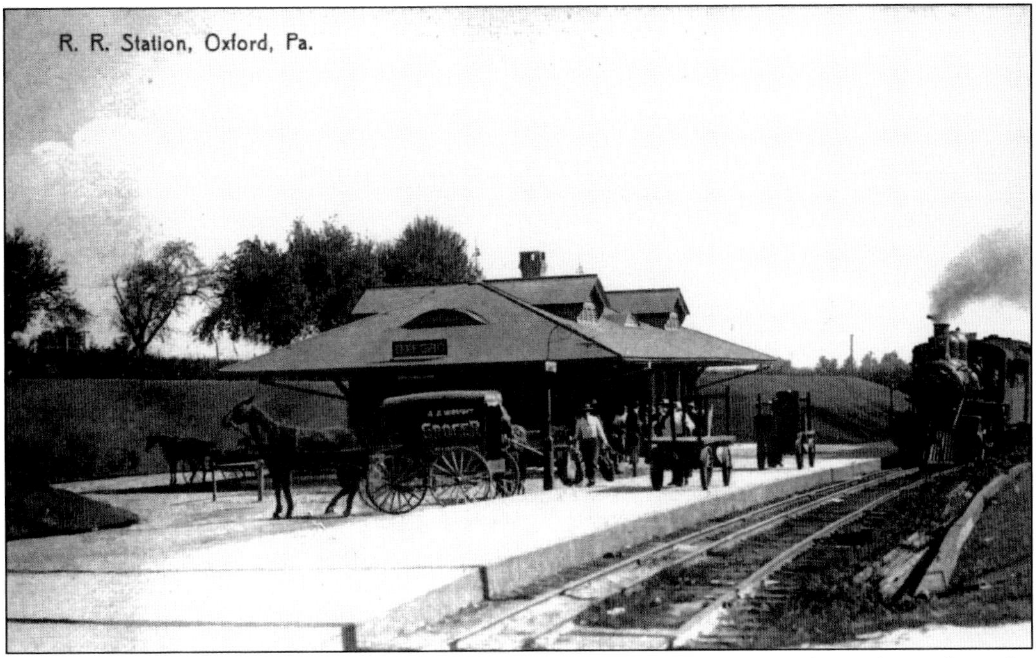

A new 65-by-20-foot brick railroad station was constructed in 1903 and was located on the north side of the tracks. The depot had separate waiting rooms for both men and women. In 1905, a stucco baggage room was added to the end of the depot. Since it was not styled to match the building, community members nicknamed it "the wart." According to a 1986 *High Line* magazine article, news agent John Good used the tracks (when regular trains were not running), for a three-wheeled velocipede that stopped at different locations than the train. The last regular passenger train service to Oxford was in 1948.

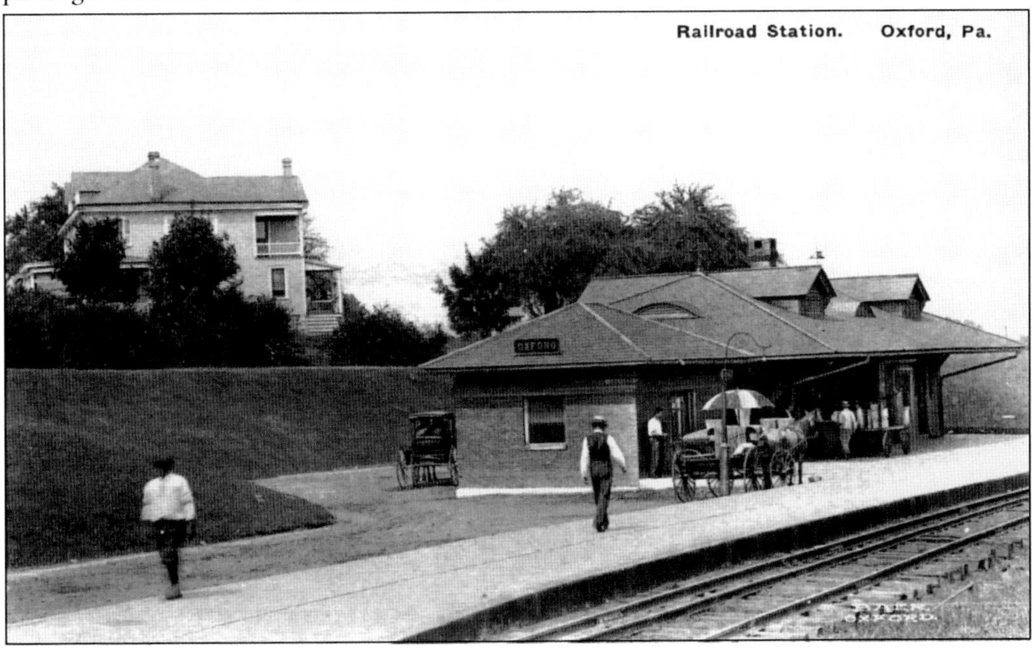

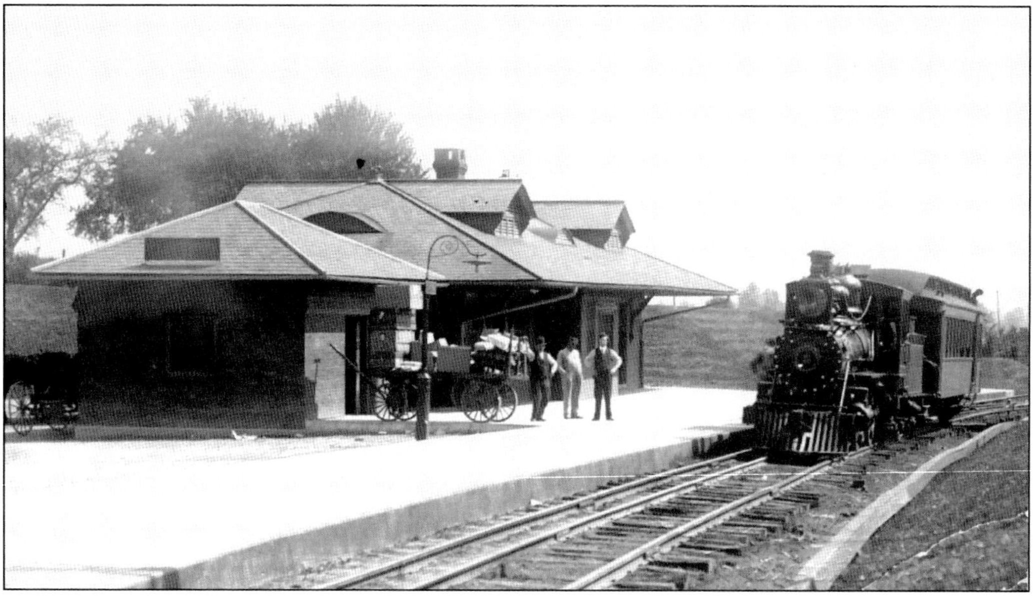

From 1890 until 1919, Oxford was also served by the narrow-gauge Lancaster, Oxford and Southern Railroad (engine seen above). The Lancaster, Oxford and Southern resulted from the reorganization and merger of the Lancaster and Reading Narrow Gauge Railroad and the Peach Bottom Railroad. Only 28 miles long, it served southern Lancaster County and western Chester County, hauling produce, animals, dairy products, and passengers. It was affectionately known as the "Peachy," the "Little, Old and Slow," or "Lost and Out of Sight," resulting from its many incidents, such as the time in 1894 when "Turkey Stops Train" was reported in the *Philadelphia Record*, or the time a gust of wind blew a passenger coach off the train. The real-photo postcard above dates from 1907–1912, while the postcard below shows the train crossing the bridge at Pine Grove in 1909.

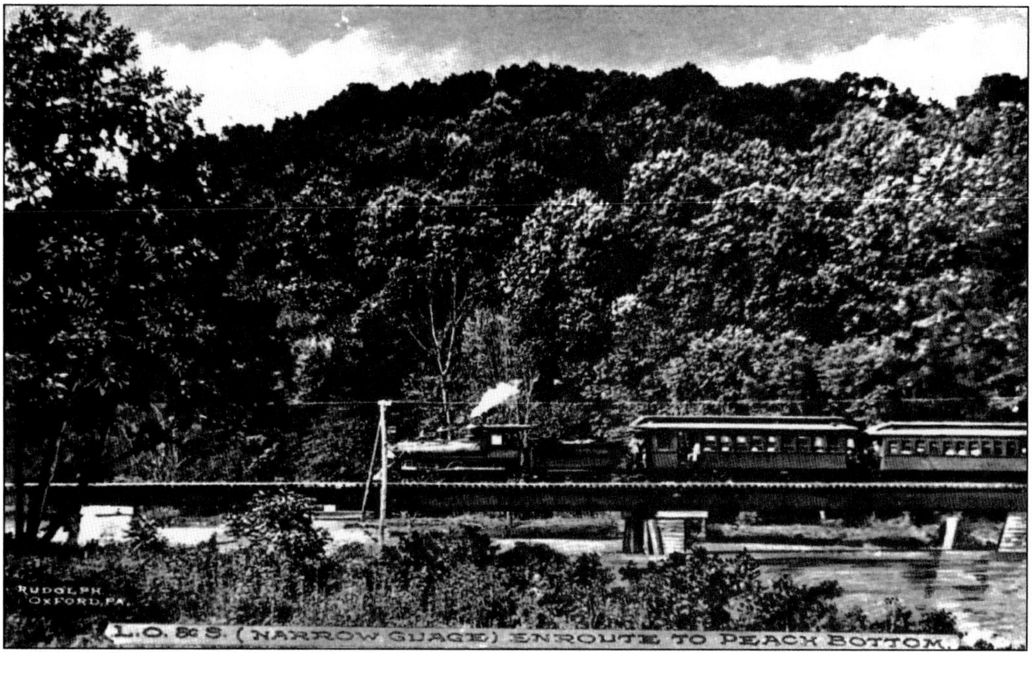

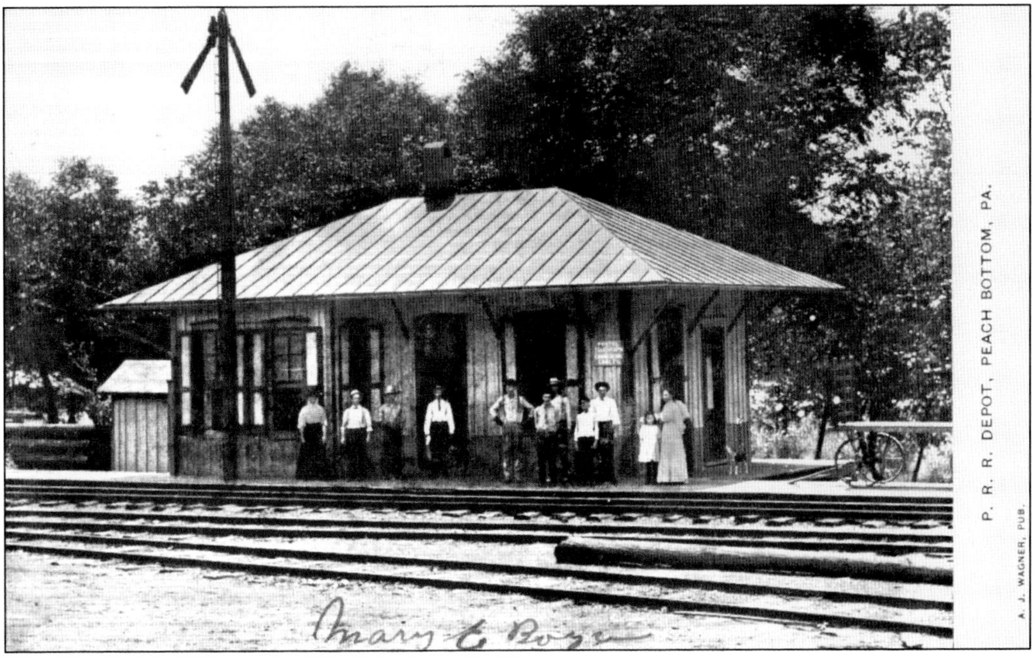

The Pennsylvania Railroad depot at Peach Bottom, Lancaster County, is seen in this 1908 postcard. Peach Bottom was the terminus of the Lancaster, Oxford and Southern Railroad's narrow-gauge railway. Between Oxford and Peach Bottom, trains made several regular and flag stops in Chester and Lancaster Counties. A few of those stops included Hopewell, Tweedale, Point Lookout, White Rock, Fairmont, Fulton House, Arcadia, and finally Susquehanna (Peach Bottom). The Unicorn-Quarryville spur line made a connection at Fairmont.

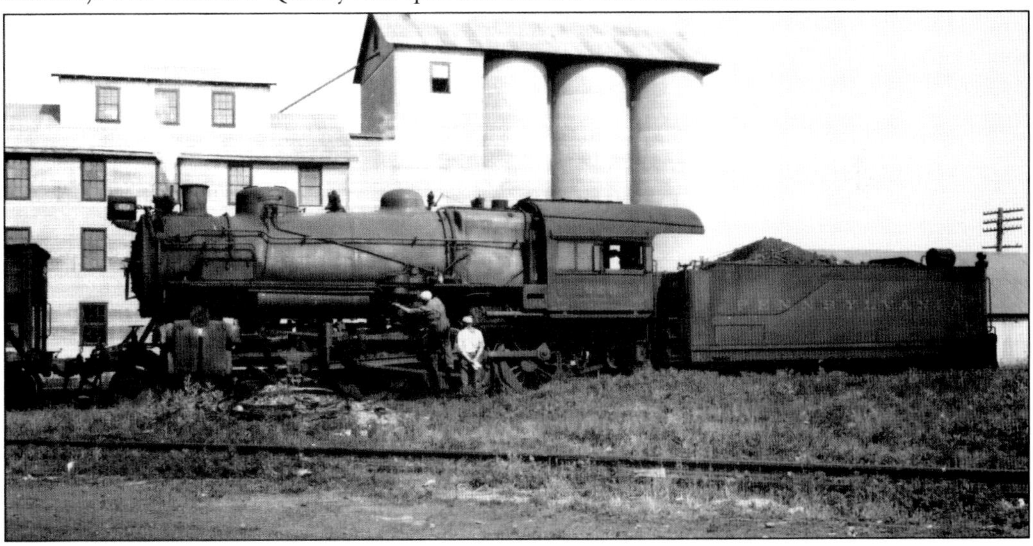

This July 14, 1946, photograph shows a Pennsylvania locomotive and coal car in front of the old grain elevator on South Third Street. The site was once W. D. Alexander's bone mill (pre-1884) and later George B. Passmore and Son's Oxford Milling Company, established in January 1888. Passmore sold the mill to the Eastern Milling and Export Company in 1901. It lasted into the second decade of the 20th century, at which time it was sold to Samuel Weigel. From that time until it closed in 1985, the Weigel family operated the mill.

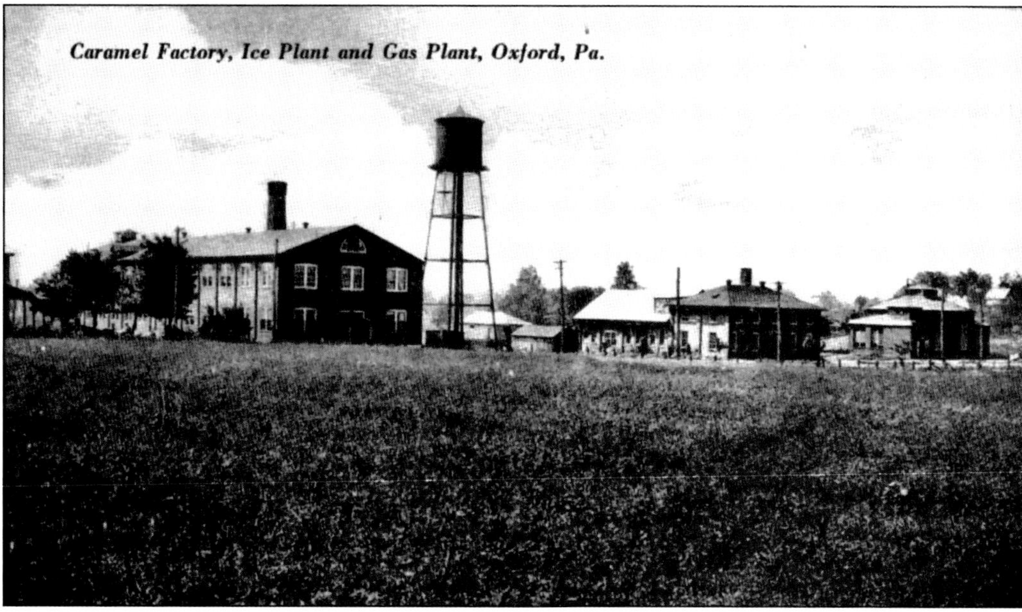

Oxford has been associated with candy for over a century. The W. F. Parker and Company factory was constructed during 1891 and finished and ready for machinery by December 16, 1891. The original proprietor was Willard F. Parker of Philadelphia. It was a self-contained operation, with the first floor containing the packing and wrapping departments. Over 100 girls and women were under the supervision of Gertrude Smith. The building was heated with steam and lit with electricity. Total employment was 200, with no one under 14 years of age. On Wednesday afternoon, April 20, 1892, the first batch of caramels were turned out and shipped all over the world. Milk for the first caramels came from the dairy of Lyburn Whittaker, an East Nottingham farmer. An early advertisement states "smart girls make as high as $7 a week." The company was later incorporated in 1894 as the Oxford Caramel Company with capital of $100,000 and 50,000 shares.

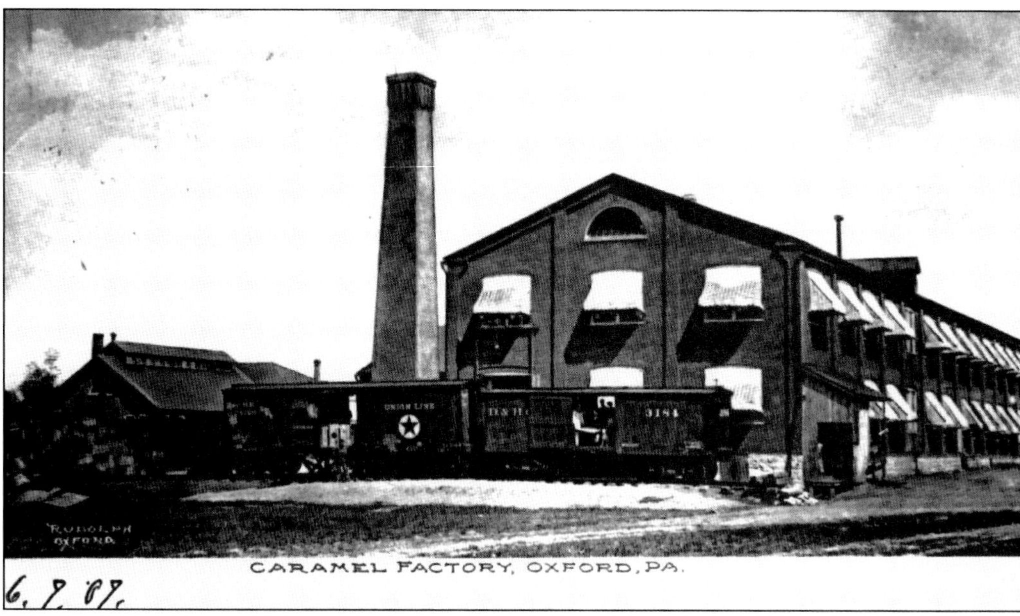

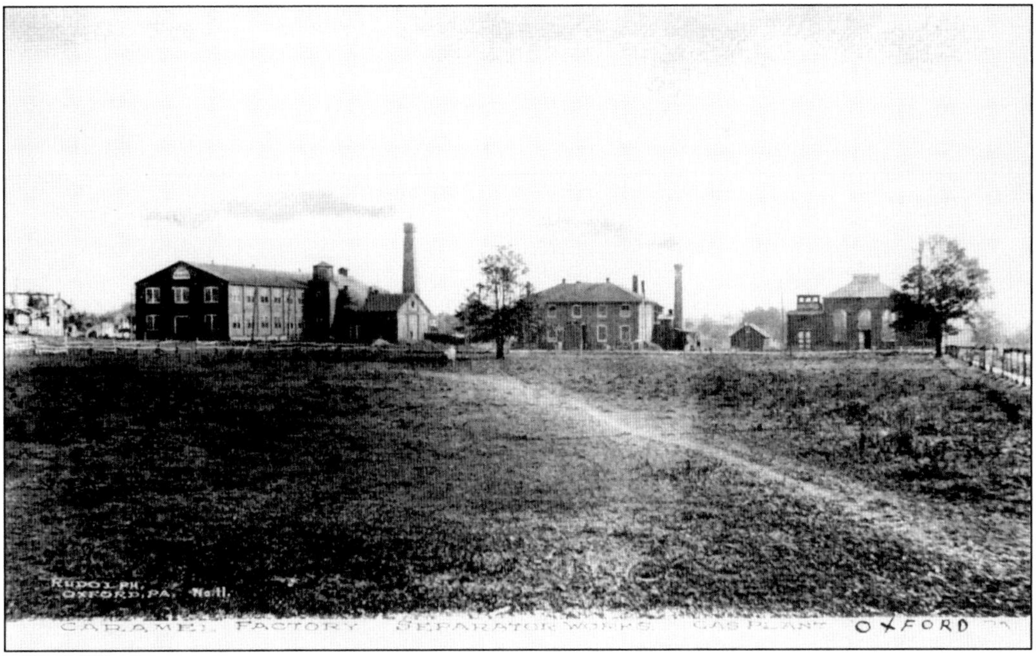

In 1898, the operations passed to the (Frederick) Breisch-Williams Company and, later, to Daniel F. Lafean of York, who represented the American Caramel Company. Later W. F. Burling moved his caramel candy factory from Philadelphia to Oxford and employed over 500 workers. The operation, known as the Oxford Confectionary Company, fell victim to the depression and, in 1929, the factory was purchased by John H. Ware Jr. and continued operation until 1933. In 1936, the facility was sold to the Cabinet Manufacturing Company, but in 1947, was destroyed by fire. The building was located on the southwest corner of South Street and Franklin Avenue. The postcards show the buildings along South Street, the Caramel Factory, and on the right, the Golden Rod Separator Company and Oxford Gas Works. In 1910, the Williams Caramel Company issued 30 distinctive baseball cards (E103 series) and in 1921, the Oxford Confectionary Company issued 20 baseball cards (E253 series).

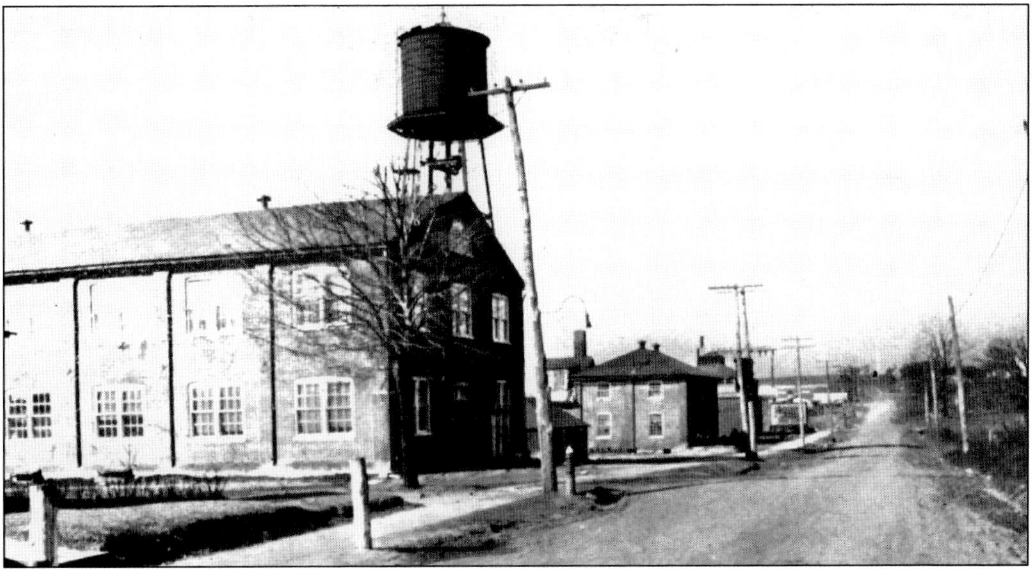

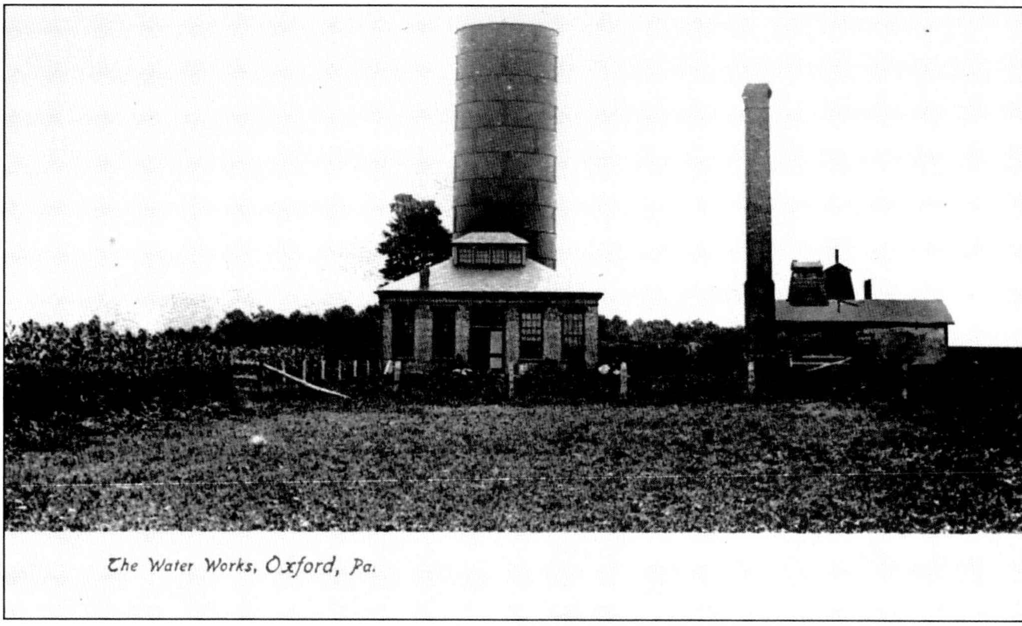

The west branch of the Big Elk Creek was the source of the running water that came to Oxford in 1870. The Oxford Water Works was located three-quarters of a mile north of town and included a reservoir. The operation included the laying of pipes and the installation of fire hydrants. Water arrived in town 30 minutes after it left the waterworks. Later water was supplied from artesian wells, the deepest being 543 feet. The 1894 board of trade stated, "While Oxford, owing principally to her high elevation, has always been regarded as a healthy town, her mortuary record has been considerably lowered since her water supply has been rendered above suspicion." The top postcard dates from 1907, and the bottom postcard from 1917.

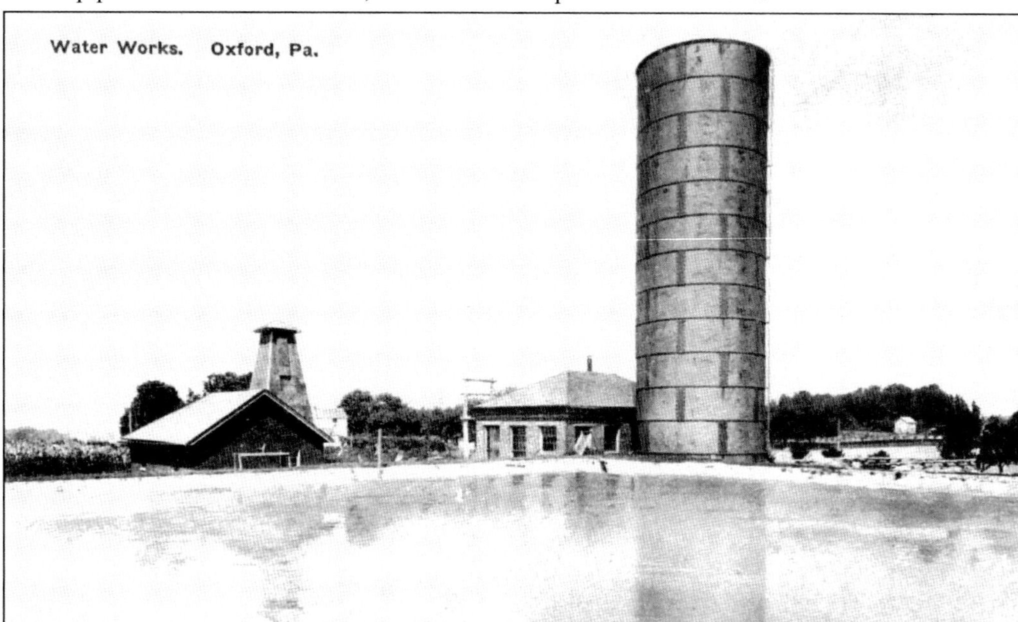

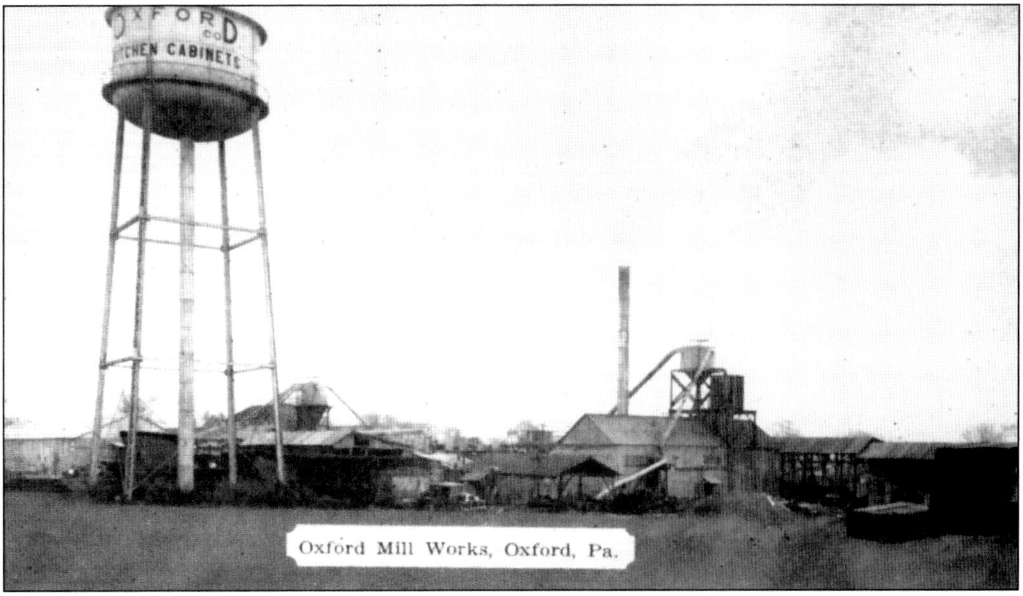

When the Central Mill Works was destroyed by fire in 1947, a new woodworking facility was built on South Third Street. By 1949, it was known as the Oxford Mill Works, and it was the largest industry in Oxford (and the only one of its kind in Chester County). Its slogan was "Direct from the forest to you," as the wood was cut within a 30-mile radius and delivered to its own sawmill. After the wood was treated, it was made into kitchen cabinets and dinette sets. Frank J. Michaels was the president at the time. The site was formerly known as the Oxford Flooring Company.

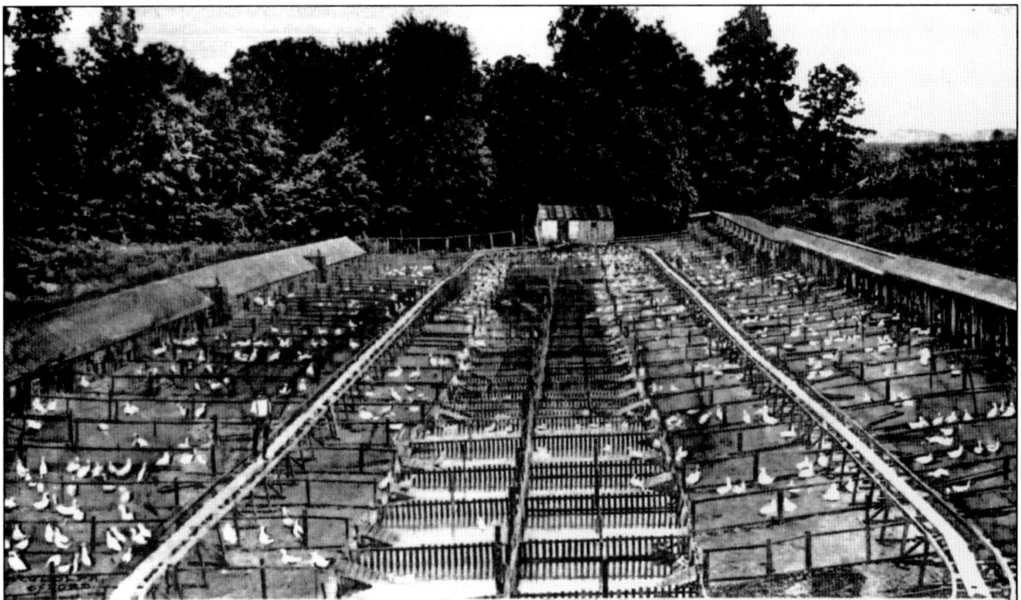

In 1898, investors D. H. Menough, J. D. Burn, and R. A. Walker purchased 13 acres of land from Dr. J. K. McKissick just north of Oxford. They started the Oxford poultry farm (also known as the Duck Farm) and used part of the farm to grow celery, which was used to feed the ducks. By 1916, the operation went up for public sale.

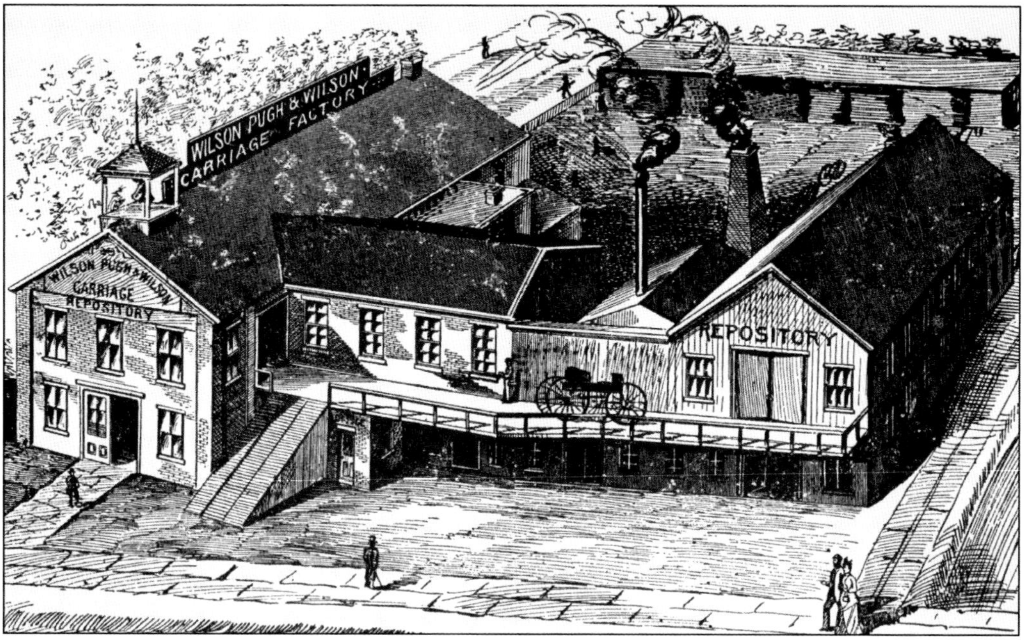

Wilson, Pugh, and Wilson Carriage factory was located next to the Presbyterian church at the corner of Coach and Pine Streets. The illustrated woodcut above was taken from a pamphlet published in 1903. In operation since 1863, the carriage manufacturing firm of Wilson Brothers and Company was dissolved in 1908. In 1882, a 35-by-100-foot two-story building with basement was erected on the site. A blacksmith shop adjoined the building. The carriage shop property was sold to W. R. Smith, with the title being passed on January 1, 1920. In 1929, J. Henry Wilson was involved in the automobile business. The site of the carriage works is now the middle of Lancaster Avenue and Coach Street.

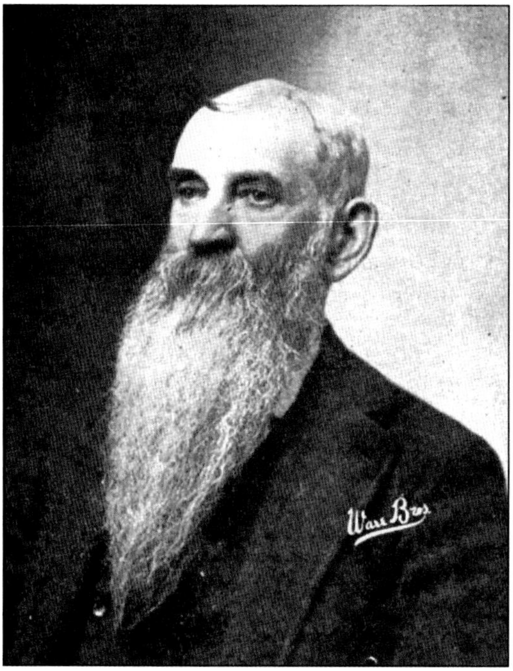

Samuel W. Wilson was born in Elk Township on April 28, 1839. He learned his carriage-making skills with W. J. Marchbank of Brick Meeting House, Cecil County, Maryland. In 1863, he moved to Oxford and formed a partnership with F. V. Johnson. In 1872, Evan P. Baily bought out Johnson. Baily and Wilson continued until Baily died in 1886, at which time Wilson ran the company alone. In 1888, Wilson went into partnership with A. Louis Pugh and his son J. Henry Wilson.

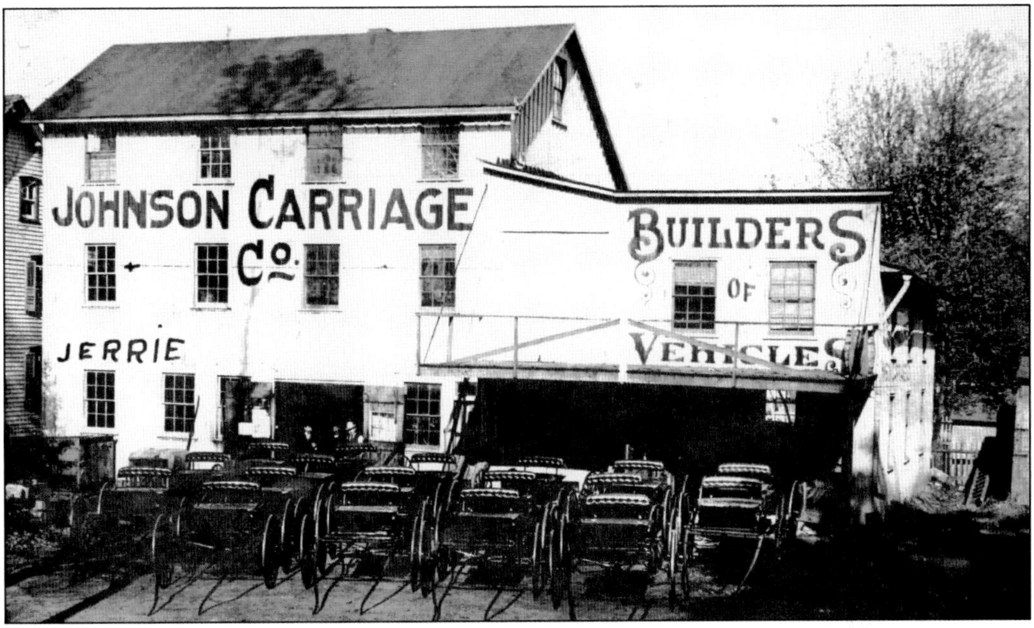

Joseph E. Johnson's Johnson Carriage Company was one of Oxford's major manufacturers of carriages, wagons, buggies, and road carts. The materials used included wood, iron, and steel; a specialty was the three-spring milk wagon. The business began on October 31, 1881, at a site on Railroad Avenue, but it later relocated to 475–477 Hodgson Street. By 1917, a new facility was being used in the manufacturing of automobile bodies. In 1920, S. J. Phillips of the American Road Machine Company in Kennett Square purchased the property for the manufacturing of truck cabs.

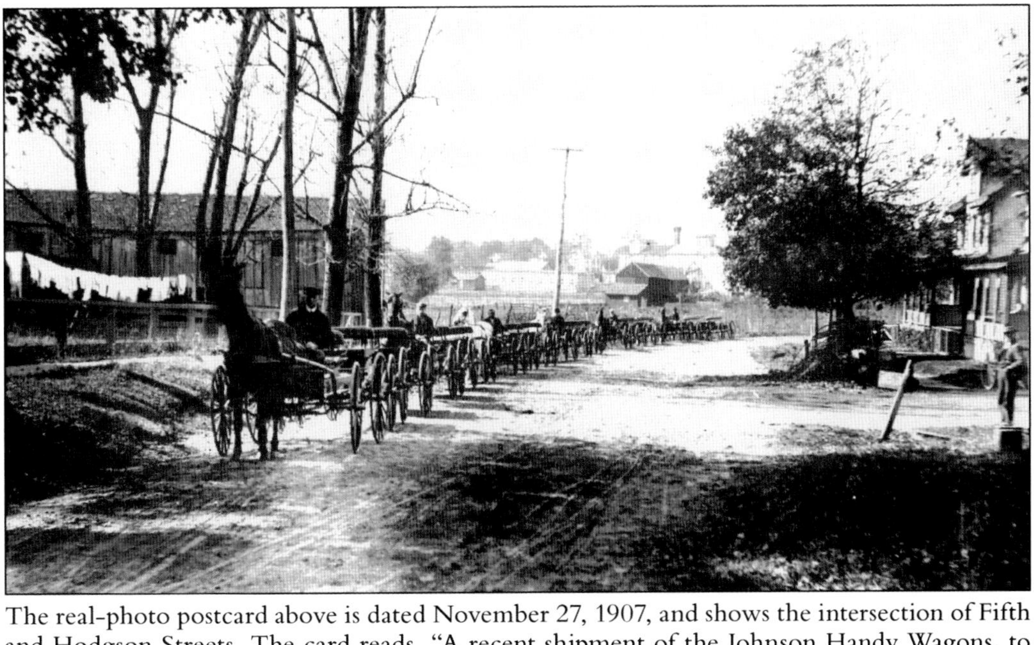

The real-photo postcard above is dated November 27, 1907, and shows the intersection of Fifth and Hodgson Streets. The card reads, "A recent shipment of the Johnson Handy Wagons, to Jos. S. Pogue, Sons and Company, Rising Sun, Md." Johnson died on July 13, 1952, at his home on South Fifth Street, at age 96. (Courtesy of Howard Steinberg.)

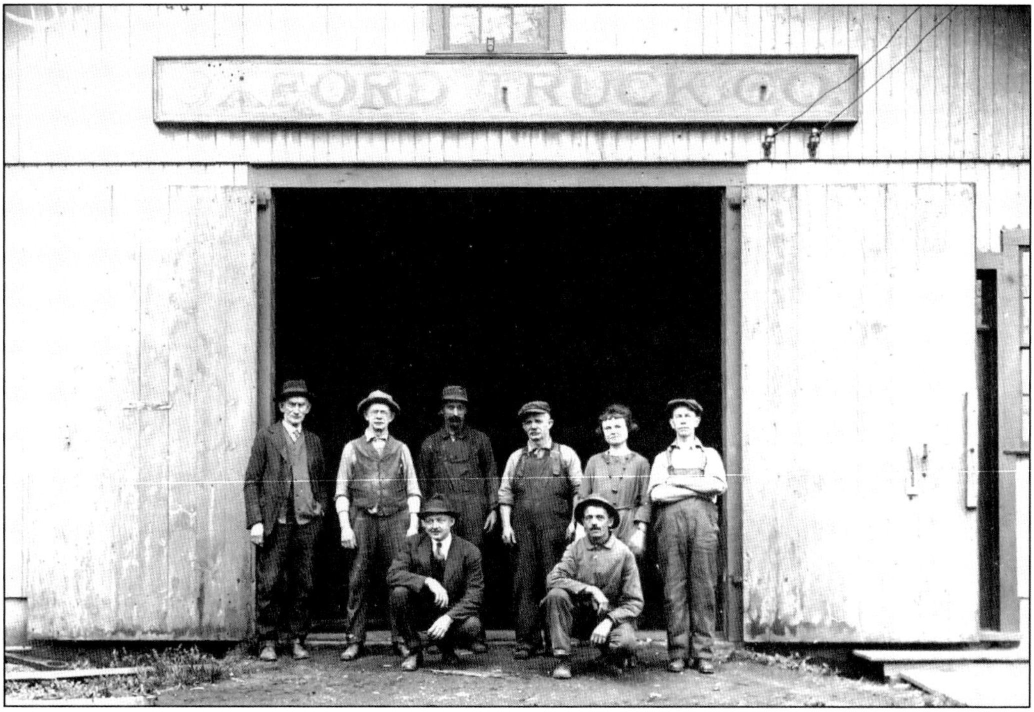

The Oxford Truck Company was the successor of Johnson's Carriage Works. In 1920, Joseph E. and Garrett E. Johnson were in foreclosure, with Thomas F. Grier and Hanson P. Passmore holding the property until S. Jones Philips of Kennett Square's American Road Machine Company took possession on November 1, 1920.

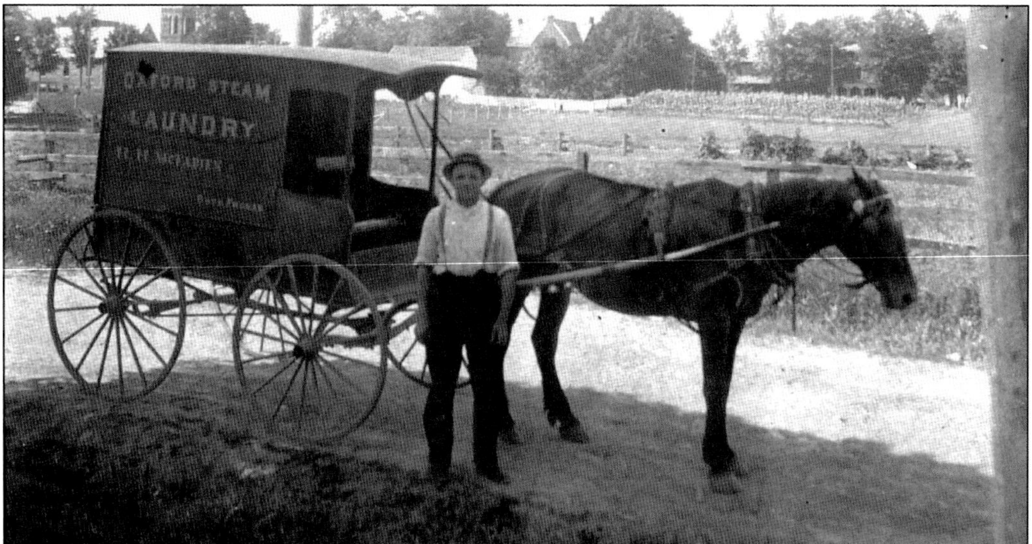

The Oxford Steam Laundry was established in 1901 and owned by R. Hayes McFadien. The laundry was located at the edge of the borough in the Big Elk Dairy buildings. The laundry had 26 different processing machines and 20 employees who cleaned four tons of laundry per week. In 1942, the laundry was destroyed by fire, the victim of faulty wiring, but reopened on Lincoln Avenue. The real-photo postcard dates from 1907–1912.

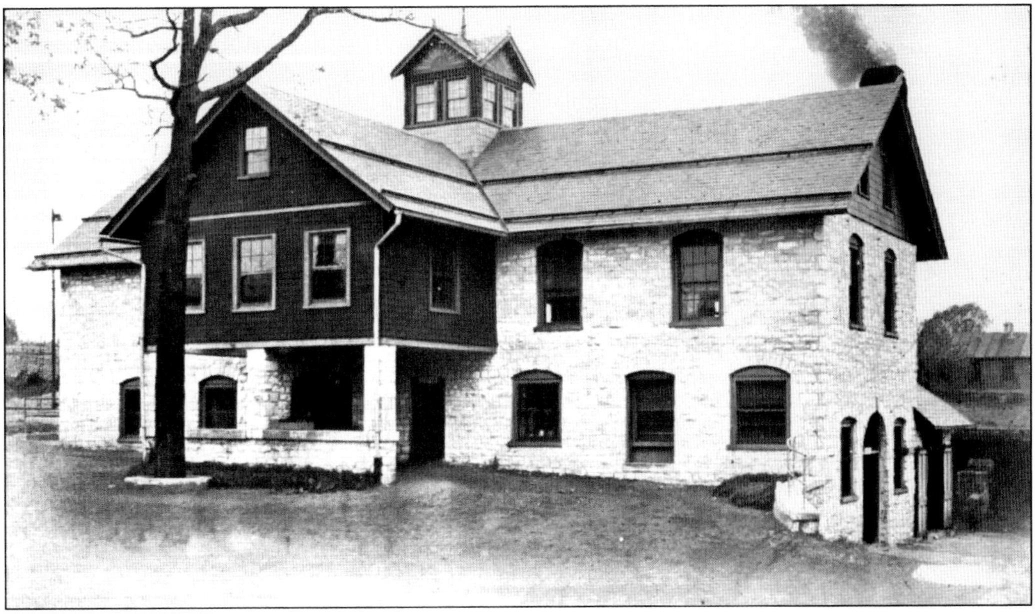

This postcard reads, "One of Abbotts up-to-date country receiving and bottling creameries at Oxford, Pa., constructed of stone, steel and cement, middle floor of reinforced concrete. Perfectly sanitary. Main Office, 1823 Filbert St., Philadelphia." The creamery was located along the railroad at North Fifth and Chase Streets.

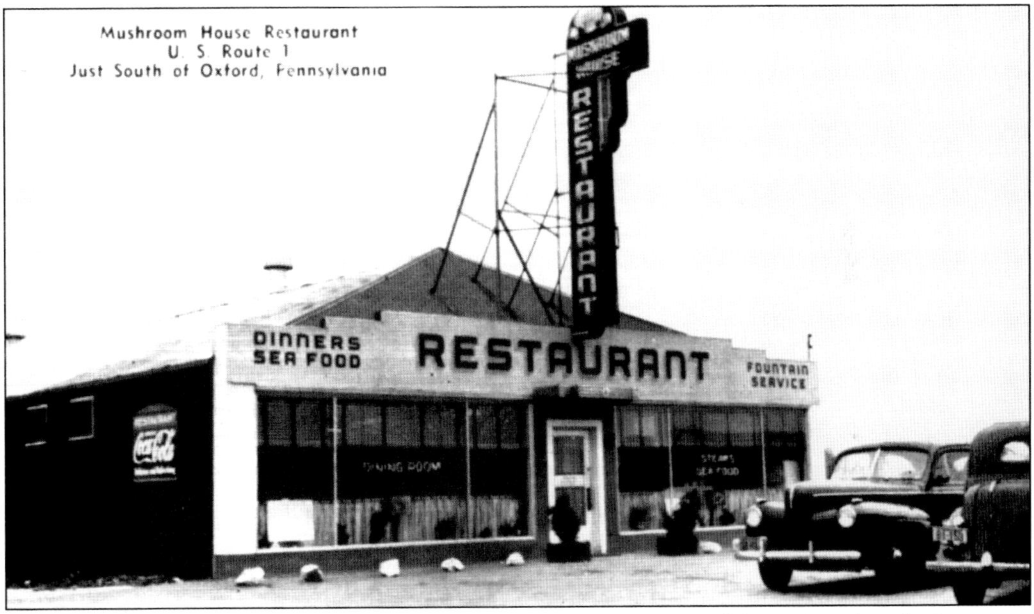

The Mushroom House Restaurant opened in May 1948 on the site of the Milton Supply Company at 2135 Baltimore Pike. Steven Vakos was the proprietor. The restaurant served full-course meals, sandwiches, sodas, and fountain delicacies. The interior was cream colored with a long light blue fountain trimmed in chrome and a green linoleum floor. From the 1960s until the early 1980s, it was the site of Campbell's Corner (a general store) where country music legends Ola Belle Campbell Reed and her brother Alex Campbell broadcast country music to over 200 radio stations in the United States and Canada.

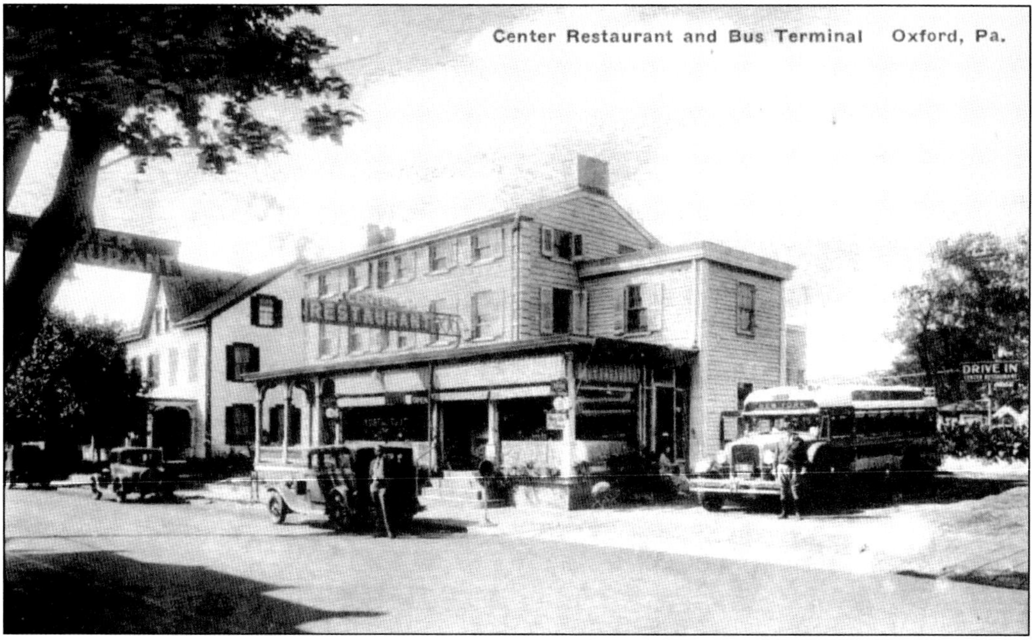

The Center Restaurant and bus terminal was located at 42 South Third Street where the Rite Aid pharmacy now stands. Chester L. Woollens purchased the property from the estate of his brother Dr. Taylor Woollens of Chicago in the late 1920s. After his own death in 1934, his wife, Florence L. Woollens, and her brother, Harry Reinhart, took over the business. Florence and Reinhart also served as ticket agents for the Safeway-Trailways and Short Line bus routes. In 1943, Trailways purchased the premises at a sheriff's sale. Florence remained as ticket agent. These two postcards date from the early 1930s.

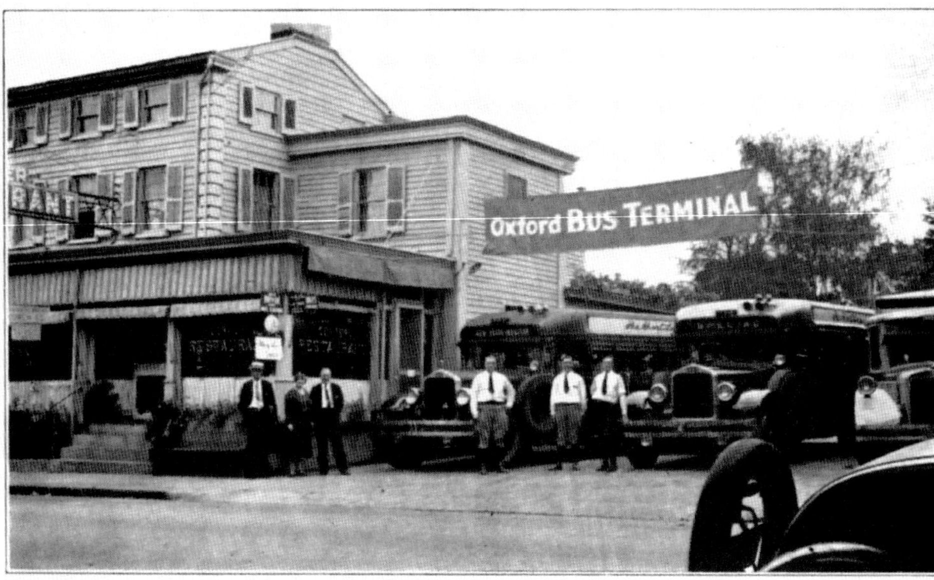

Centre Restaurant and Bus Terminal **C. L. Woollens, Proprietor, Oxford, Pa.**

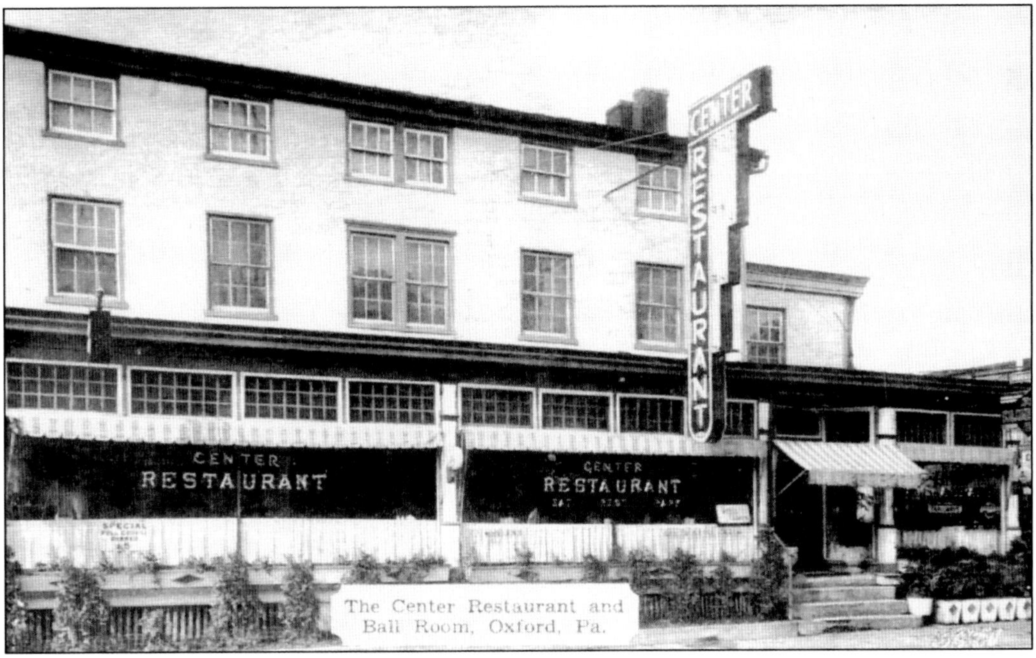

In 1952, Charles E. Adelman purchased the Center Restaurant from National Trailways. Adelman was the proprietor of the Western Auto Store located across the street. On July 15, 1954, Adelman had Oscar Roten demolish the building. The postcard dates from the late 1930s.

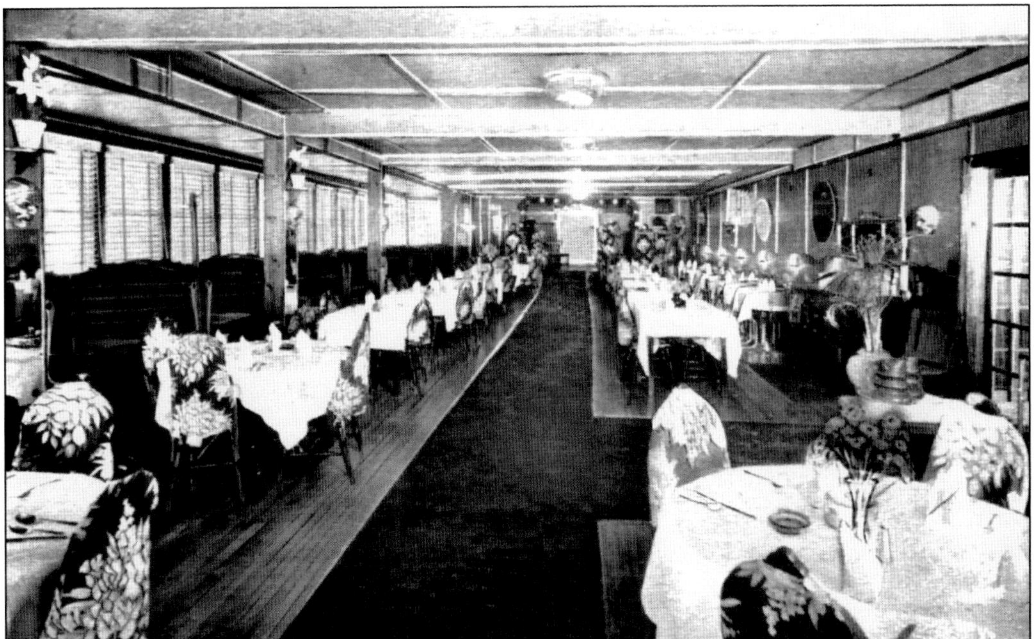

This lovely postcard shows the dining room of the Center Restaurant as it appears in 1934, when hardwood floors, furnishings, an orchestra dais, and fireplaces were installed. A loudspeaker was also installed to announce the arrival and departure of the buses in a "business-like manner."

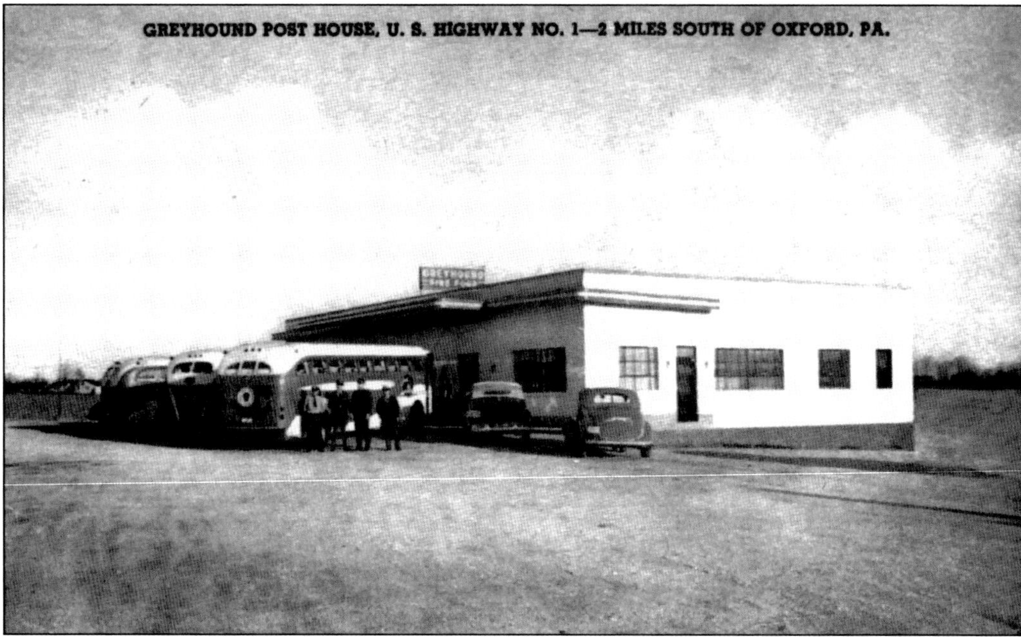

Before the era of bypasses and interstates, roadside restaurants and cafés dotted the highways of America. The Post House, located 2.3 miles south of Oxford on the Baltimore Pike (then U.S. 1), was a fine example of a roadside eating establishment. Clarence E. and Horace J. Samples were managers of the Greyhound Post House that had its grand opening on November 29, 1934. Howard R. Brown, a local contractor, helped in the drawing of the original plans. A special photographer took pictures of the interior (seen on page 49) and exterior and these were used as postcards that the Samples had printed and sold at the Post House. The building was constructed of cinder block and stucco and is still in operation today. Below is a linen postcard from the early 1950s.

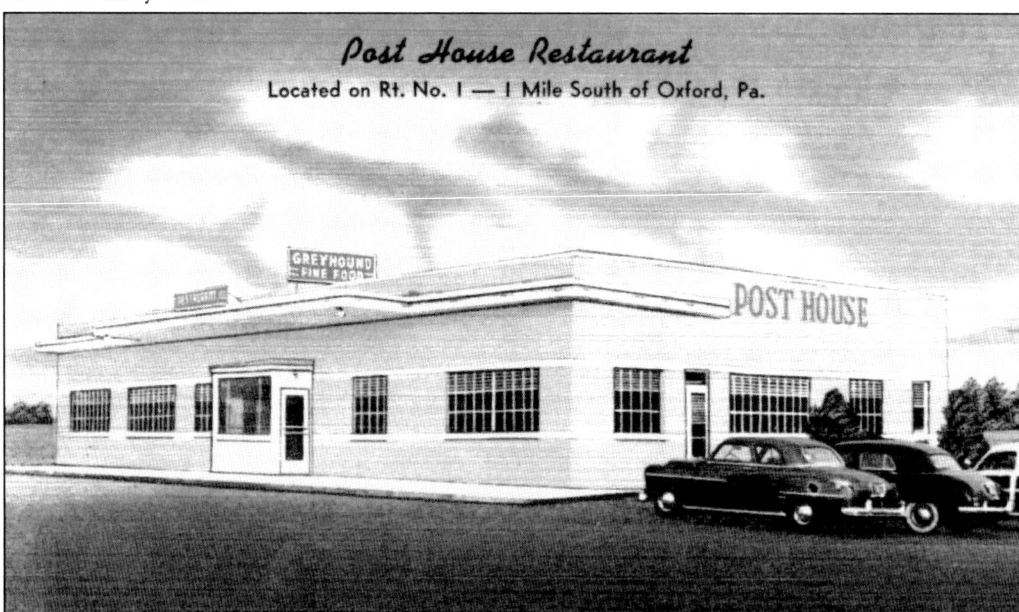

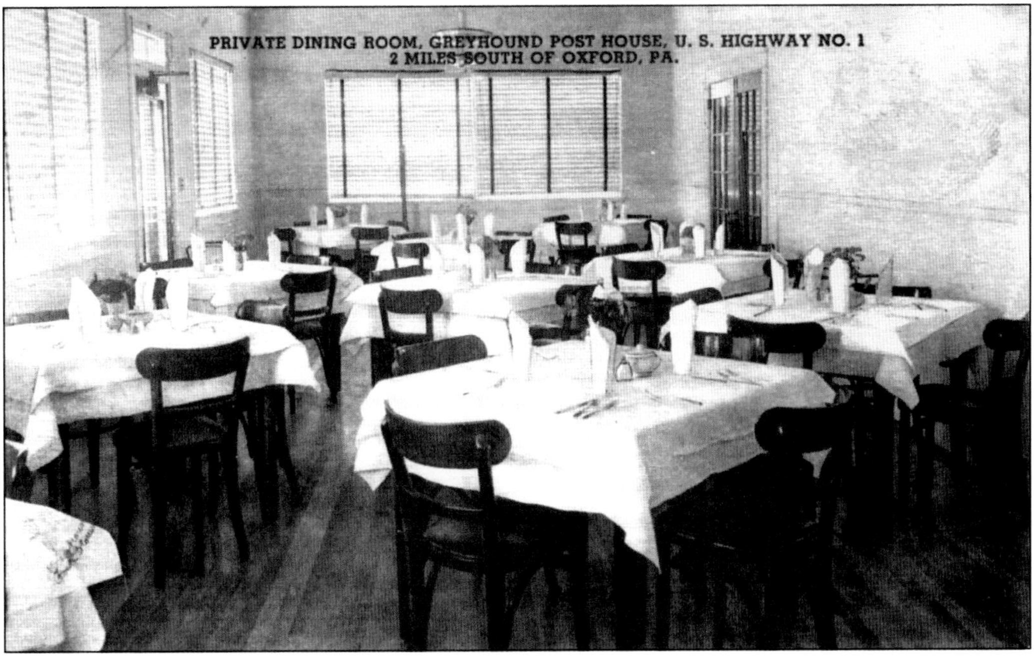

These two 1940s postcards show the private and bus dining rooms in the Post House. During its years of service, the Post House has changed hands many times. From 1946 until 1957, Clarence Samples, Frank McWhoter, and James Brady managed the restaurant. In 1957, it was sold to William Shiflett, who continued on until 1960. At that time, the Post House was sold to Ada Howery. The interior had a bus dining room seating 74 and a private dining room (shown above) that seated 65. An advertisement in 1952 stated that they served 15 complete dinners with a choice of 10 vegetables, and the prices ranged from $1.15 to $1.60 (children's platters at 75¢).

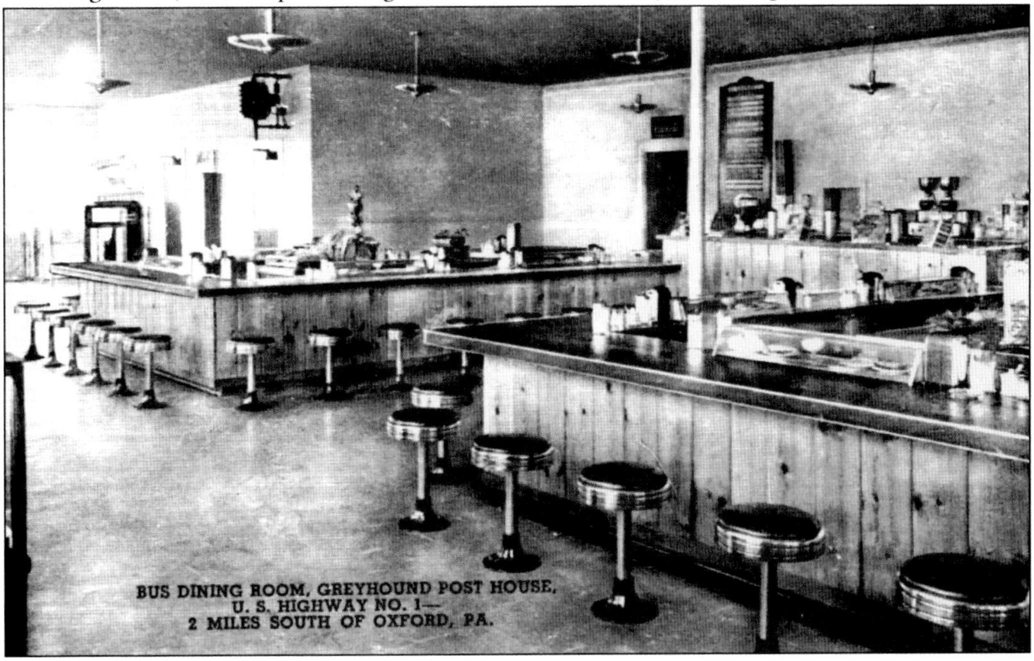

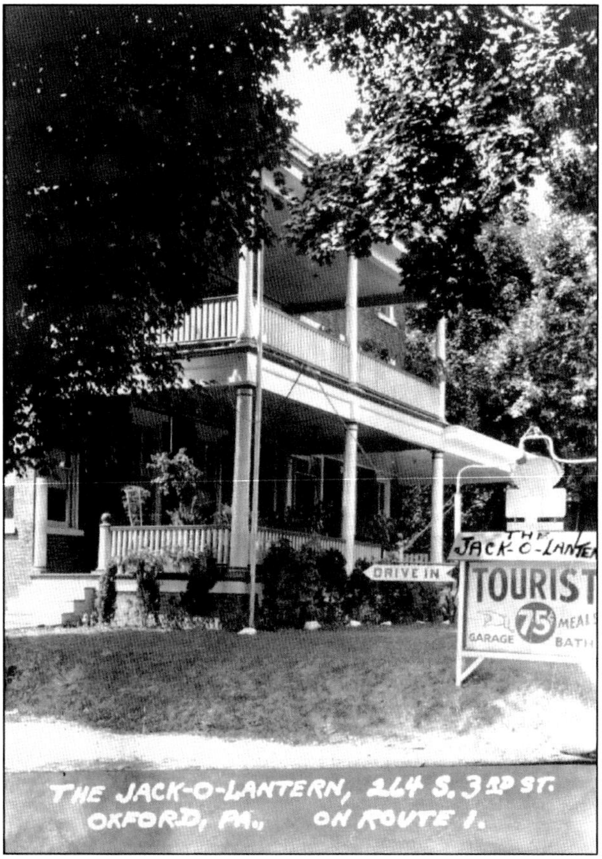

George and Ruth McMichael were the proprietors of the Jack-O-Lantern tourist home located at 264 South Third Street (now No. 276). The McMichaels also owned the Varsity Grille, located across the street. The open house for the Varsity Grille was held in October 1952 and was attended by over 500 people. Guests were served 90 quarts of ice cream, coffee, and doughnuts. The grille room was decorated in chartreuse and gray with booths and a modern counter. The Varsity Grille (seen in the photograph below) is still in operation.

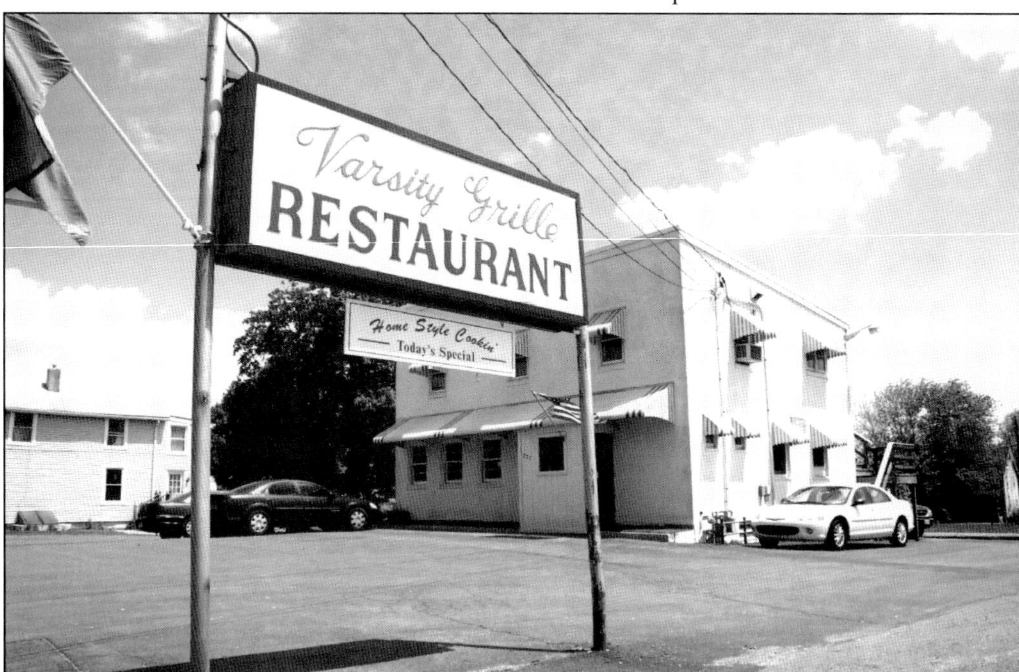

Bill and Flo Shields are shown with their son Dan in this advertising postcard from the 1950s. The Shields owned the Oxford Diner. Flo passed away in 2007 at the age of 99.

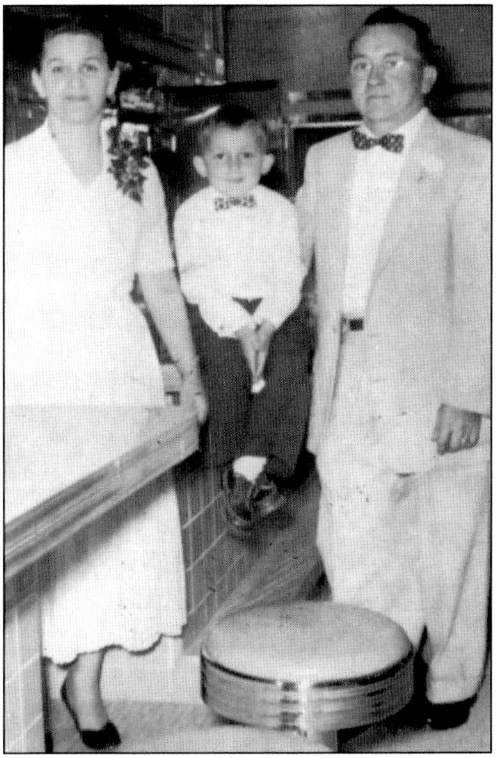

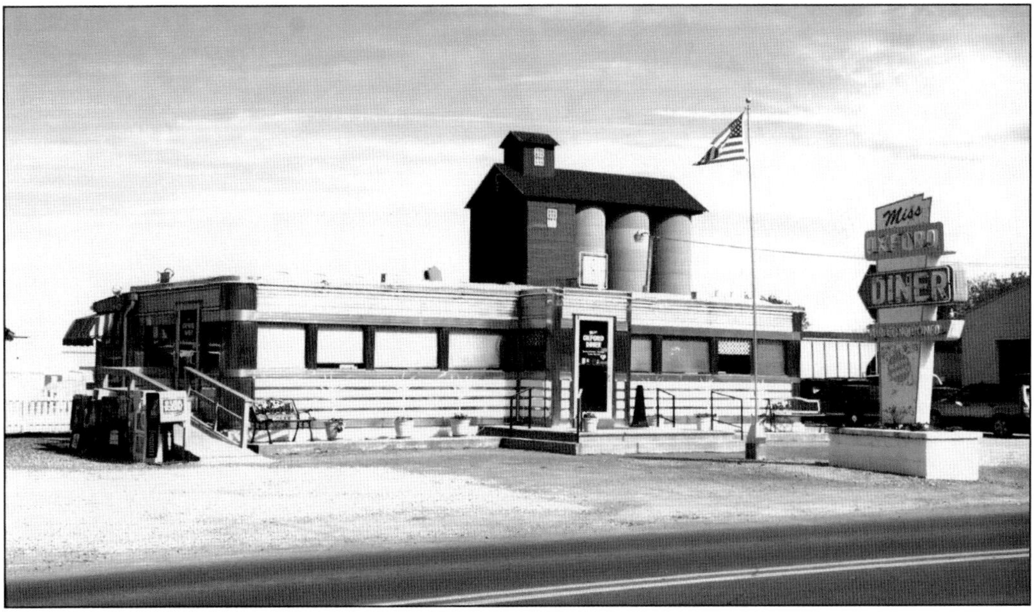

The Shields came to Oxford from Mount Union, Pennsylvania, in 1933, when Bill became manager of the diner, which was then owned by Lawrence Lattimos of Coatesville. In 1941, the Shields purchased the diner. In October 1954, the Shields ordered a new ready-built Silk City diner of stainless steel with a seating capacity for 50. It replaced an earlier diner that had been there since 1933, and they renamed it the Miss Oxford Diner. The diner is still serving food to its many loyal customers. In the background is the old mill.

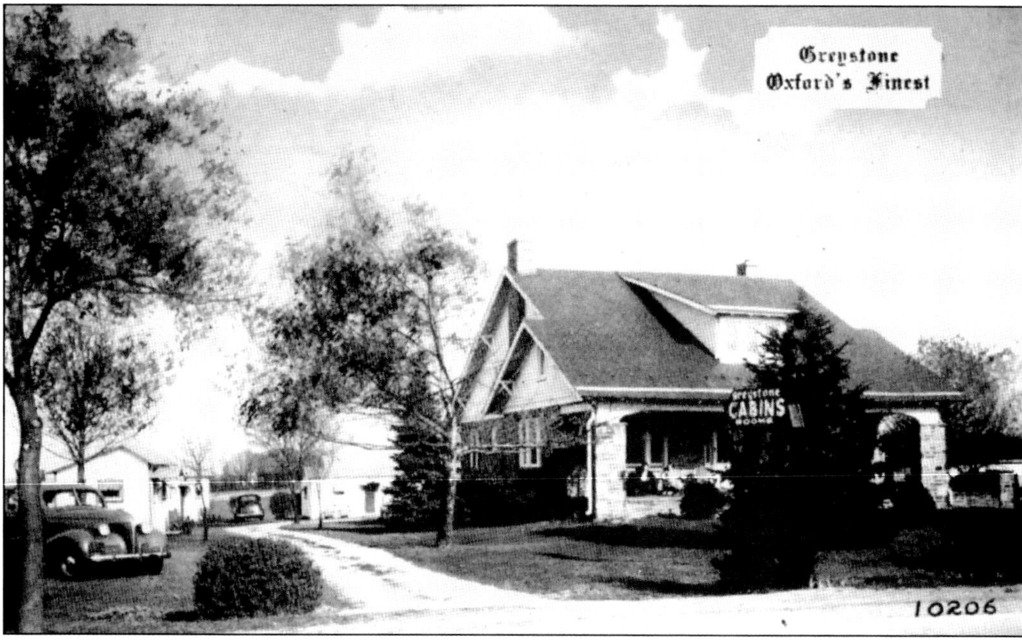

The Greystone Cabins, located at 2203 Old Baltimore Pike, was a tourist home operated by Mr. and Mrs. Howard Shea. Although called Greystone, the facing stone is a light brown color. The home is still in place at the corner of Old Baltimore Pike and Wedgewood Road. This postcard dates from the 1940s.

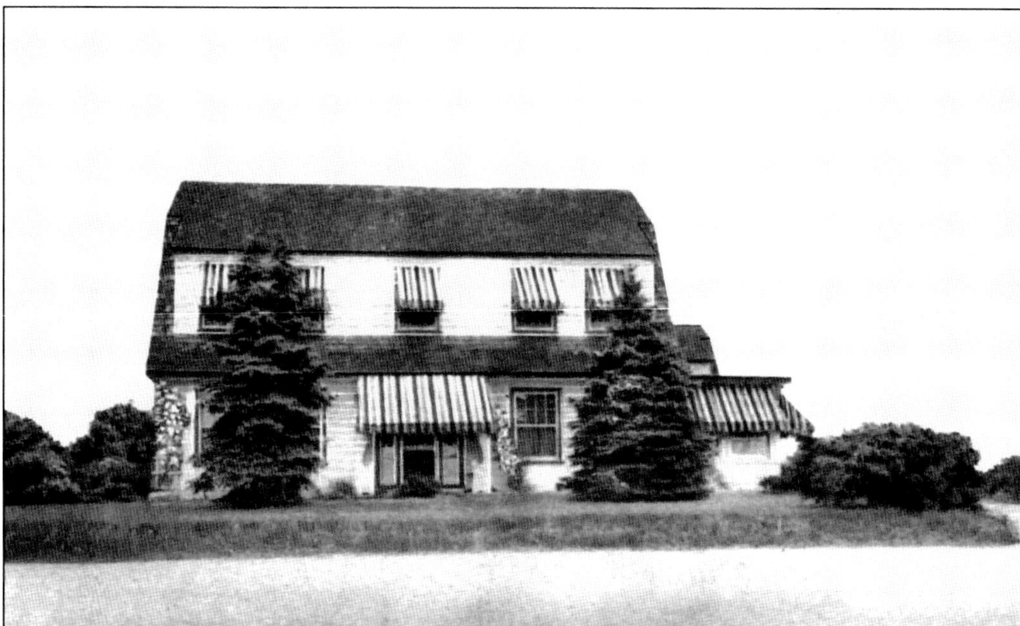

The Cozy Nook was another private residence used for traveling tourists on U.S. 1. It was located a mile south of Oxford and owned by Mrs. Paul Kavanagh. She offered rooms with a bath and breakfast, if desired. Today, it is the office of Dr. Swain-Gray, D.O., located at 2222 Old Baltimore Pike.

Three

COMMUNITY INSTITUTIONS

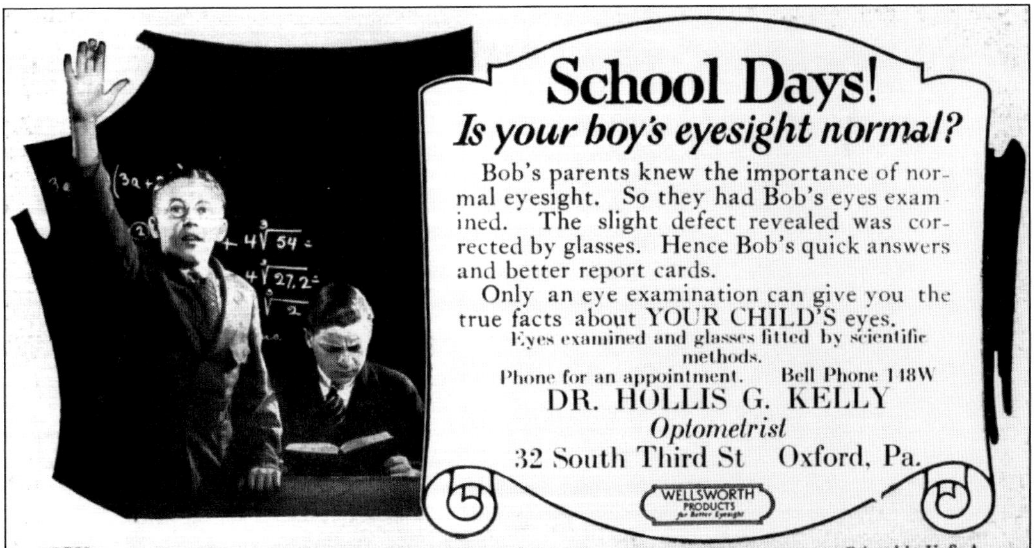

Dr. Hollis G. Kelly (1880–1960), optometrist, distributed this advertising blotter in the 1950s. Dr. Kelly's business was located at 32 South Third Street. Dr. Kelly was a member of several social organizations, including the Pennsylvania State Optometry Association, the Pennsylvania State College of Optometry, and the Union Fire Company.

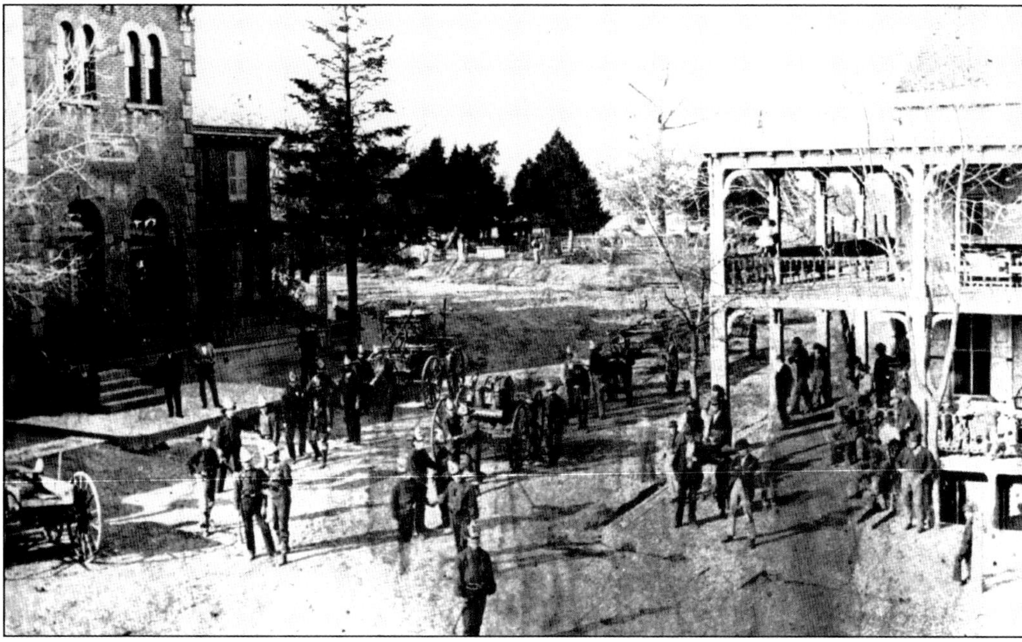

The oldest known photograph of Union Fire Company No. 1's fire equipment is shown in the top 1874 view. The men and their equipment are at the intersection of Market and Third Streets. To the right is the Oxford Hotel and, to the left, the National Bank of Oxford. The National Bank had recently built its two-story facility leaving part of the old country store to the right. The old cemetery and oak tree can be seen in the distance. The bottom photograph dates from 1881 and shows the old firehouse on the corner of South Third and Broad Streets. The fire company was organized on Monday, February 6, 1871, by a group of 21 men meeting in the store of Showalter, Matthews and Company on Third Street. They met "for the purpose of organizing a fire company for the preservation of property in case of fire." The motto of the Union Fire Company is "Prompt To Save With Spirit To Subdue." (Above, courtesy of Union Fire Company No. 1.)

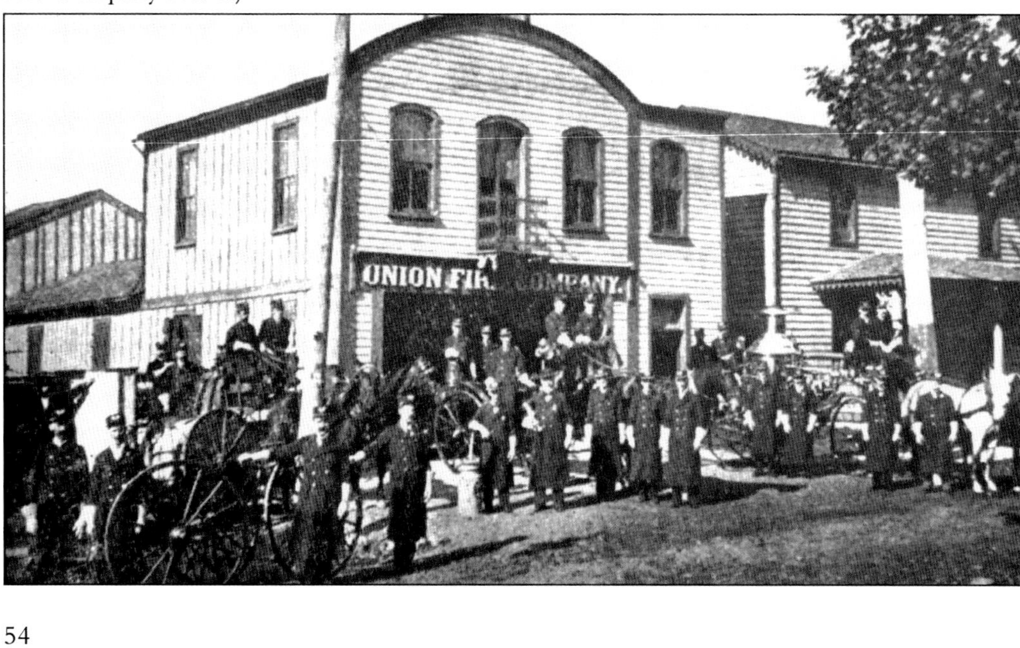

Oxford's Fire Department.

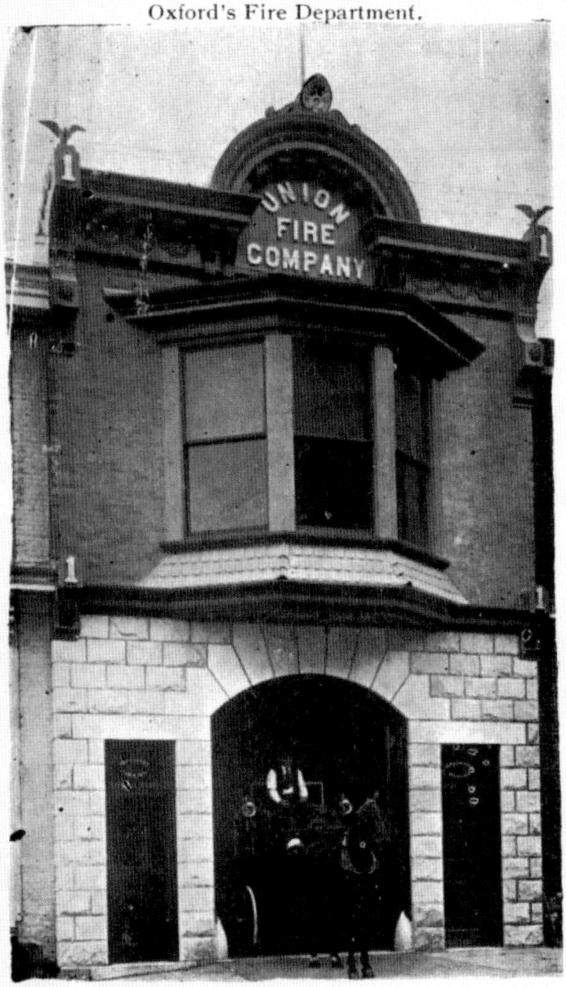

YOURSELF AND FAMILY

are cordially invited to contribute to a postcard surprise, to be tendered Mrs. John Spence, Oxford, Pa., in honor of her birthday. Kindly mail card so as to reach Oxford not later than Saturday, August 10, 1907, so that the cards can be presented to Mrs. Spence on her birthday, August 11.

The Union Fire Company received its charter in 1872. In 1874, a two-story 20-by-50-foot building was constructed at the northwest corner of South Third and Broad Streets on land donated by J. M. Cresson Dickey (1848–1908). Before the construction of the firehouse, equipment was stored in the Oxford Market House (now the site of the Masonic building). The first president and fire chief was George E. Jones. The first real pumper, a Silby steamer, was purchased in 1880 for $3,000. In 1901, the fire department moved to its new home at 324 Market Street, as shown in this postcard. It was a two-story 20-by-100-foot structure with rock marble on the first level, Pompeiian brick on the second story, and capped with a galvanized circle cornice.

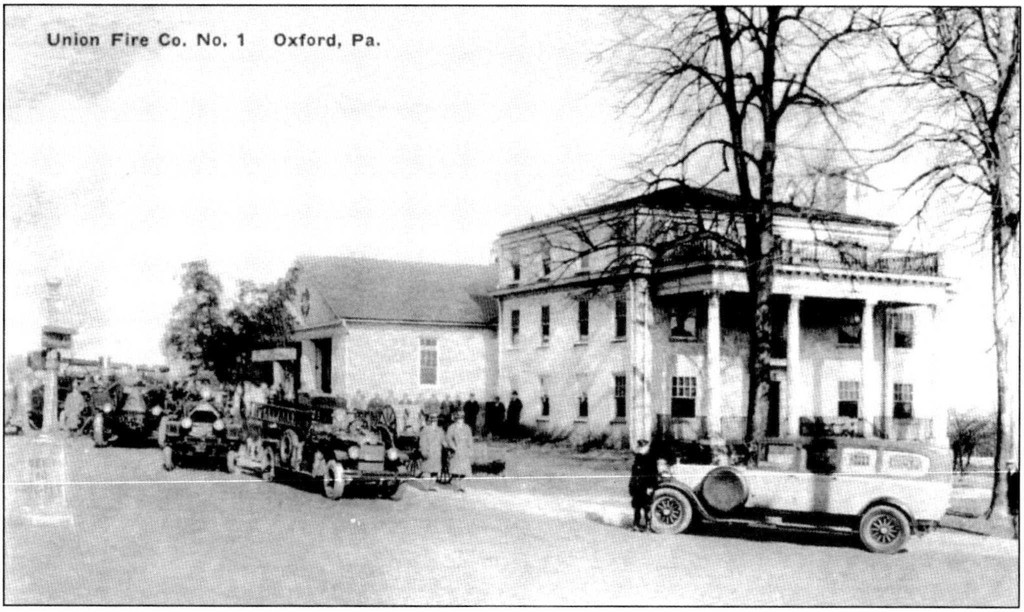

In 1922, the fire department purchased the grounds and three-story Italianate mansion of the Rev. Samuel R. Dickey at 309 Market Streets for $21,000. From 1922 to 1924, the mansion was completely remodeled and an addition constructed. The fire company held a reception and inspection of the new facilities in February 1923. It included piano and vocal solos during the day, a performance by the Oxford Concert Band in the evening, and tearooms on the third floor. In 1977, the mansion was demolished and a new complex erected with only the porch and pillars preserved.

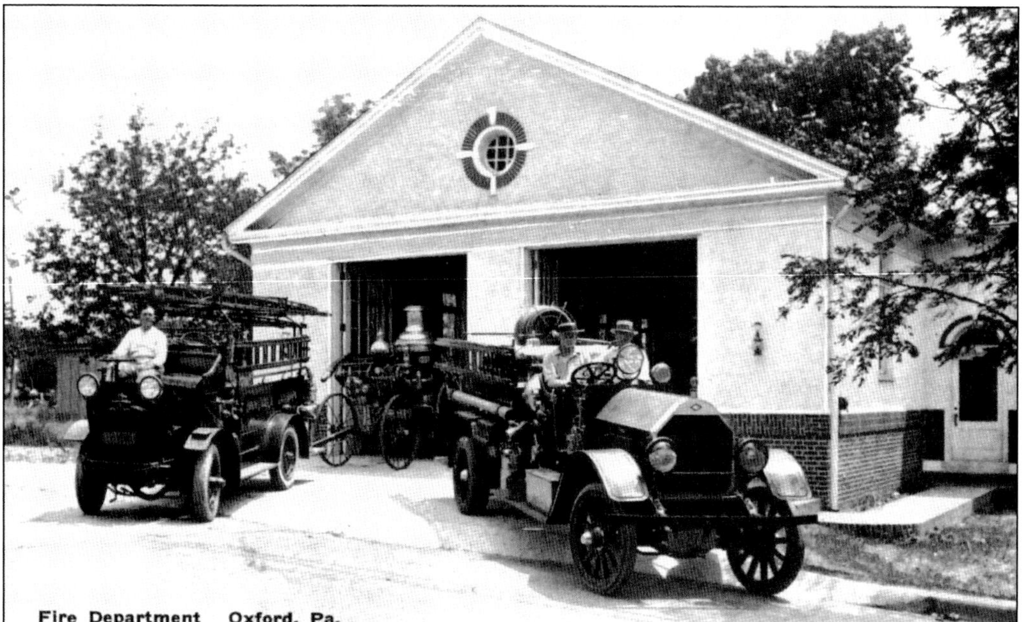

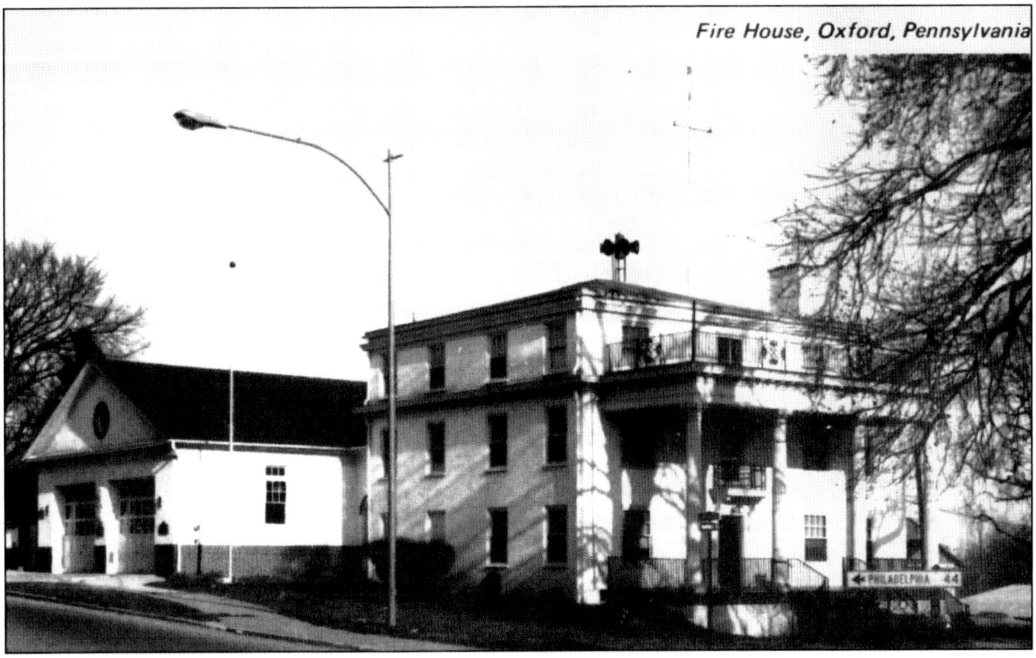

In 1933, "F. G. Wilson gave the company a Willys-Knight automobile, which was turned into a fire chief's car by virtue of putting a bell on the front and a stack of buckets and fire extinguishers on the running boards." Note the sign for Philadelphia—44 miles—in the postcard. At the time, Lincoln Street was U.S. Route 1 going north.

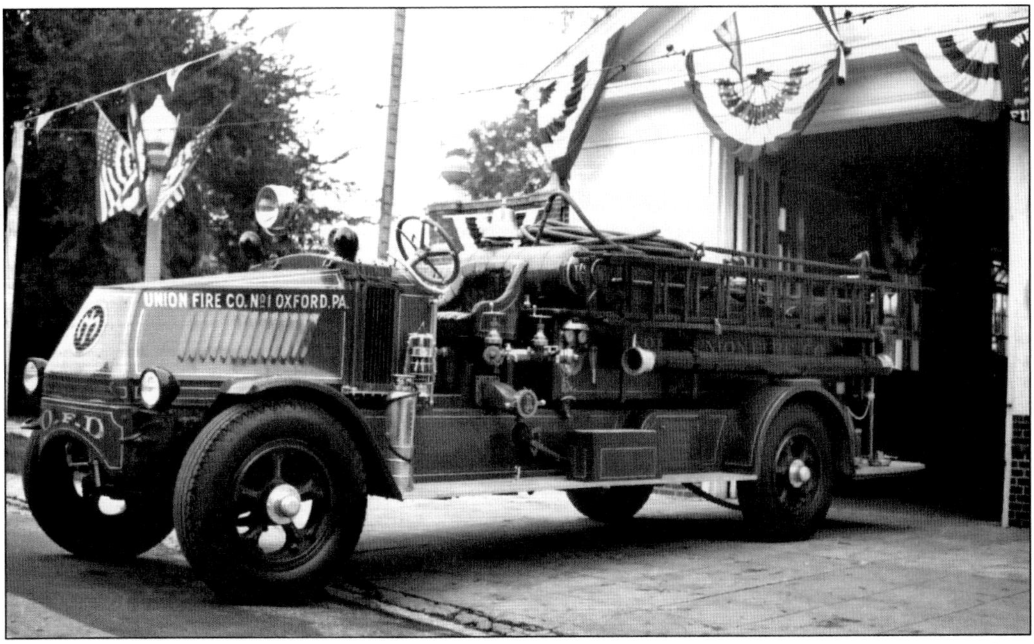

This real-photo postcard shows the 1927 *Bulldog* Mack Pumping Engine. The engine had 157 horsepower and cost $11,000. The pumper was purchased from the Mack Truck Company of New York City with part of the receipts from the 1927 firemen's carnival. The engine was presented to the public on October 20, 1927.

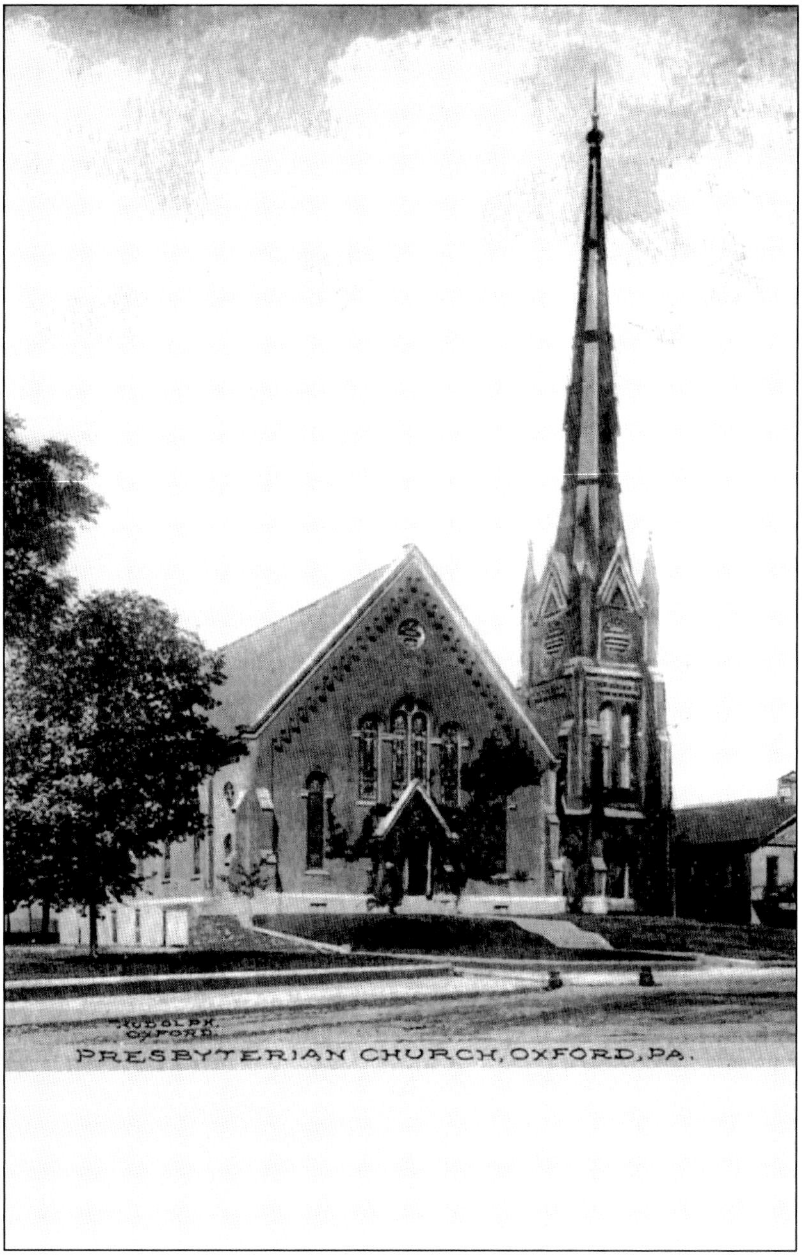

The Presbyterian Church in Oxford was organized on October 27, 1754, under the direction of Rev. Alexander Géllatly, the first pastor. The first church (known as the Sessions House) was built of log and situated on the green at Third and Pine Streets. A brick building was constructed on the same site about 1796. In 1833, another brick church was built on the site of the future 1866 church and enlarged between 1850 and 1852. In 1865, the 1833 brick church was demolished when construction began on a new sanctuary. The imposing neo-Gothic brick church was dedicated on September 13, 1866, when Rev. Frank B. Hodge (1863–1868) was pastor. The 100-by-55-foot church had a spire of 162 feet and cost $35,000. The church was also incorporated in 1866. The most famous ministers of the 19th century were Rev. Ebenezer Dickey (1796–1831) and his son Rev. John Miller Dickey (1831–1856).

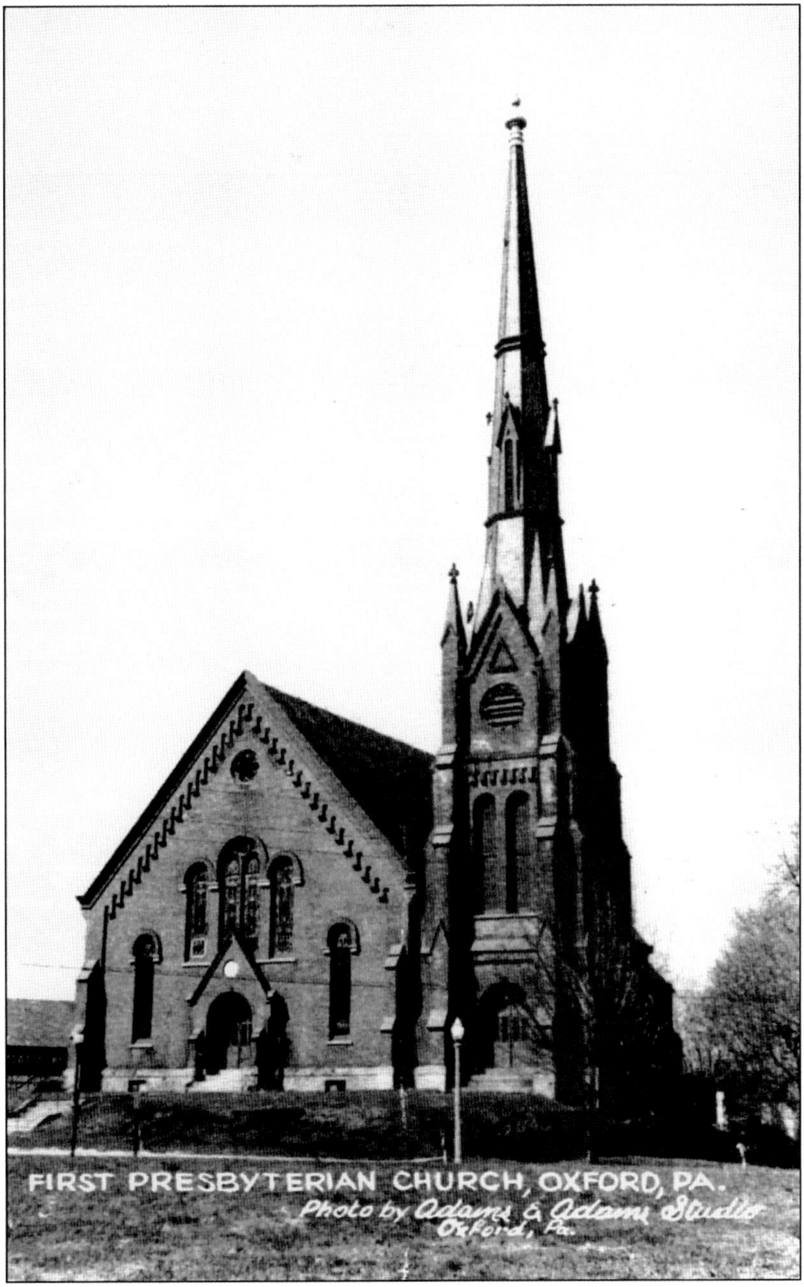

A new bell from Baltimore was installed (known as the "Belle of Baltimore") in 1875. In 1885, a new three-story brick parsonage was completed, with the contract going to Abner E. Stiner of Kennett Square. A pulpit and a large pipe organ, built for the church by Johnson and Son, were installed by January 1897. An opening ceremony was held on February 19, 1897, with Prof. D. D. Wood, a renowned organist from Philadelphia; Miss M. B. Wilson, the church organist; and a choir and soprano soloist. A six-alarm fire struck the church on May 28, 1989. Damages were severe, with 100 firemen from 15 departments attending. The structure was demolished in 1990, and a new sanctuary was constructed shortly afterward. Fortunately, the tower and steeple were saved.

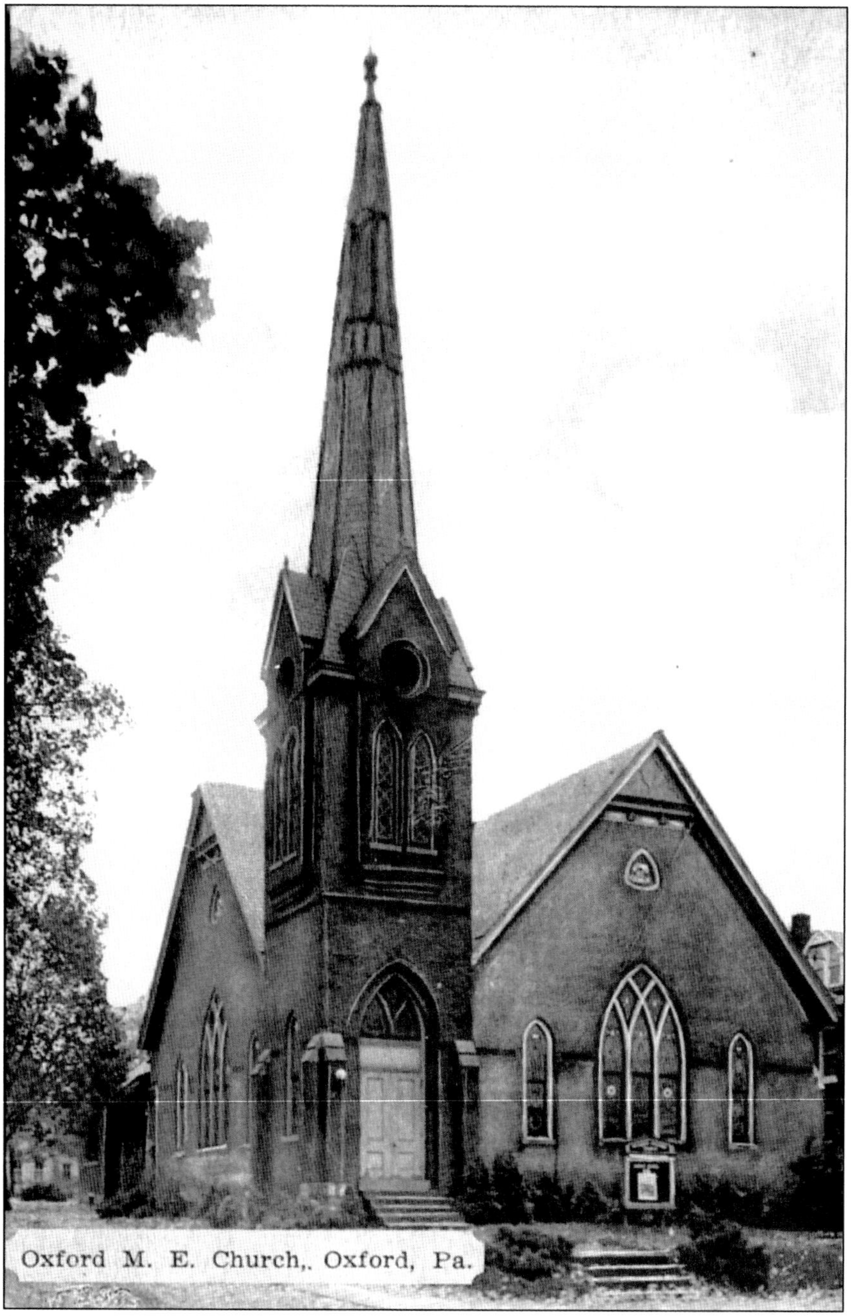

The Methodists have been in Oxford since the 1820–1830 period. Early in 1851, 20 members gathered and established a church under the direction of Rev. Jonas Bissey (1809–1851). They purchased a lot on South Third Street and constructed a one-story 40-by-60-foot brick church. Rev. Francis B. Hodgson (1805–1871) of the Philadelphia Annual Conference dedicated the new church. Reverend Bissey died in the pulpit while giving a sermon on August 17, 1851. By the early 1880s, the church was no longer adequate for the congregation's needs, so a 60-by-200-foot lot at the corner of Market and Addison Streets was purchased. An adjoining lot of 50 by 185 feet was also purchased for a hitching ground.

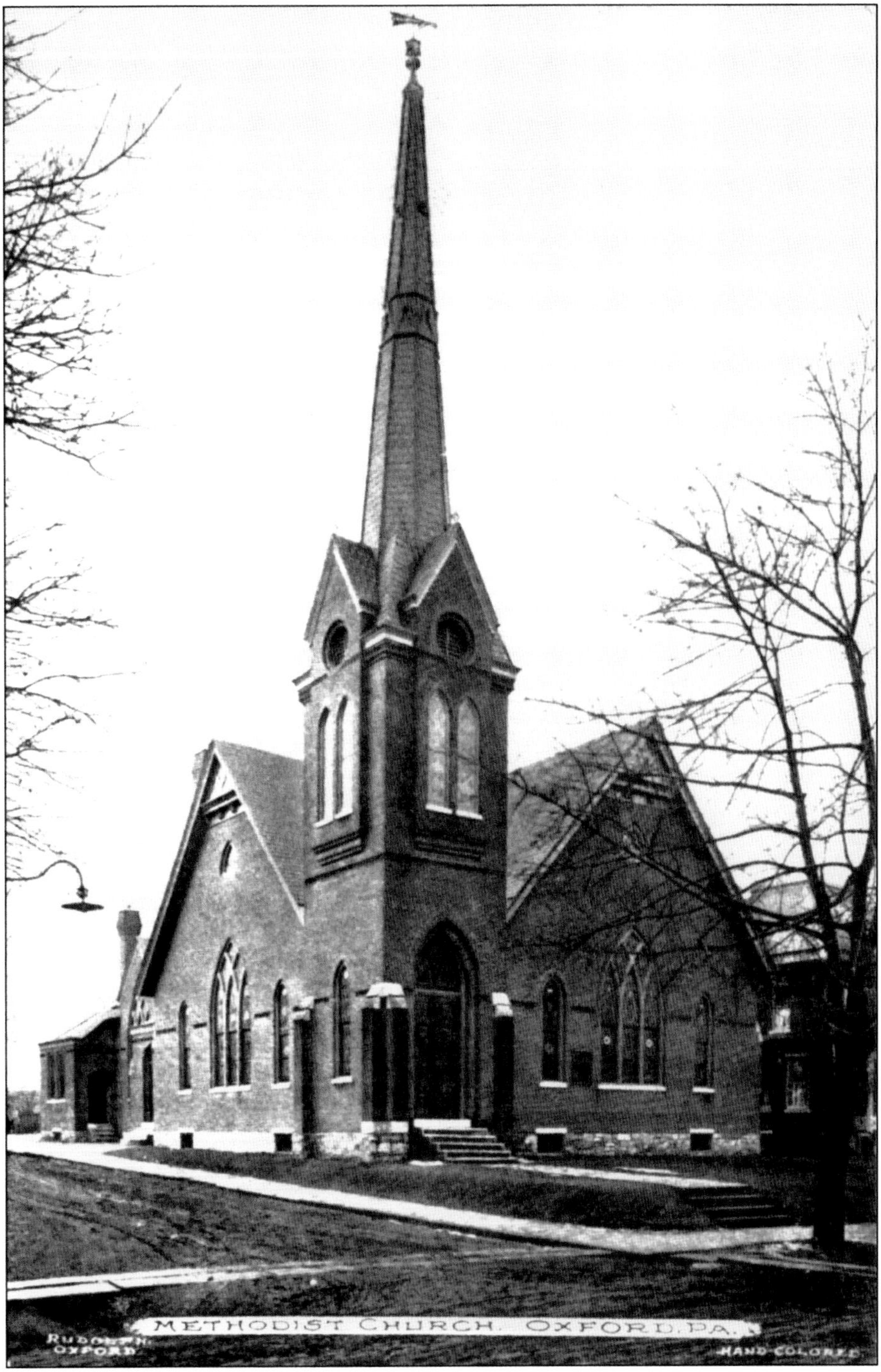

On August 20, 1885, a cornerstone was laid for the new brick and stone church. On March 7, 1886, the facility was dedicated under the auspices of Elders William Swindells and William Banford. Membership at the time was 185. Milton Walker of Oxford was the contractor for this project. On February 28, 1904, when Rev. N. B. Master was pastor, the church was able to burn its mortgage. The South Third Street church was then sold to the Baptists.

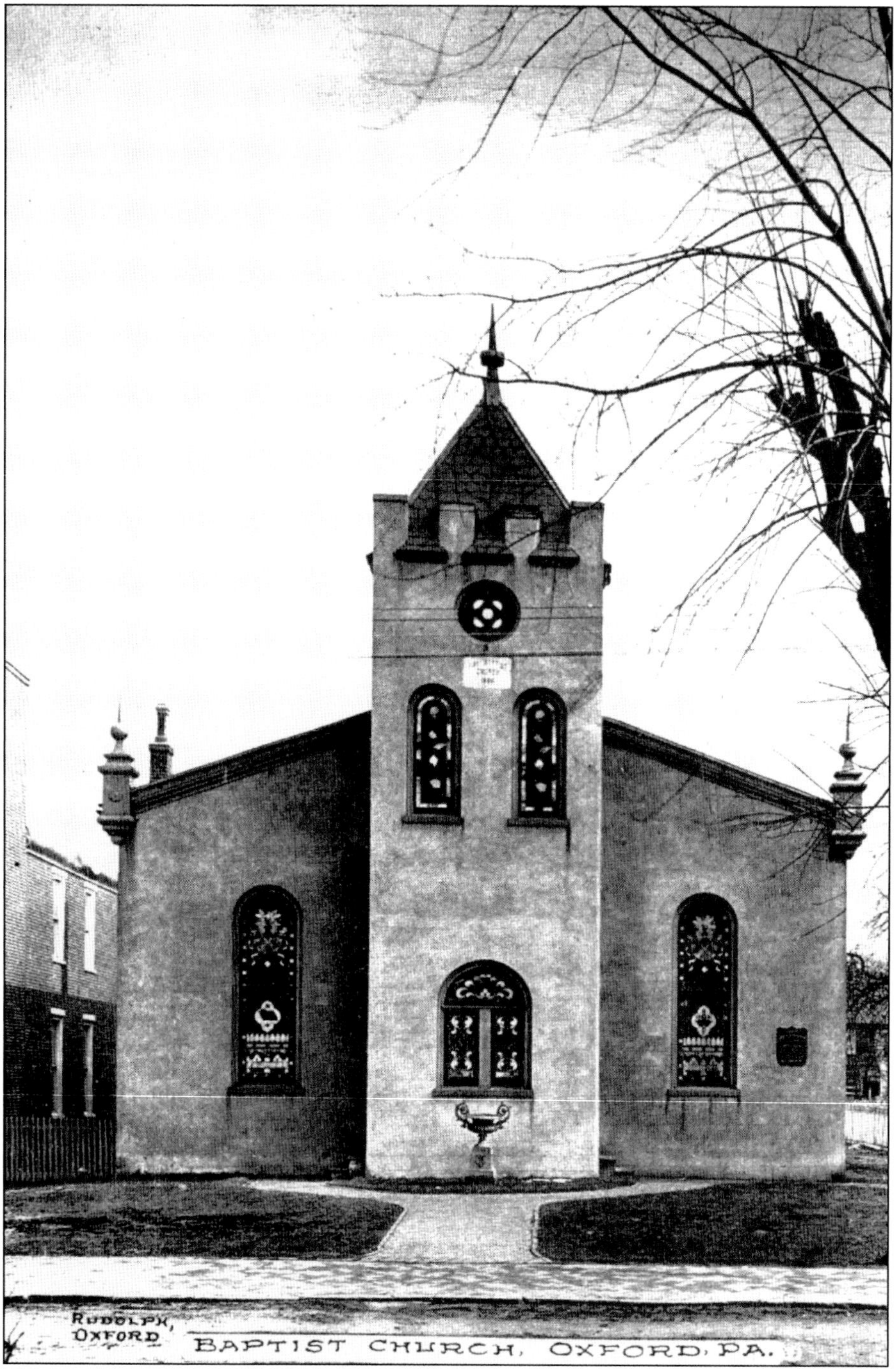

The Baptists purchased this facility on South Third Street from the Methodists in 1851 for $2,475. In November 1895, the building was improved with the addition of new pews and an enlarged vestibule and tower with two doors. By 1906, the church was serviced with electricity. Church services were held in this building until 1926, at which time the church purchased the United Presbyterian Church on the corner of Sixth and Addison Streets. The old 1851 structure was later incorporated into a commercial store.

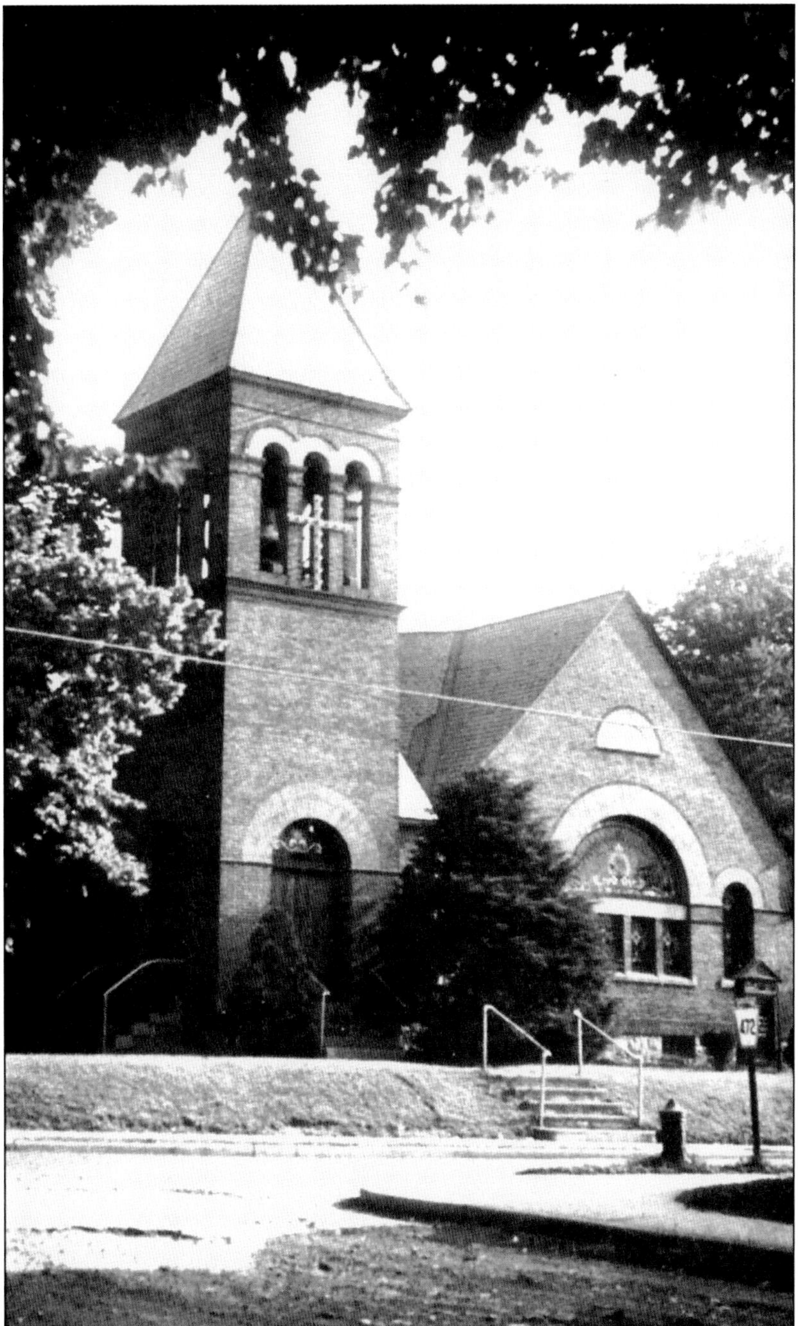

The United Presbyterian Church was formed after a split with the Presbyterians. In 1851, a small brick church was constructed at Sixth and Addison Streets for $3,000 with Thomas Sloan as contractor and Richard McDonald doing the brickwork. On August 18, 1893, the cornerstone of a new facility was laid. Milton Walker had the contract to build the brick church. It cost under $12,000, had a slate roof, and seated 500. The beautiful new church building was dedicated on Sunday, March 11, 1894, with Rev. C. H. Robinson of Baltimore giving the address. On January 7, 1927, the building was rededicated as a Baptist church.

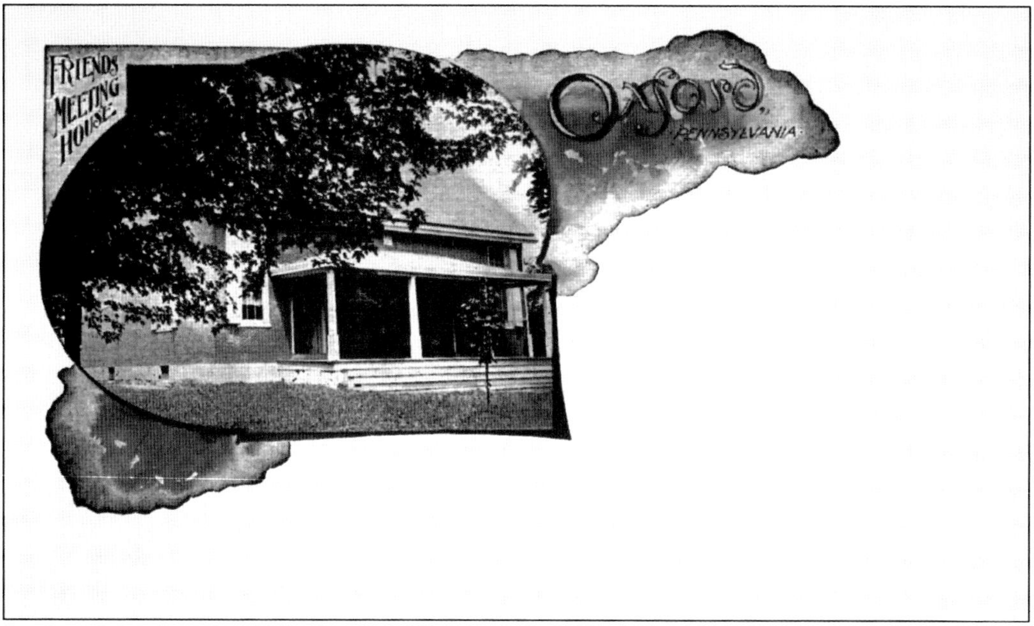

The first meeting of Friends was held in the home of George B. and Elizabeth B. Passmore on June 4, 1876. For several years thereafter, meetings continued to be held in the homes of members. By 1879, a Hicksite meetinghouse had been constructed on South Third Street at a cost of $2,357.76. The lot was 200 by 300 feet, with half being donated by Dr. J. M. Dickey and the other half purchased for $500. Joseph B. Bonsall of Elk Township did the brickwork, and Luke Oswald of Oxford did the carpentry. The first meeting was held on November 9, 1879. In September 1881, a school was opened with Arthur H. Tomlinson as principal. In 1906, an iron fence was added around the property, and, in 1909, a Young Friends' Association was organized.

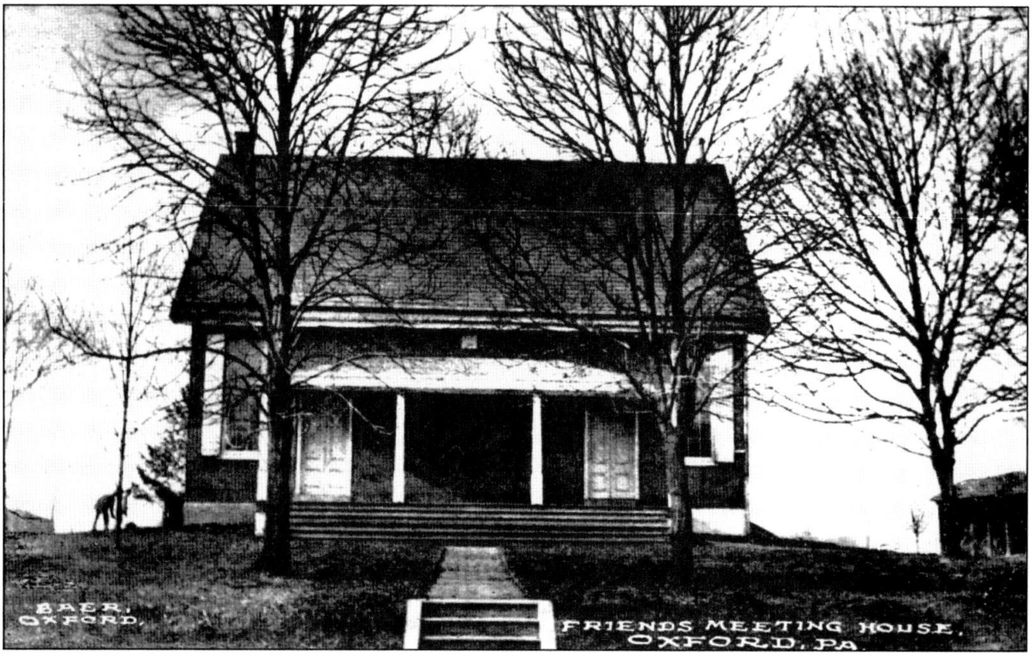

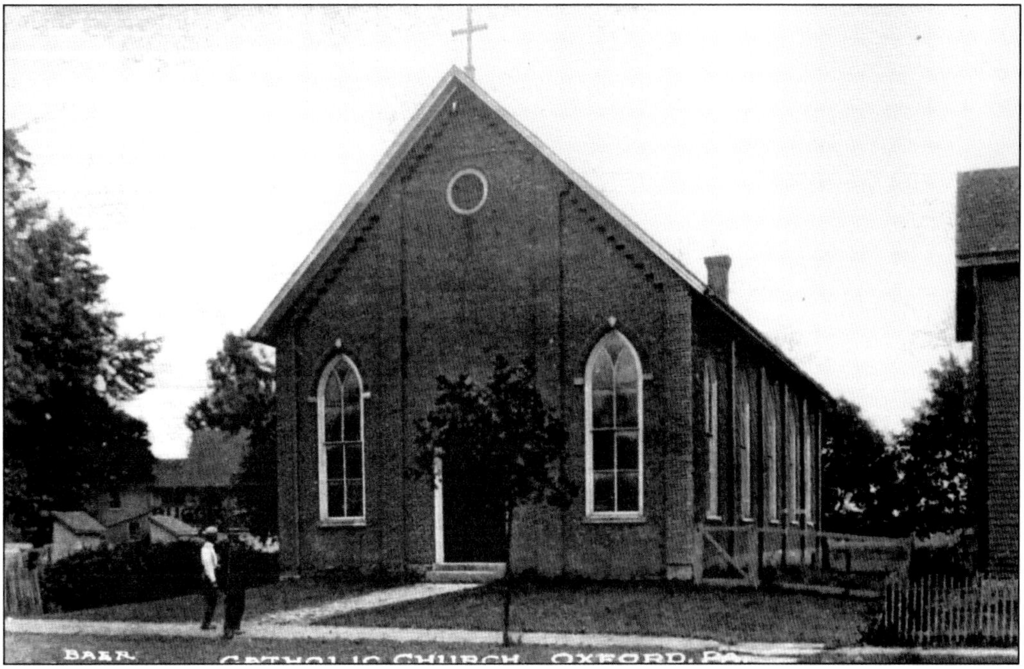

The Catholic Church acquired a lot on Broad Street near Fifth Street that was donated by D. Timoney. The cornerstone of the church of the Sacred Heart was laid on August 1, 1877. The brick 36-by-70-foot building had a stone foundation and a slate roof. The contractors were George E. Jones and Milton Walker of Oxford, with masonry work by George Curry. Father James F. Kelly of West Grove and Father Kallen of Baltimore held the first Latin services on July 29, 1877. The church moved to a new facility on Limestone Road in 1983. The Community Bible Fellowship is now using the Broad Street structure.

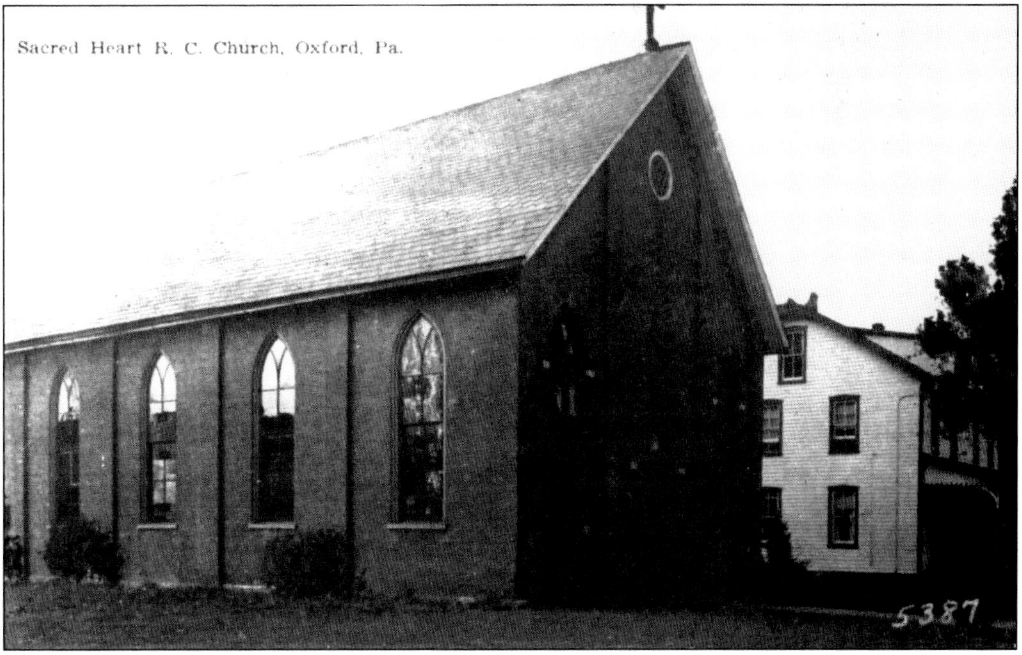

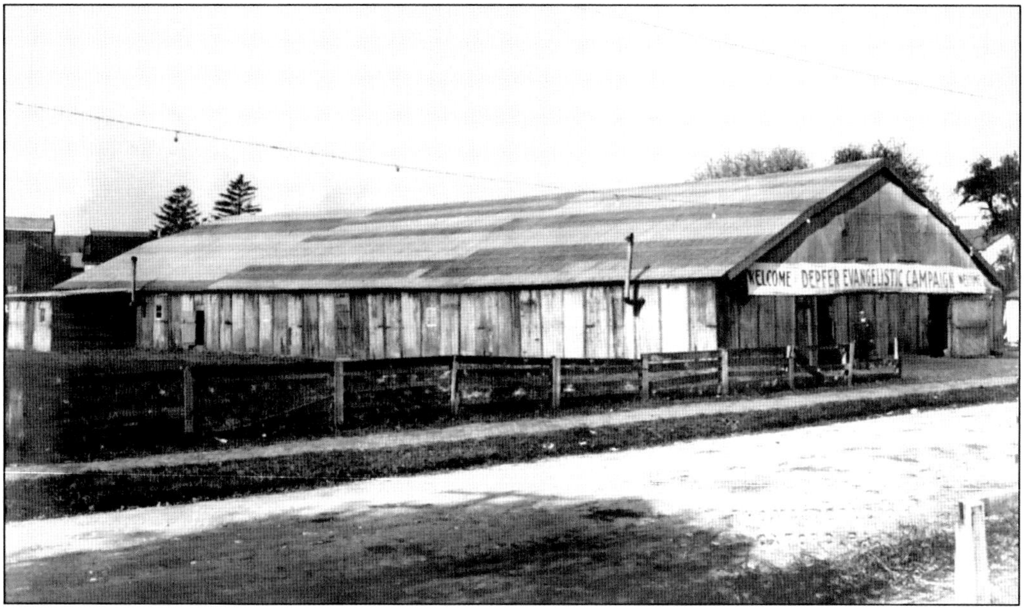

Little is known about these two real-photo postcards dating from 1907–1912 (the bottom produced by Dora E. Thomas). The banner over the front door of the building in the top postcard reads, "Welcome Depfer Evangelistic Campaign Welcome." A September 1902 newspaper article mentions that evangelist Rev. J. B. Ellison would be conducting an impressive service with music and a male choir in Oxford Park (located near the railroad tracks at Mount Pleasant Road and South Third Street). His preaching included a sermon on "The Home Prepared for You." According to research done by John T. Bradley, Rev. H. A. Depfer gave an "evangelistic address" at Lincoln University in 1916. During this period of religious fervor, such evangelistic services were common throughout the United States, and there is no doubt that Reverend Depfer also preached in Oxford.

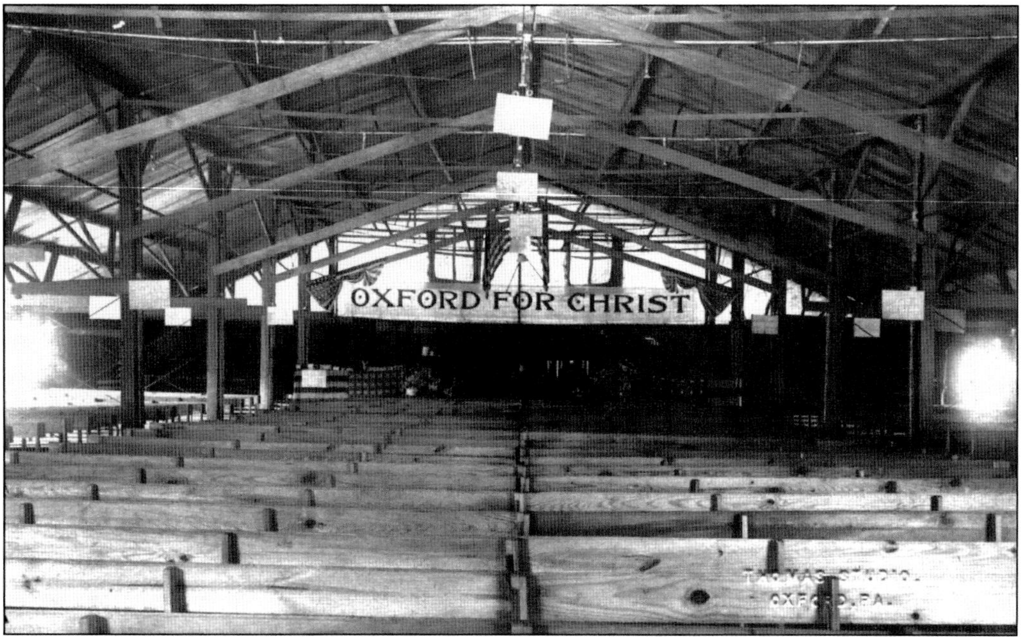

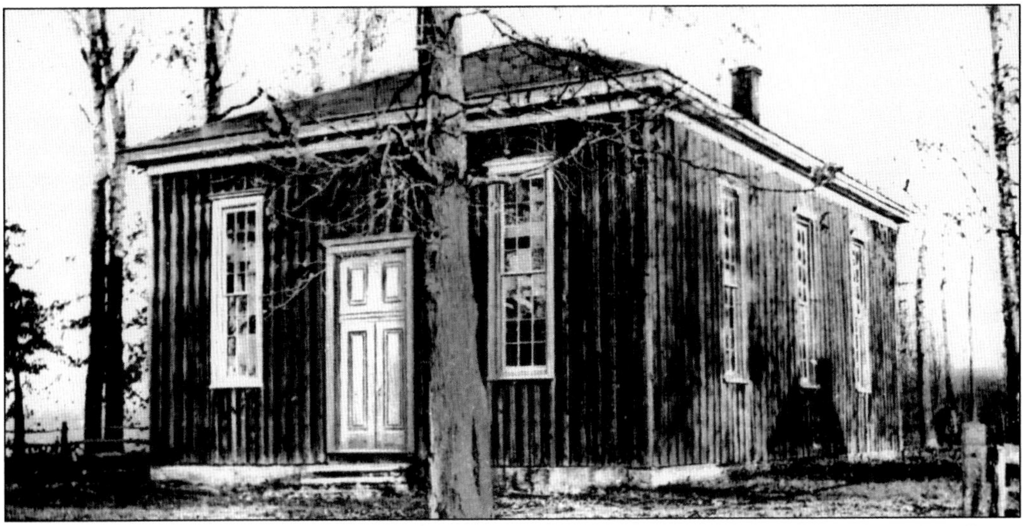

Originally located on Bethel Road not far from Roney's Corner, the "Old Bethel" chapel was built in 1833. During the winter of 1859–1860, a second building was constructed. Old materials and slate roofing obtained from Peach Bottom were used. The chapel was torn down in 1907, and a new church building (as shown above) was dedicated on August 25, 1907. In March 1942, the church was sold to Mr. and Mrs. Harry Senderling, who had the building moved to their property nearby on Bethel Road. After sitting vacant for several years, it was rented to another church group.

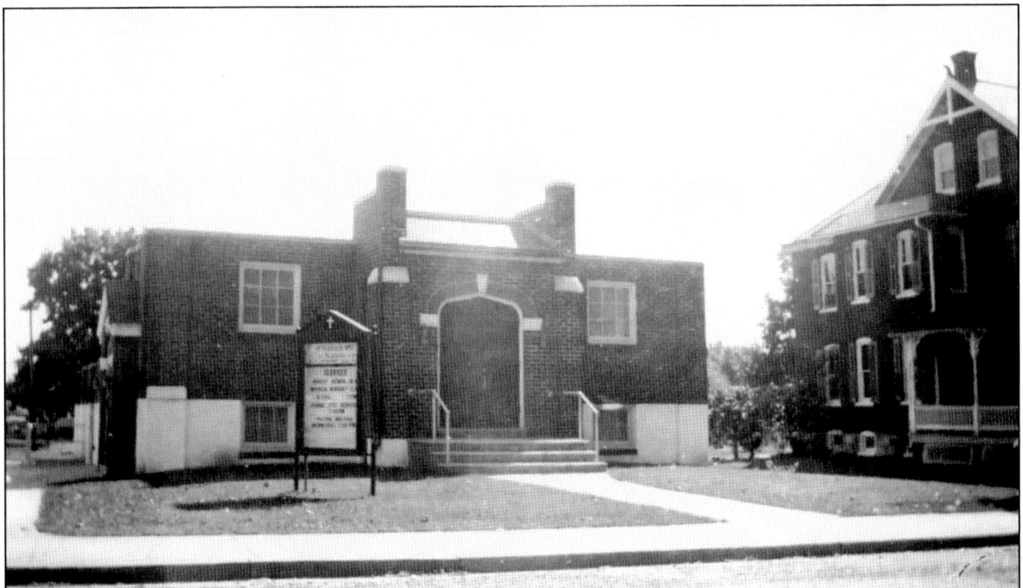

This rare early-1940s real-photo postcard shows the Church of the Nazarene located on the corner of Locust Street and Penn Avenue. On September 2, 1929, the church was organized under Rev. J. T. Maybury, with Rev. George W. Andrews as the first pastor. In the beginning, the congregation met in various places. Work began on a church in 1941, with only a basement structure completed. The semi-completed church (seen here) was dedicated on August 23, 1942, with services held in the completed redbrick church on Easter afternoon, April 4, 1948, under Rev. Arthur C. McKenzie, pastor.

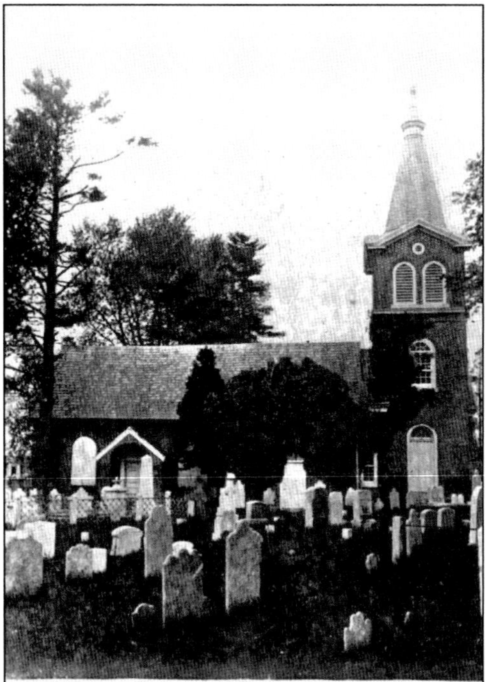

TRINITY CHURCH, OXFORD, PA.

Although once attributed to Bethel Road, Oxford, the 18th-century Trinity Episcopal Church is actually located at 6901 Rising Sun Avenue in Philadelphia. Nevertheless, the 1860 and 1873 Chester County maps do show an "African Church" on Bethel Road. Known as the Calvary American Methodist Episcopal Church, it was constructed in 1852 on ground donated by Rev. Henry Jones. Bishop Payne, along with the first pastor, Reverend Herbert of Baltimore, dedicated this early African American church. In August 1892, church members held a 40th anniversary celebration in Johnson's Grove opposite the church. Former Maryland slave Thomas Spencer Myers (1822–1904) is buried in the old cemetery that still remains today. Myers was a skilled veterinarian and employed by Dr. D. W. Hutchinson.

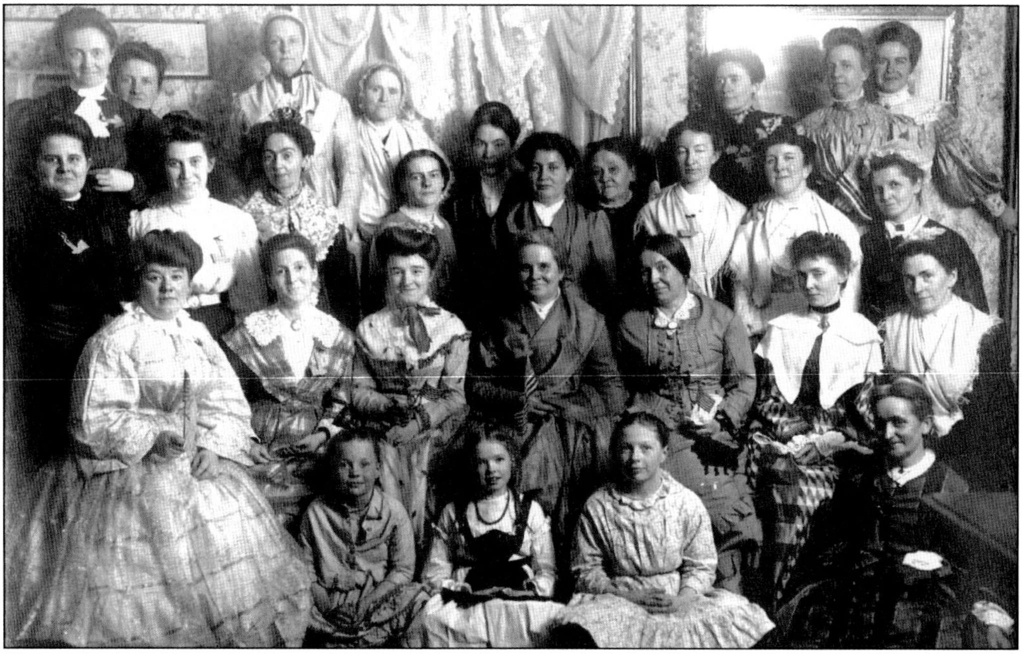

The International Order of the King's Daughters and Sons was founded on January 13, 1886. It is still a vital organization today, being an international and interdenominational organization of Christian men and women whose slogan is "Look up not down, Look forward not back, Look out not in, Lend a hand." This *c.* 1900 photograph shows a group of the Oxford King's Daughters. It includes many members of the Pugh family as well as ladies named Kirk, Wright, Passmore, Reynolds, and others.

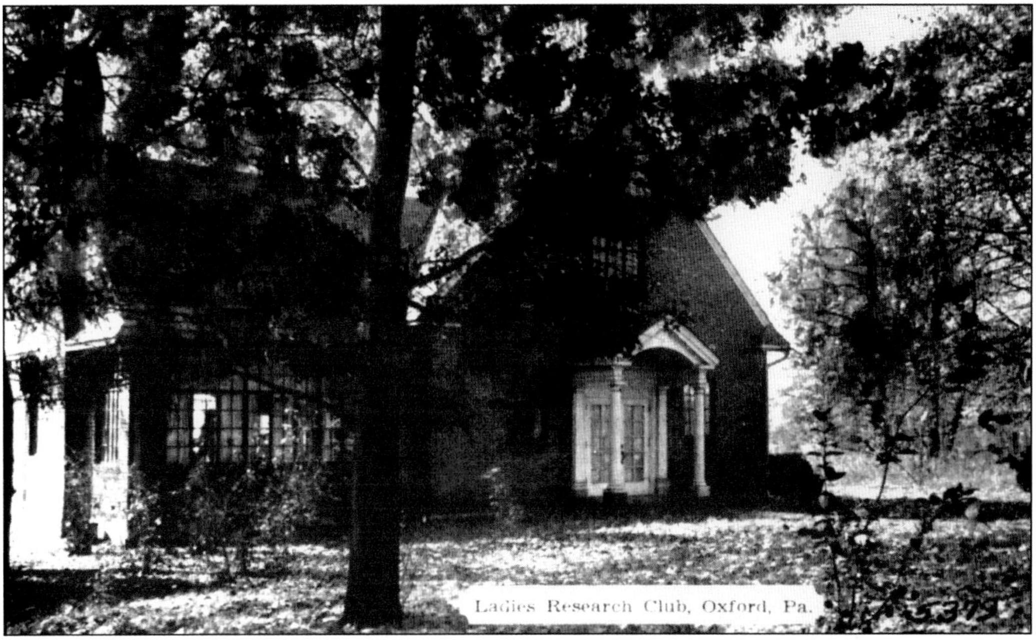

Several ladies' social clubs existed in Oxford before 1879, one of which was called the Research Club of Oxford. In 1891–1892, Dr. Ella S. Webb organized a travel club, and by 1893–1894, it was reorganized as a literary and civic organization. In 1905, Mrs. J. M. Cresson Dickey was president. The organization built a new clubhouse on Locust Street in 1929. The old Research Club building is now the Oxford Senior Center.

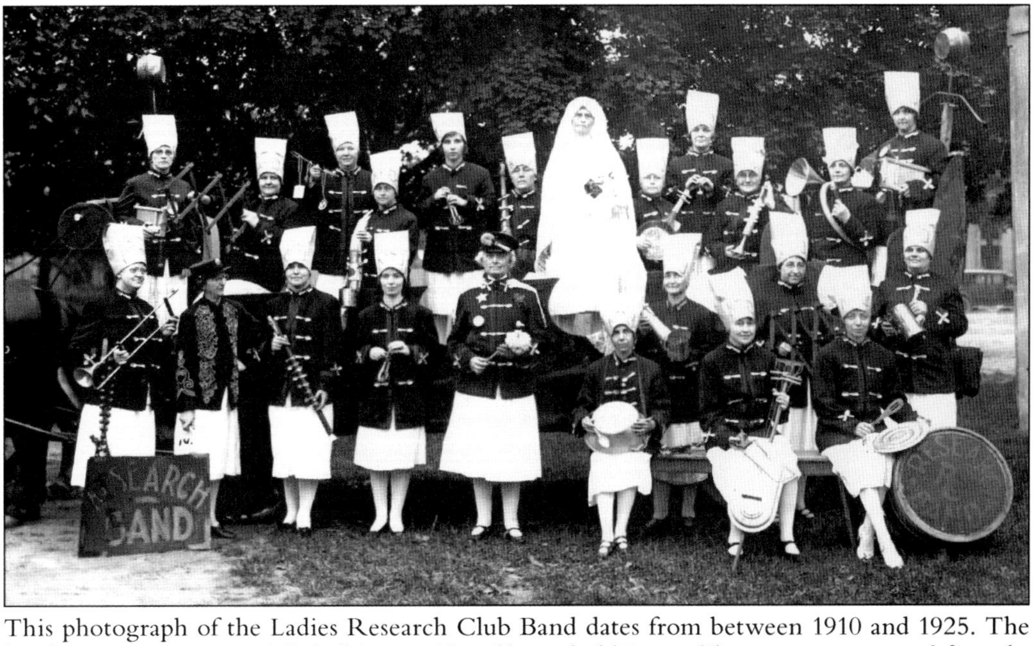

This photograph of the Ladies Research Club Band dates from between 1910 and 1925. The band instruments are a delightful assembly of household items, like spoons, pans, and funnels. Note the decorative spoons on their uniforms and the hats made from paper bags. (Courtesy of the Chester County Historical Society.)

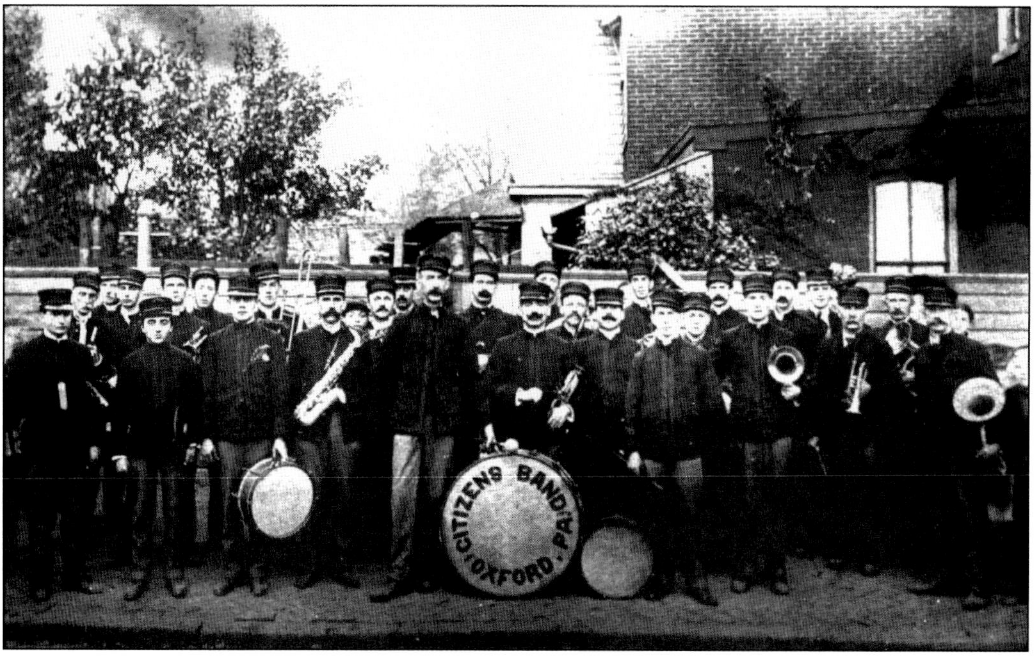

The Oxford Citizens Band was formed in 1894 when it merged with the Citizens' Brass Band of Oxford, which was formed before 1879. In 1905, the band was reorganized with president Samuel J. Janney, leader Joseph E. Johnson, treasurer Garrett E. Johnson, and assistant leader G. F. Collins. In 1916, the band moved to new quarters over Brown and Caldwell's meat store on Market Street, with Clarence Samples as director.

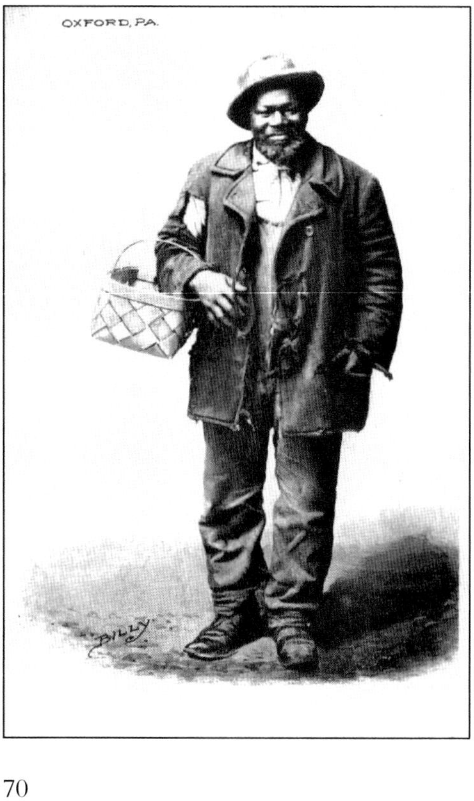

Billy was a well-known figure around town at the beginning of the 20th century. He sold produce by going door-to-door with his characteristic basket. George M. Rudolph published this postcard in 1904.

In 1910, Franklin Emig sold the old Gem movie theater to Joseph G. Crowl. Crowl built a new 36-by-100-foot brick and concrete theater on the site. Opening night of the Oxford movie theater was on September 7, 1911. The theater sign reads, "Censored Pictures and Photoplay Theater." The movie showing at the time of this 1912 real-photo postcard below was a western, *The Oath of His Office*, a silent film directed and starring Gilbert M. "Broncho Billy" Anderson (1880–1971). The poster of coming attractions advertises *Lost Three Hours*, a comedy starring Augustus Phillips. The building was torn down in 1922, and another theater was built elsewhere. Wilson's Garage on South Third Street distributed the advertising postcard on the right; it also included a picture of a famous movie star on the verso. The theater was also known as the Oxford Opera House.

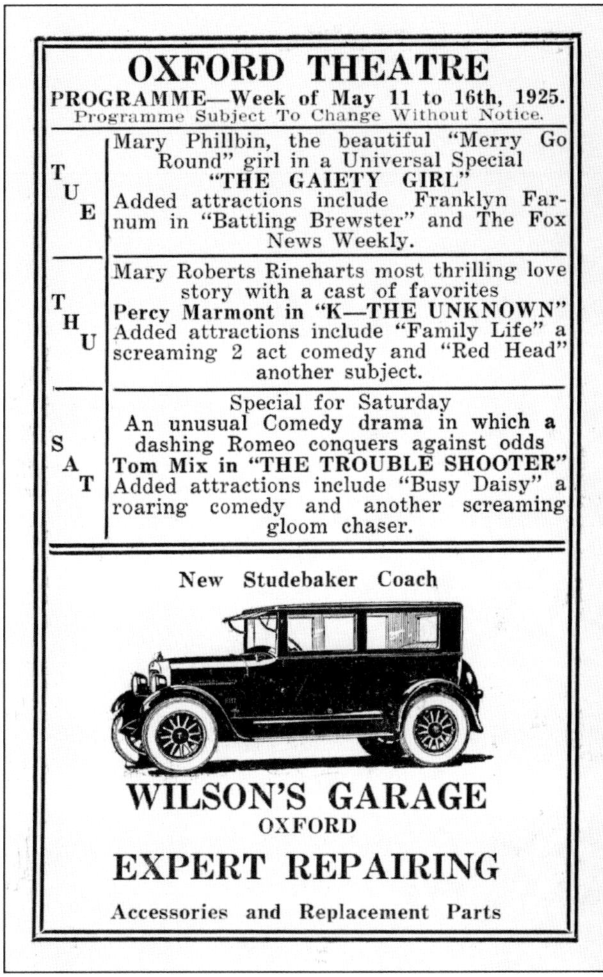

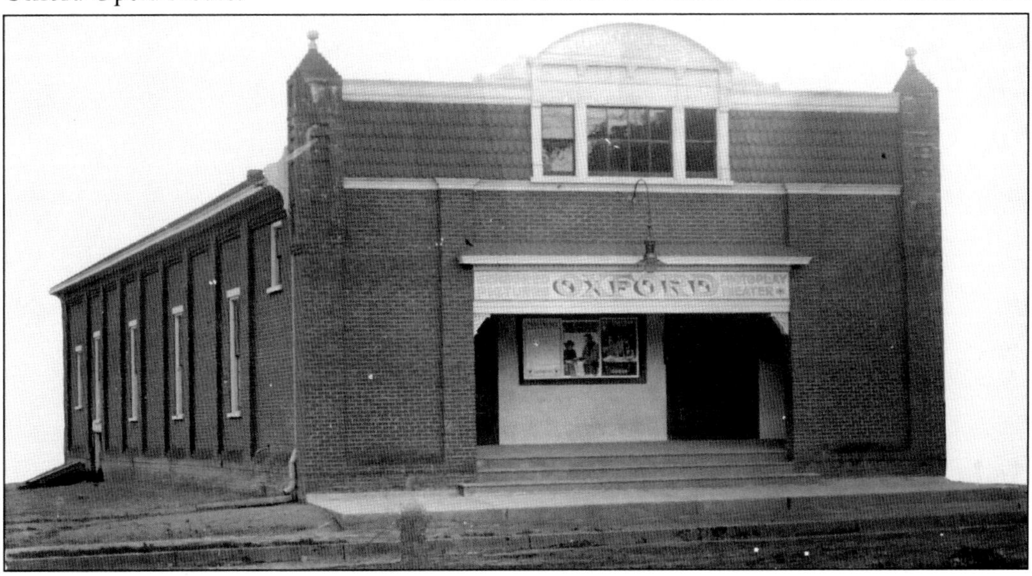

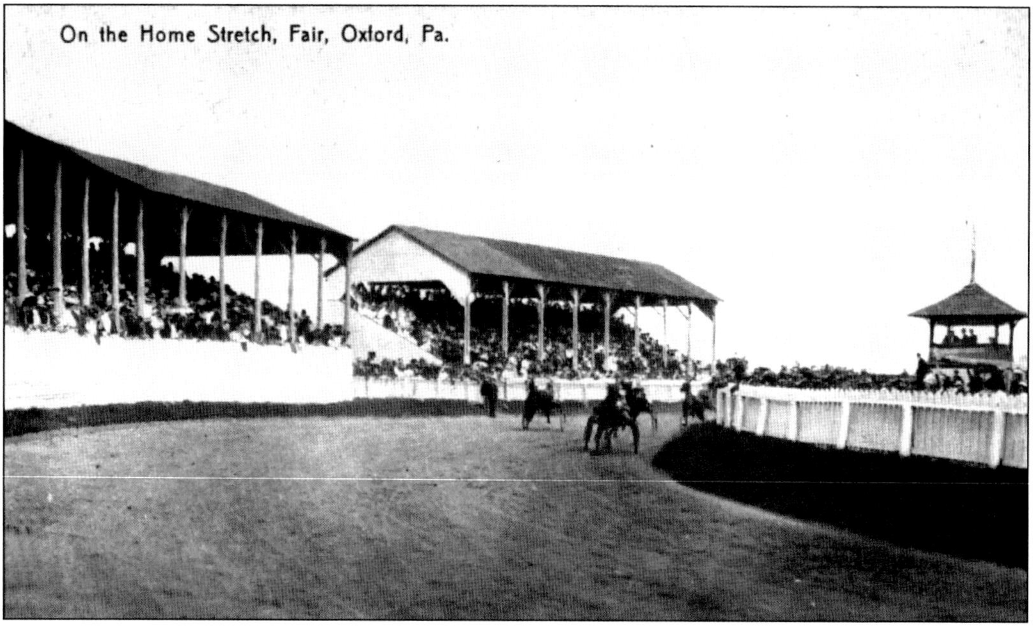

The Oxford Agricultural Society was organized in 1870, with J. Lacey Darlington as president. The new fairground was located on 20 acres purchased from James Rutherford. At the first fair in the fall of 1870, 30,000 people attended, with proceeds at $3,606.89. The Oxford Fair was only held in the fall, but in 1872, a spring fair was added. In 1915, the fairs ceased to exist. Finally, in 1919, the buildings were torn down and most of the lumber sold. At that time, Al F. Wheeler purchased the property (located on the land between Park Street and Wheeler Boulevard) to use as his circus winter quarters.

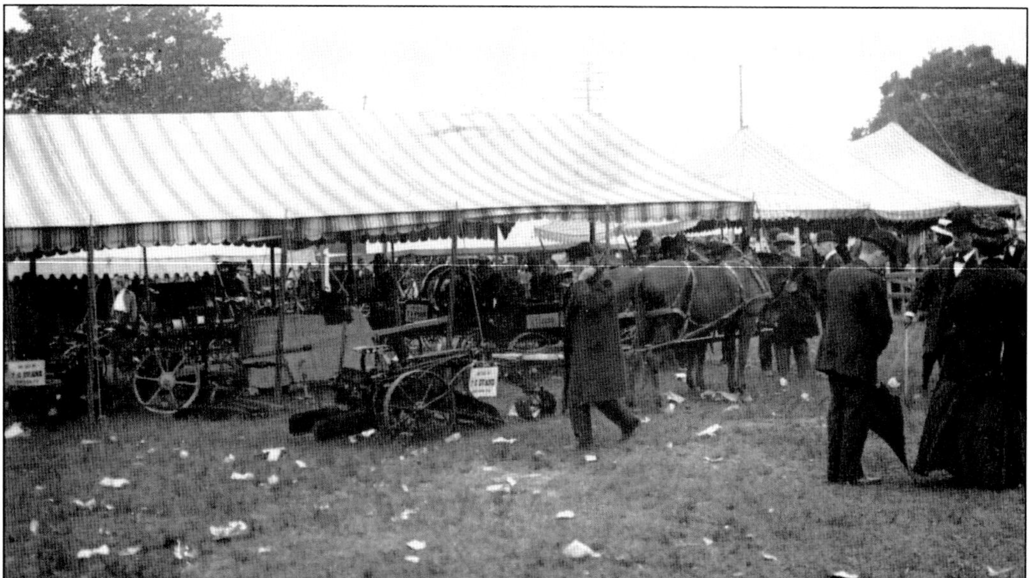

This interesting real-photo postcard from 1910 shows a group of men admiring various pieces of farm machinery. The signs on the front pieces of equipment read, "On Sale By F. G. Evans West Grove Pa." (Evans was a local area farmer). The fair was most famous for its horse racing, but like today's farm shows, there were competitions for the best jellies, handiwork, cakes, and pies.

In 1908, Al F. Wheeler began using Oxford as the winter quarters for his "Wheeler Bros. New Model Shows" and "Downie & Wheeler Circus." He went out of business in 1919 but then operated the circus again from 1929 to 1933. The real-photo postcard at the right shows the winter training building. Cap Snyder stayed with the Wheeler animals. Capt. Henry R. Snyder billed himself as the world's greatest lion tamer, although his lion, Spitfire, was really an old lion with no teeth! During the winter, local kids would visit "Cap" to hear his adventurous yarns. Later Al F. Wheeler became a real estate manager, and he sold the fairground as building lots. He passed away at his residence on Pine Street in 1957. (Courtesy of Howard Steinberg.)

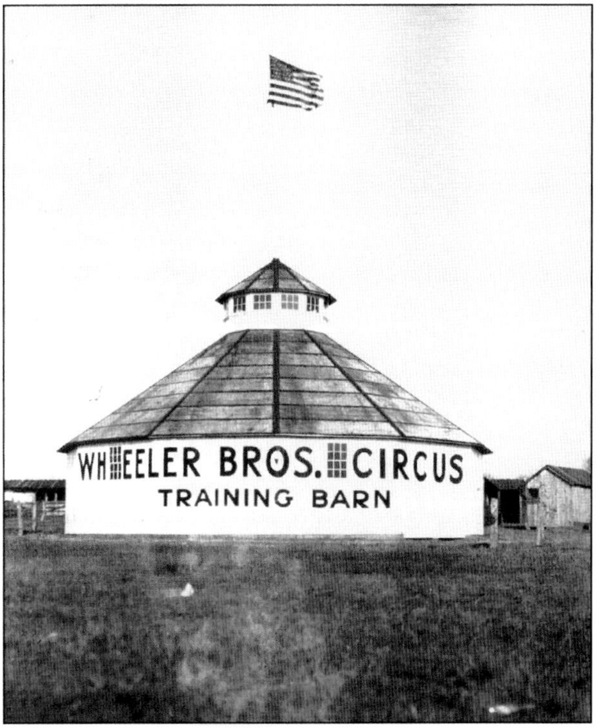

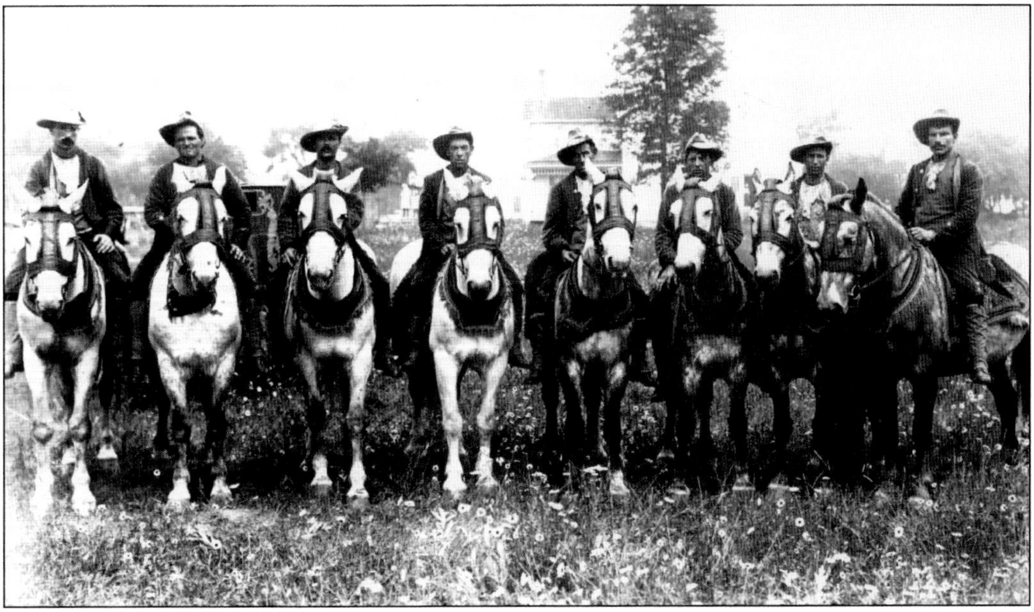

The Wheeler Brothers New Model Shows and Downie and Wheeler Circus traveled the length and breadth of the East Coast. The real-photo postcard above shows members of the circus on horseback. When the circus came to town for its shows, it was always an exciting time. Four elephants drew the bandwagon, and shows were held on the fairgrounds. A newspaper article from 1905 relates that one night two elephants that were chained to a tree on Rev. Samuel Dickey's property pulled up the tree and went on an excursion of their own choosing before being recaptured.

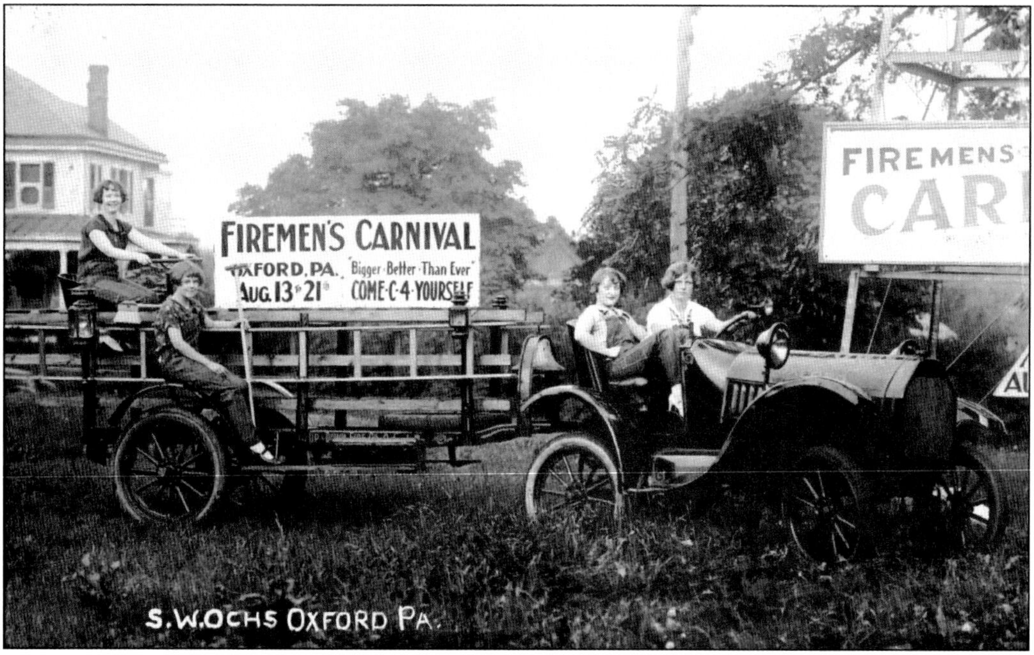

The Oxford Fire Company was known far and wide for the carnivals it held as fund-raisers and community events. Patrick Doyle, an honorary fire company member, suggested a Liberty Carnival be held on July 4, 1909, with the profits equally divided between the fire company and the Oxford Community Band. The carnival proved to be a great success with the gross receipts at $609.61; by 1927, the carnival grossed $32,000. Samuel W. Ochs, who lived at 37 South Fifth Street, was the photographer for both of these real-photo postcards advertising the 1927 carnival. (Above, courtesy of Howard Steinberg.)

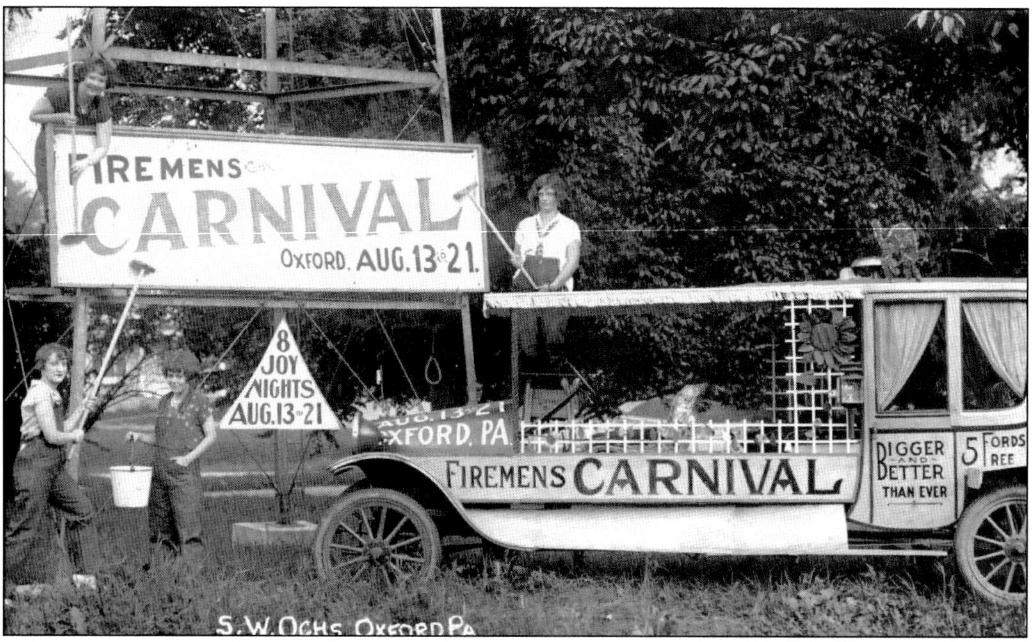

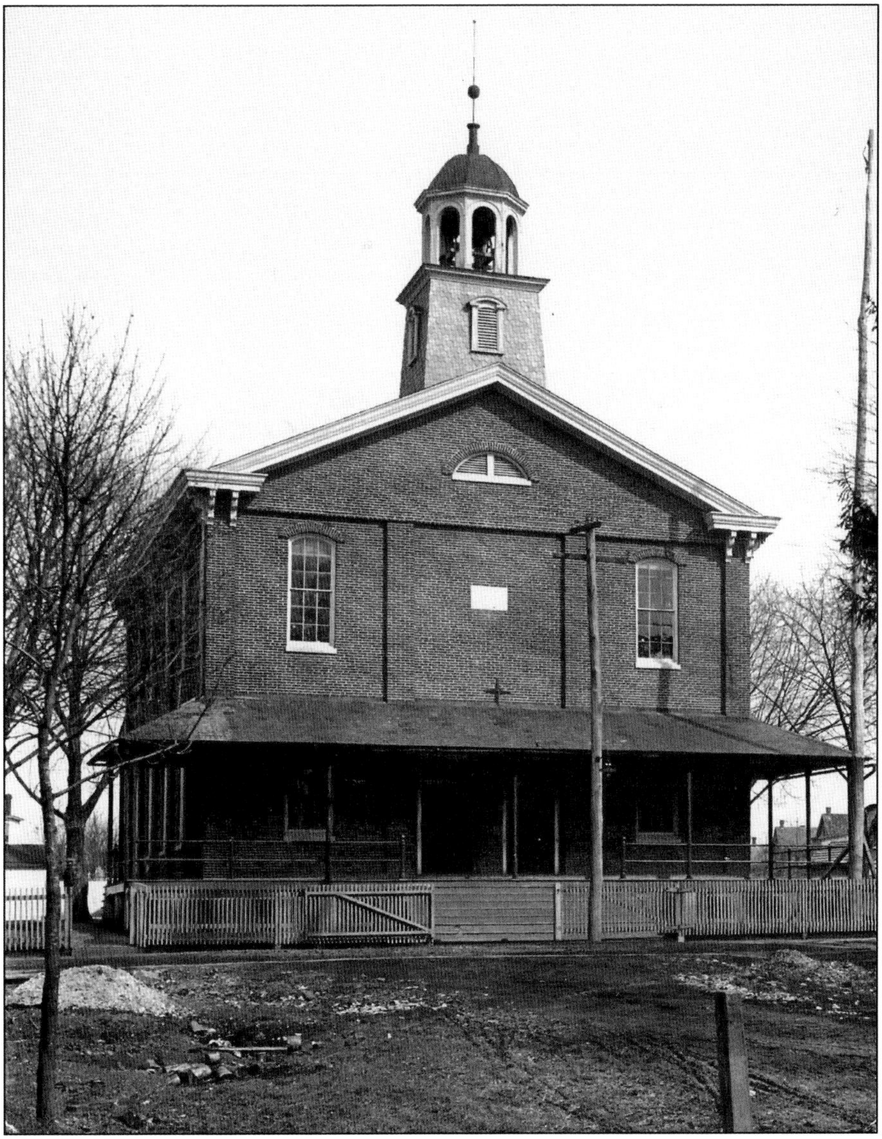

The history of education in Oxford began about 1790, when a small log house under the direction of Masters Wilson and Parke was built in a field that is now part of East Market Street. A continuation of that school occurred in 1814, when William A. Walton established an academy in a two-story brick house at the west end of Oxford. Later, in 1837, Rev. John Miller Dickey established the Oxford Female Seminary located on the west side of Third Street between Market and Locust Streets. Thomas D. Bell was the first principal. The seminary operated into the late 1870s at a new location on North Third Street after 1858. In 1851, the Oxford School Board was organized, and by 1868, the two-story brick Union School building had been erected at Fifth and Hodgson Streets, as seen in the photograph above. The roof was slate and had a 40-foot cupola. All 12 grades were accommodated, with four teachers and four rooms devoted to the four school divisions—primary, secondary, grammar, and high school. H. F. Pierce was the first principal, earning a salary of $75 per month.

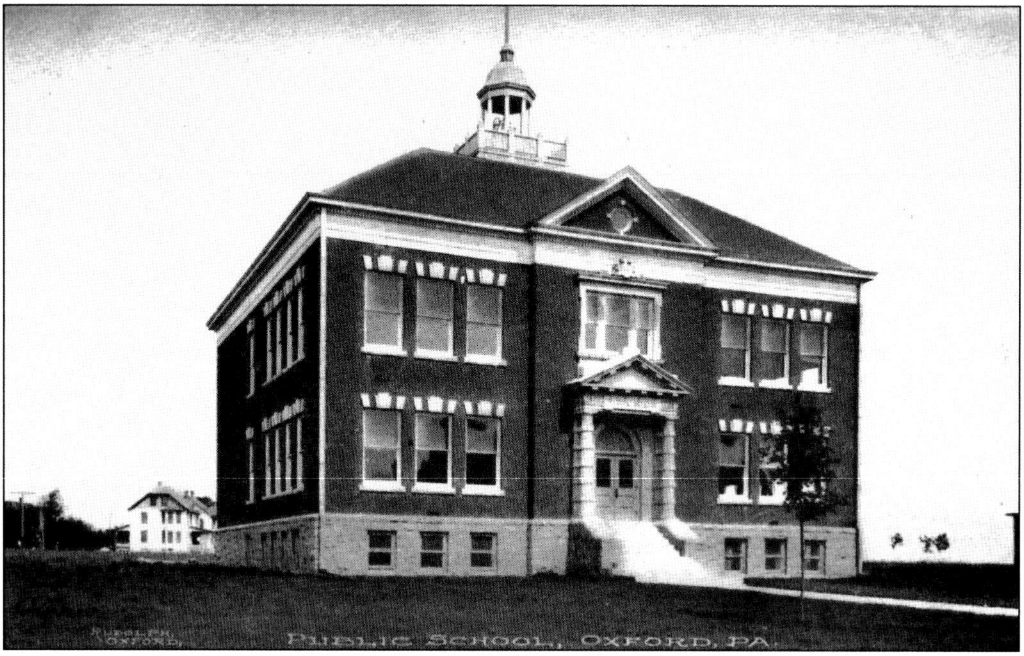

To handle the growing school-age population, an additional school was constructed on Fifth Street in 1904–1905. The two-story brick building was 62 by 65 feet and built by Walker and Gibson at a cost of $18,000. Two wings were later added, the north wing costing $12,700 in 1915, and the south wing in 1925. The first principal of the high school was Ralph L. Johnson, who served from 1903 until 1907.

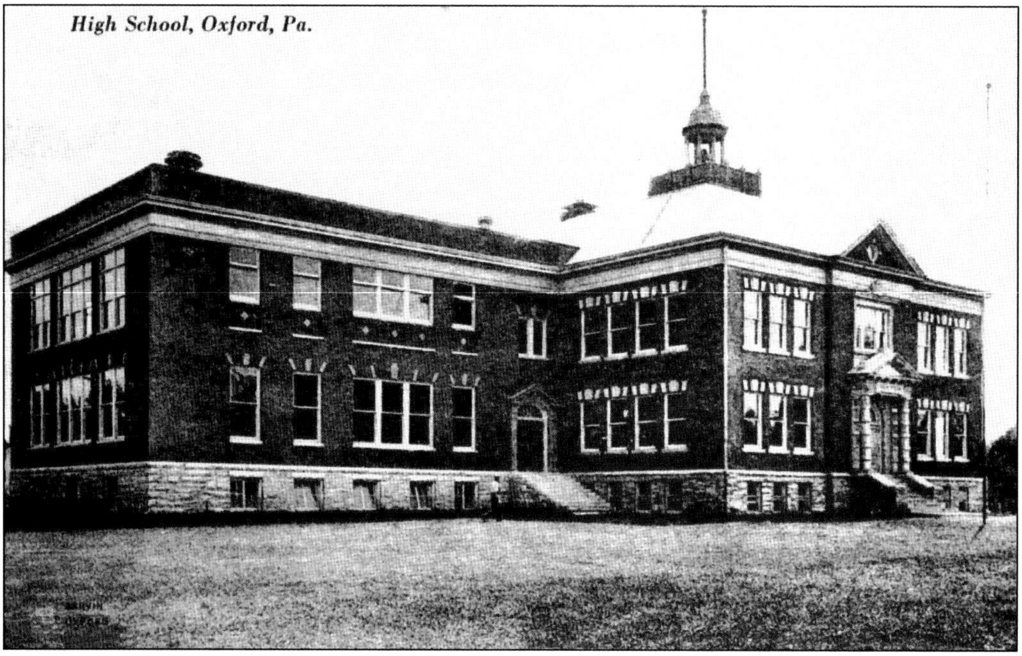

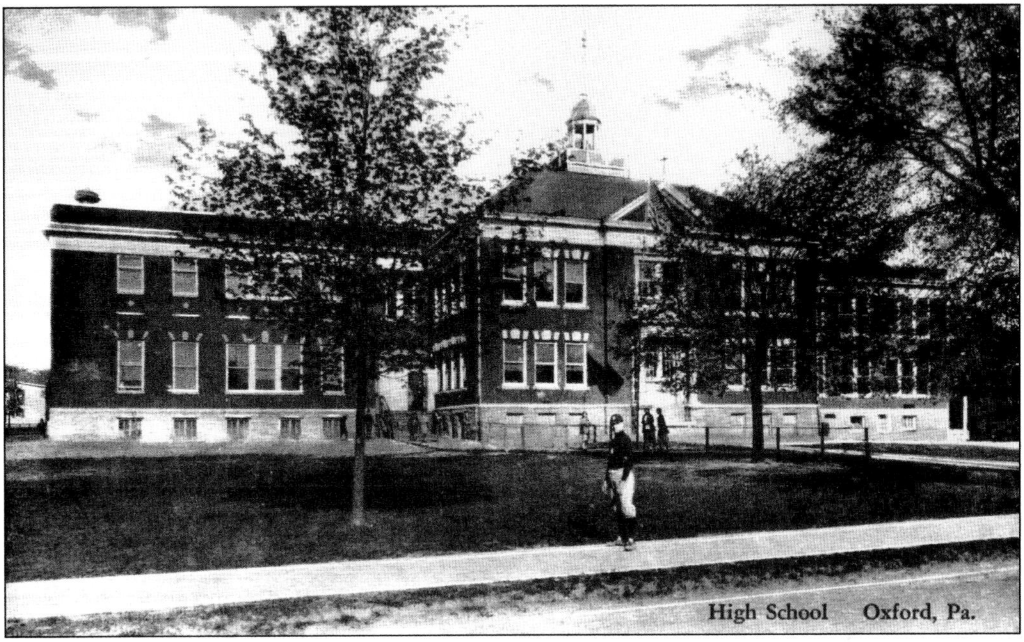

A lone baseball player poses in front of the high school in the early 1930s. During the late 1890s, Oxford was also home to Oxford College, a preparatory school for law, medicine, pharmacy, and business, located in the Ewing Building at 41 South Third Street. It was under the direction of M. L. Bittenbender and J. C. Wagner.

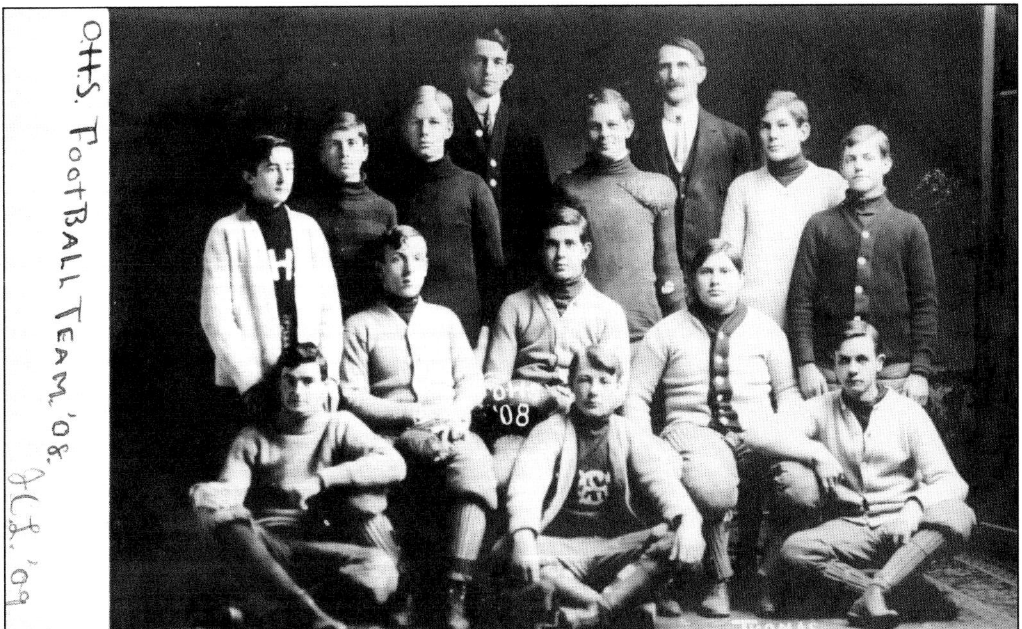

The Oxford High School 1908 football team defeated West Grove 5-0 in the opening game of the season on October 3, 1908. The students on that winning team included the following: Miller, Smith, Alexander, Buckalew, Pitt, Robert, Sharp, Broomell, Woodside, Urbine, and Stubbs.

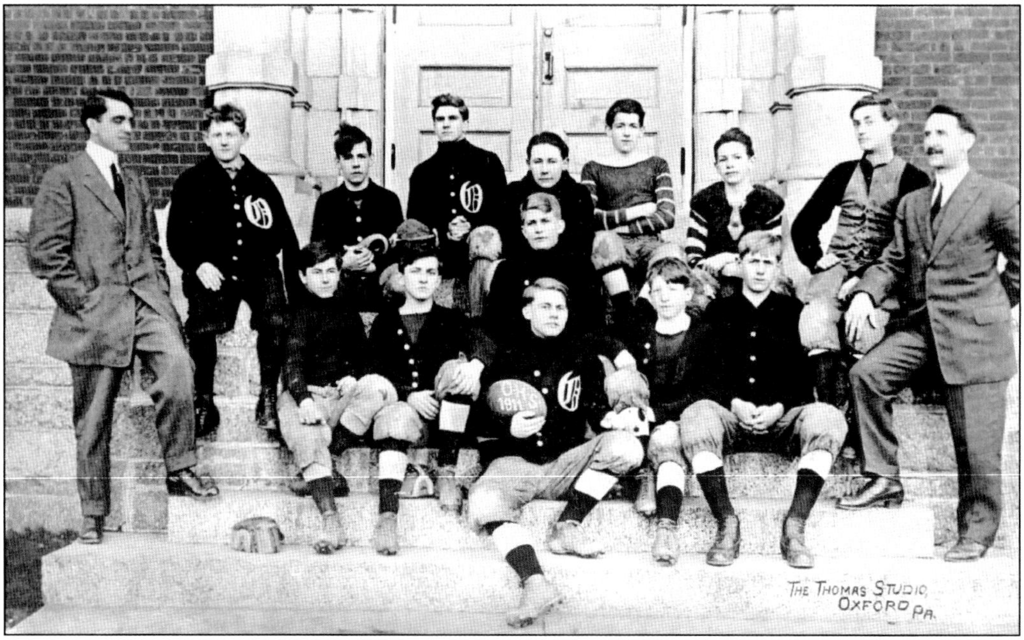

Many dinners were given in honor of the Oxford High School 1911 football team. An especially delightful dinner occurred in early 1911 and was given by Principal Elmer E. Hess and his wife at their home. The guests included Dwight Wentz, Carl Hansen, William Alexander, Frank Harrison, Howard Brown, Mark Keeley, Howard Samples, Ernest Janney, Henry Snodgrass, Paul Turner, Ervin Ochs, Wendel Caley, Wilson "Iron Mike" O'Daniel, and David and Barton Mackey. (Courtesy of Howard Steinberg.)

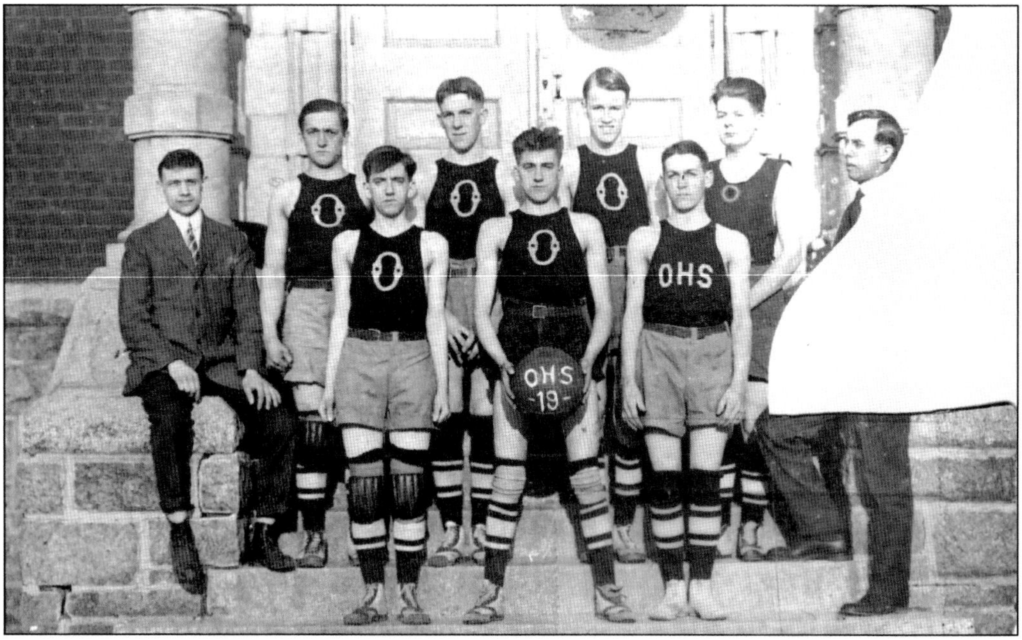

The Oxford High School 1919 boys' basketball team may have included the following students: Becker, forward; McCormick, forward; M. Evans, center; H. Evans, guard; Melrath, guard; and McCullough, substitute.

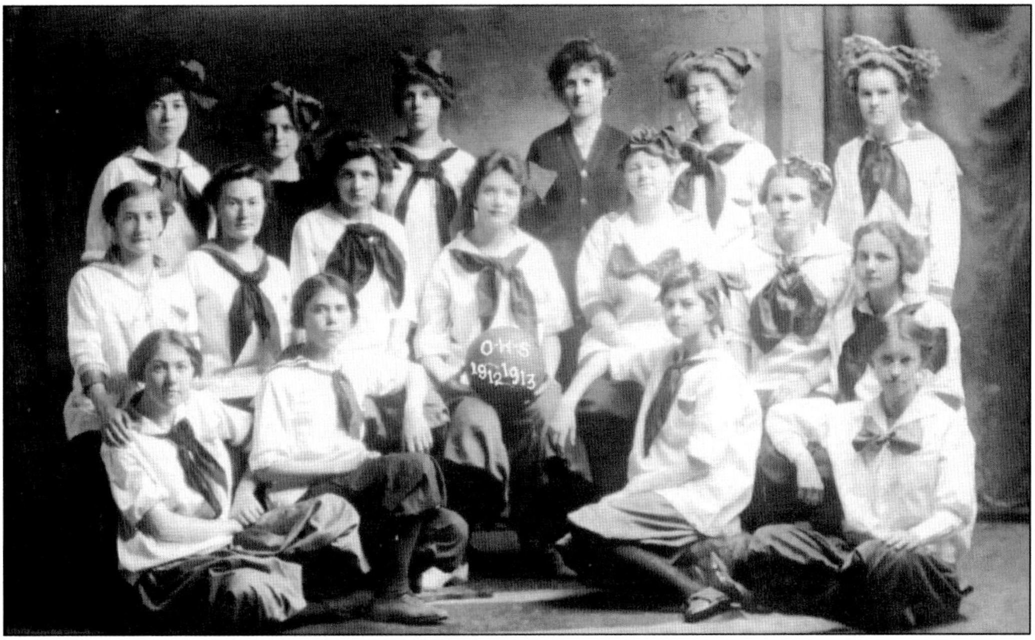

The Oxford High School 1912–1913 girls' basketball team is shown in this real-photo postcard. The 1913 class motto was *Nur Ein Anfang*, "only a beginning." The class colors were gold and black, and the class flower was the yellow tea rose. (Courtesy of Howard Steinberg.)

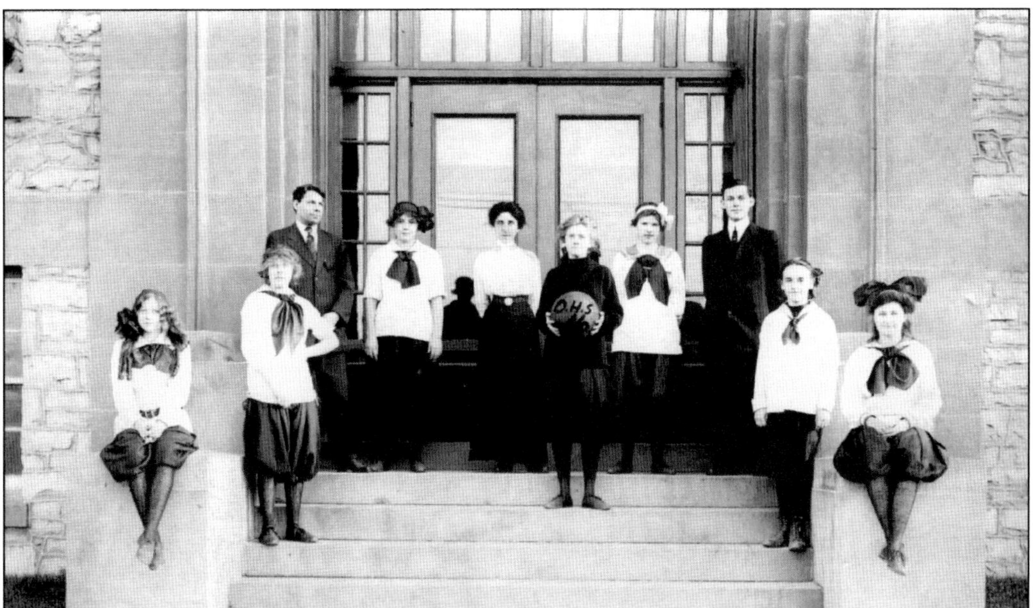

The Oxford High School 1916 girls' basketball team (pictured here), and the boys' basketball team both played games in Quarryville on Saturday, March 4, 1916. The girls team beat Quarryville 14 to 8, while the boys team lost 16 to 46. (Courtesy of Howard Steinberg.)

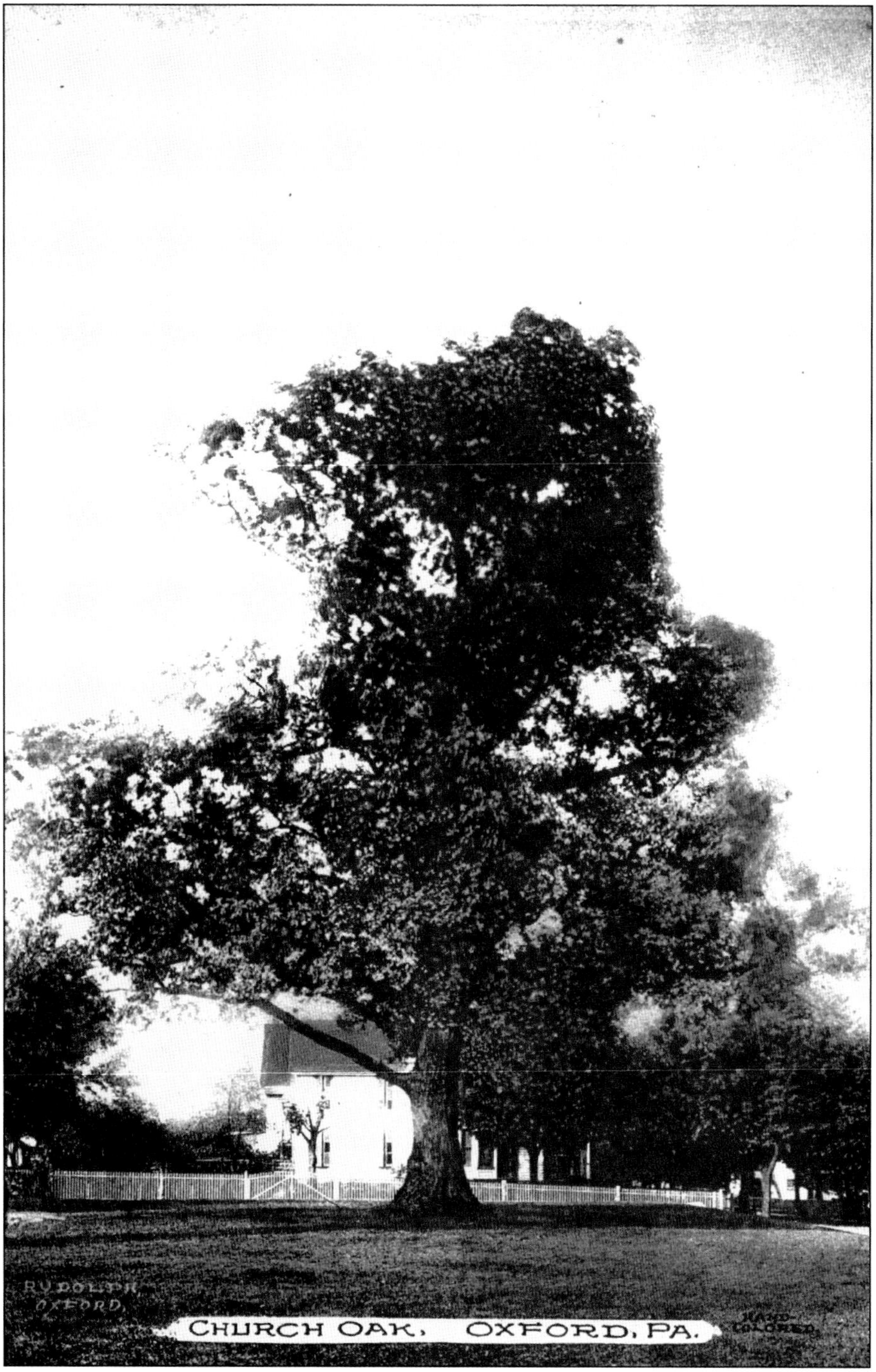

This was one of the original Penn Oak Trees, in existence since the time of William Penn in 1682. Because the first Presbyterian church was built near this tree it has been called the Church Oak or Presbyterian Oak (at the time, there were five oak trees on the green). The surviving tree was struck by lightning several times and survived but was eventually felled by disease and cut down in November 2007.

Four

Area Residences and Street Scenes

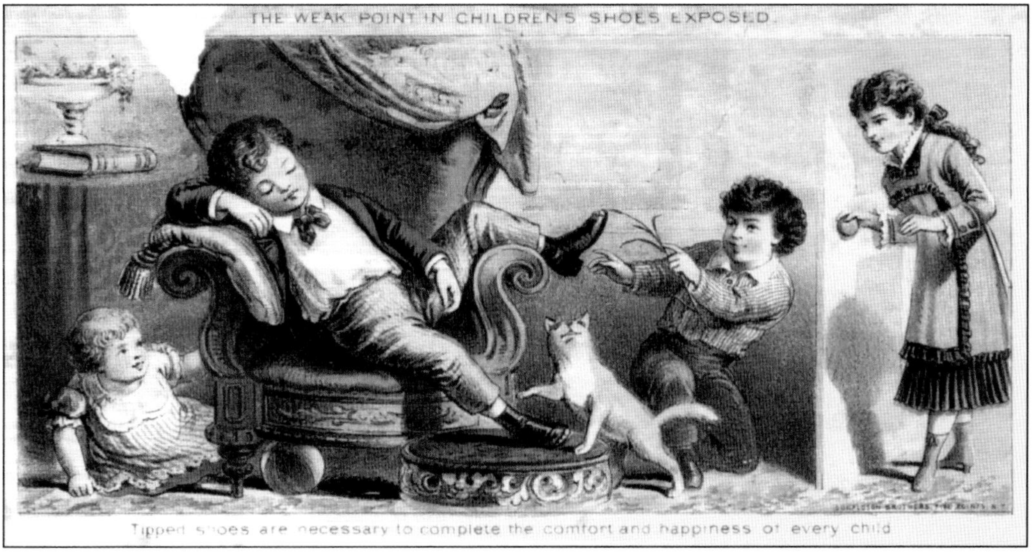

Ruth and Emma Passmore distributed this advertisement in the late 19th century. The back of the advertisement states that they had "a complete assortment and stock of Ladies', Misses' and Children's shoes, Exclusively. The only store of its kind in Oxford. Tipped shoes a specialty, at the lowest prices." The eccentric Passmore sisters moved to Oxford from East Nottingham Township in 1874, conducting their millinery business from several locations, with the last move to the Dickey Building in 1894. For many years, the sisters lived at 33 North Third Street.

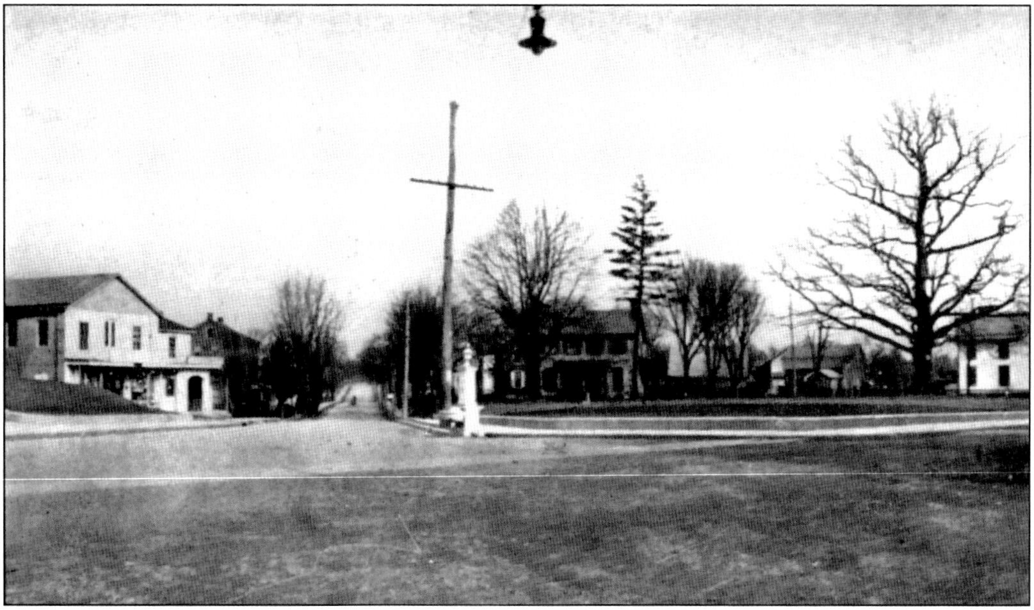

The building at the far left was the site of the Wilson Brothers and Company Carriage Works. It was established in 1863 and is shown in this early-1920s view. It was located at the southwest corner of Pine and North Third Streets. Across the street is the public fountain, and to the right, the old oak tree. In 1929, John H. Ware Jr. purchased the property of N. P. Alexander on Pine Street (see page 87) and used part of the property to construct his boulevard (Lancaster Pike).

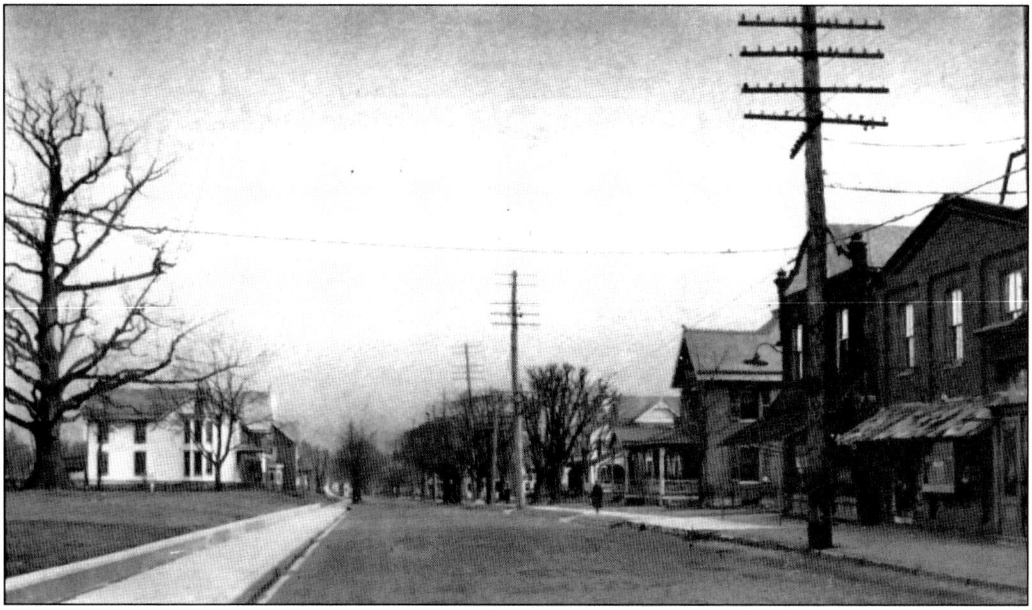

This postcard looks north on North Third Street, with the old oak tree on the left and several business establishments on the right. The building on the far right was the site of the post office before it moved into the Masonic building in 1904. The building to the left was Charles Parker's Arcade Building that housed Walter D. Biddison's movie theater and bowling alley around 1908 and his tattersall in 1911.

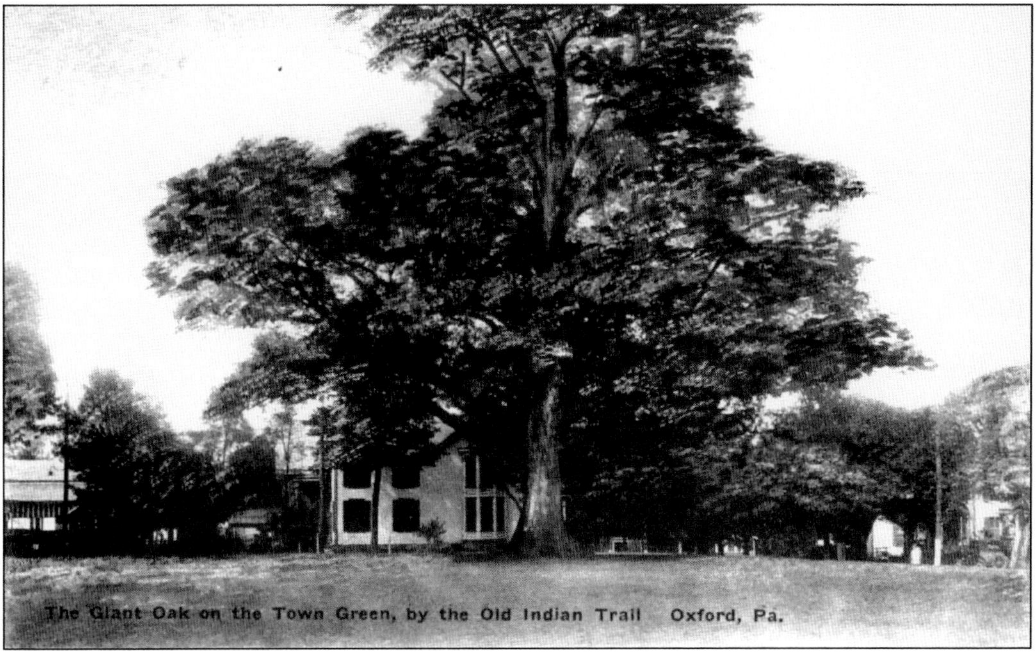

The postcard above shows the town oak and the public green. The postcard below shows the only public fountain in Oxford. It was erected on May 29, 1897, at the corner of Pine and North Third Streets, from a donation by the Christian Temperance League of Oxford. It was made of iron and ornate in style, and manufactured in New York for a total cost of $200. It was topped with a vase and had three drinking faucets—for man, horse, and dog.

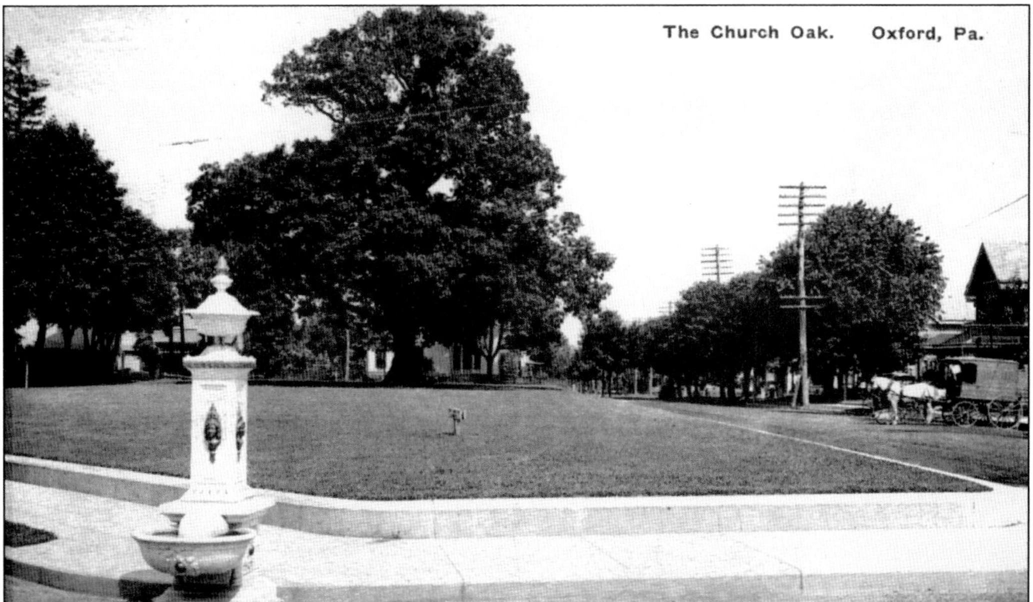

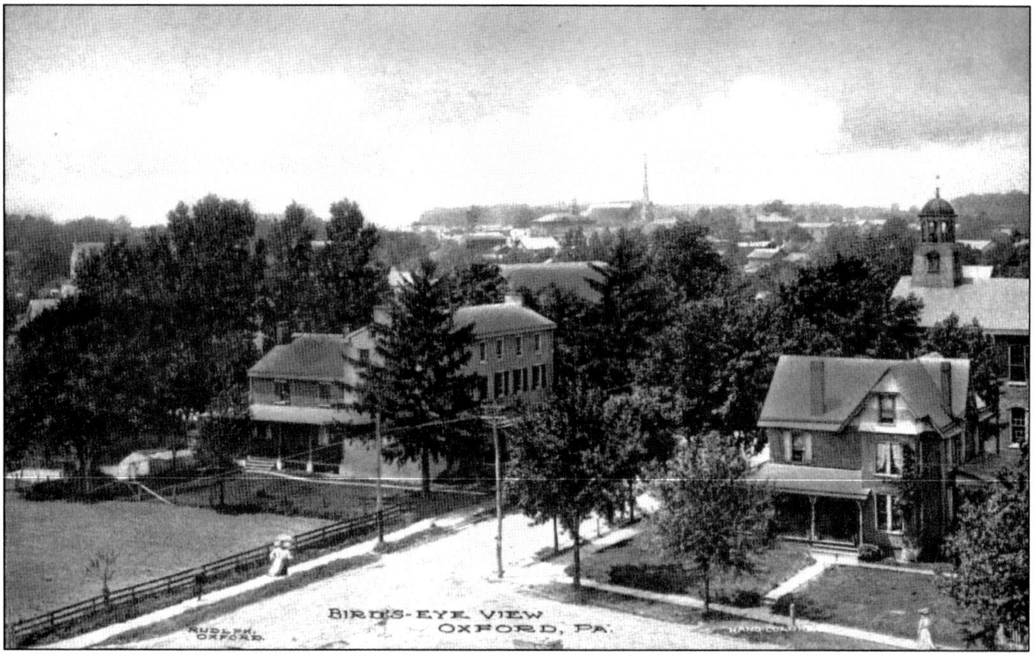

This 1908–1910 view looks northwest from the corner of Fifth and Hodgson Streets. On the right is the bell tower of the Oxford Public School building that was constructed in 1868. The school contained all 12 grades and served that purpose until a high school was constructed in 1906. The three-story house on the left was built by Isaac Boyd in 1859 and is still standing. On the 1883 Breou's map of Oxford, it is listed as the Home for Friendless Children and Philadelphia Orphan Asylum. In the background is the steeple of the Presbyterian church.

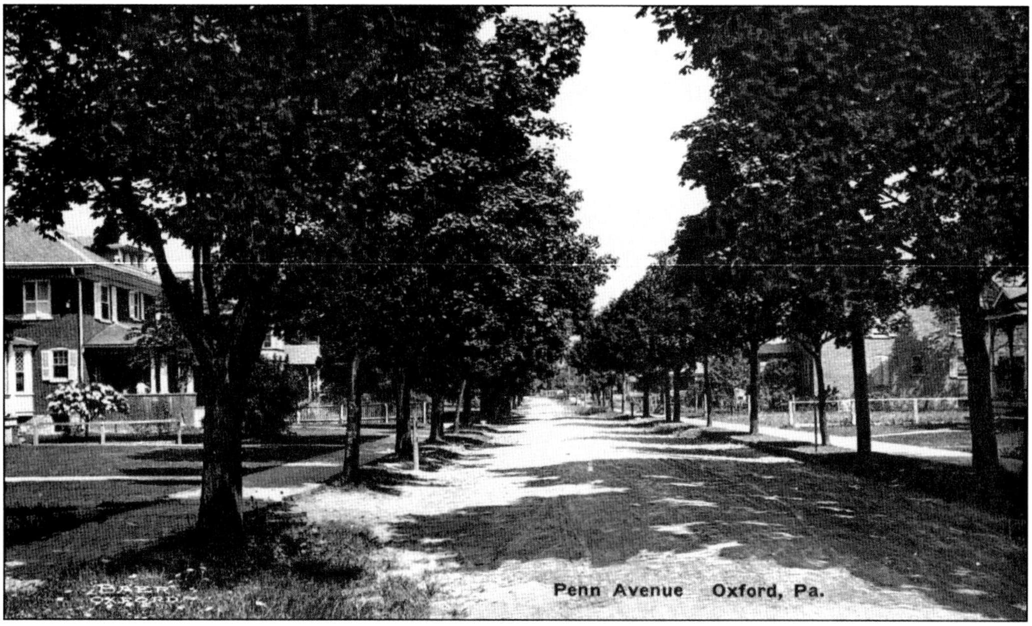

Penn Avenue was said to have a lock on the women's suffrage movement, as most of the presidents, vice presidents, and secretaries of every women's organization in Oxford lived there. This view looks north with 230 Penn Avenue on the left.

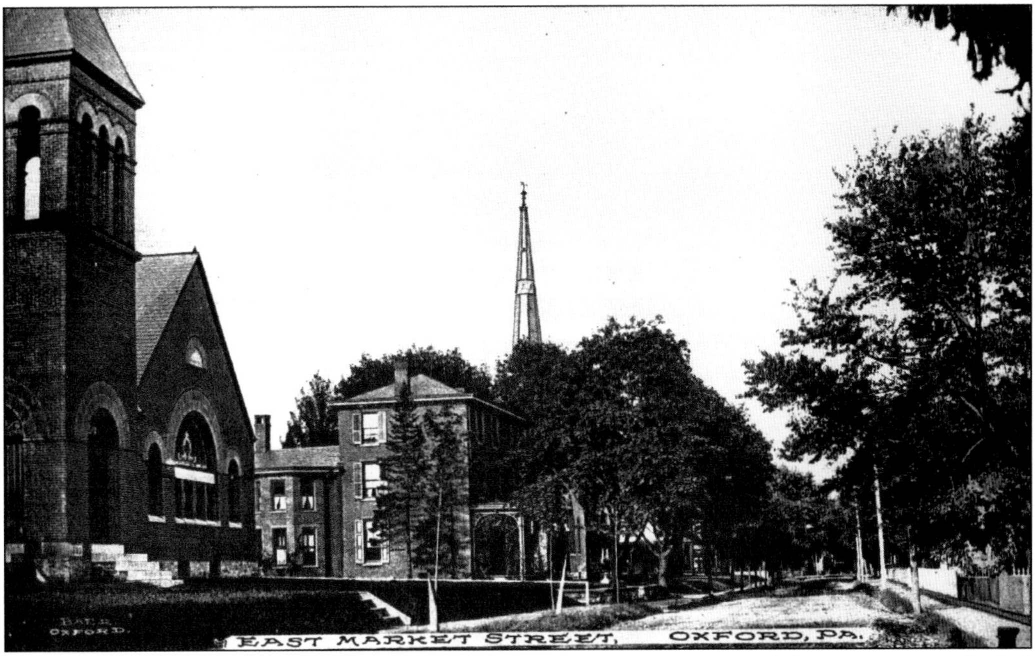

This 1910–1912 Baer postcard shows Market Street looking west toward downtown. On the left is the old United Presbyterian Church, which became the Baptist church in 1927. The three-story residence next to the church was the Steele residence, now a parking lot. The steeple of the Methodist church is visible in the center of the postcard.

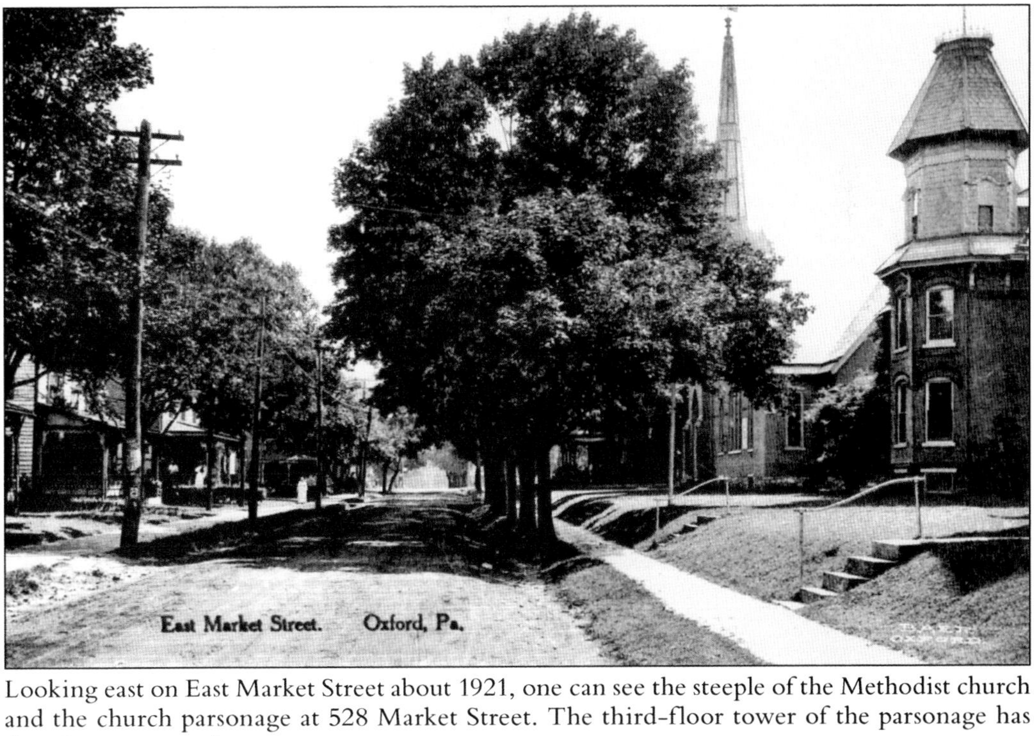

Looking east on East Market Street about 1921, one can see the steeple of the Methodist church and the church parsonage at 528 Market Street. The third-floor tower of the parsonage has since been removed.

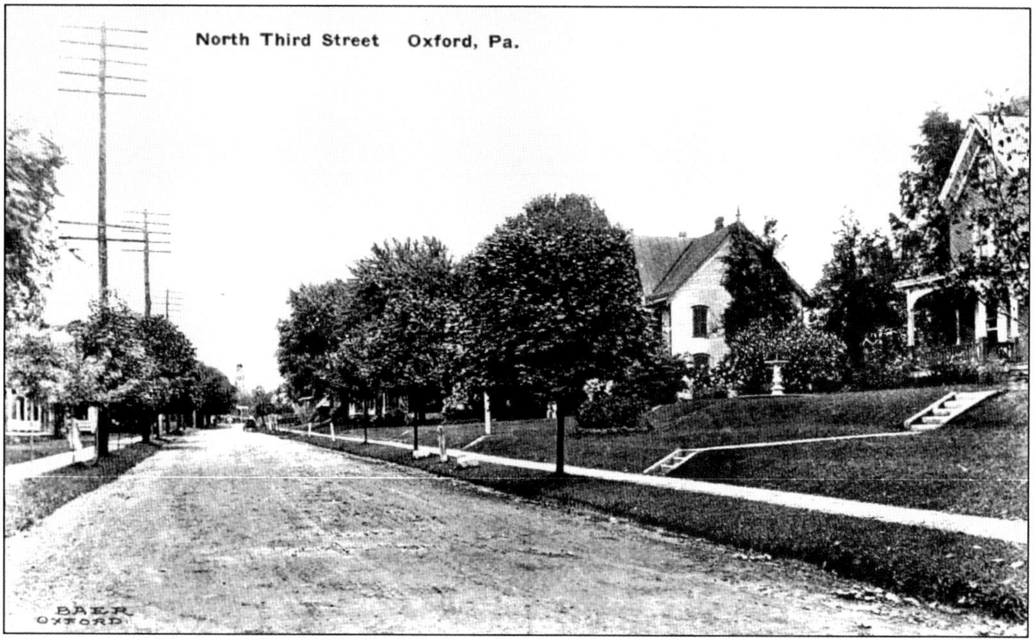

In 1893, street numbering appeared in Oxford. The 100 block of North Third Street is shown in this row of houses. In the distance, one can identify the tower of Oxford Hall. The house at the extreme right is located at 118 North Third Street, and the house to its left is No. 104. The house across the street is at either 105 or 109 North Third Street.

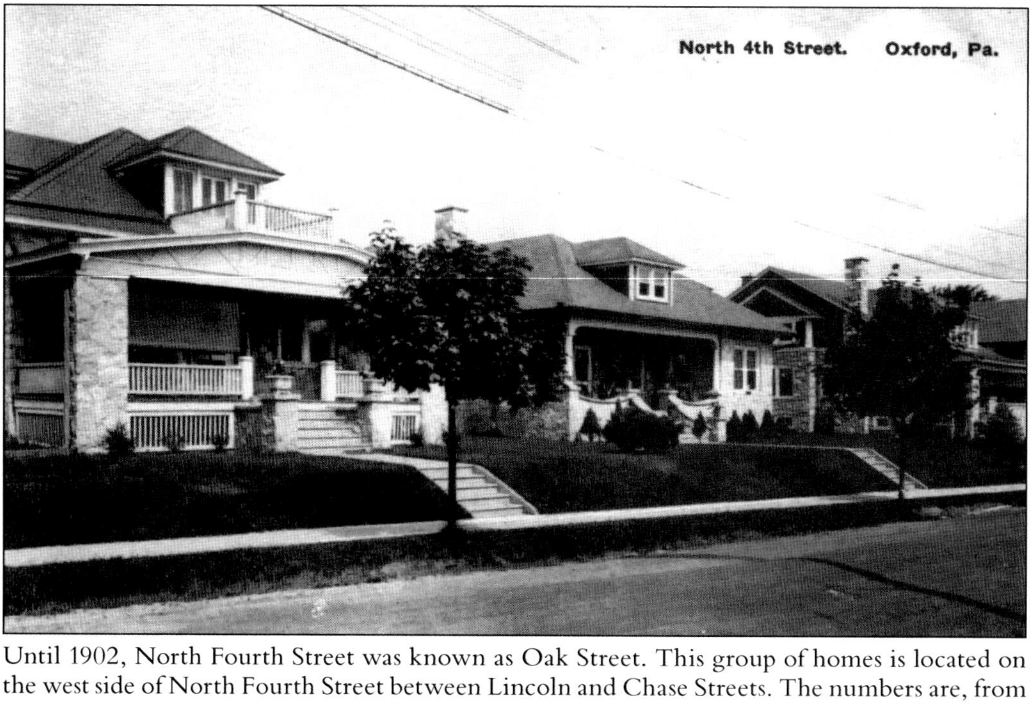

Until 1902, North Fourth Street was known as Oak Street. This group of homes is located on the west side of North Fourth Street between Lincoln and Chase Streets. The numbers are, from the left, 48, 54, 60, and the roofline of 66 North Fourth Street.

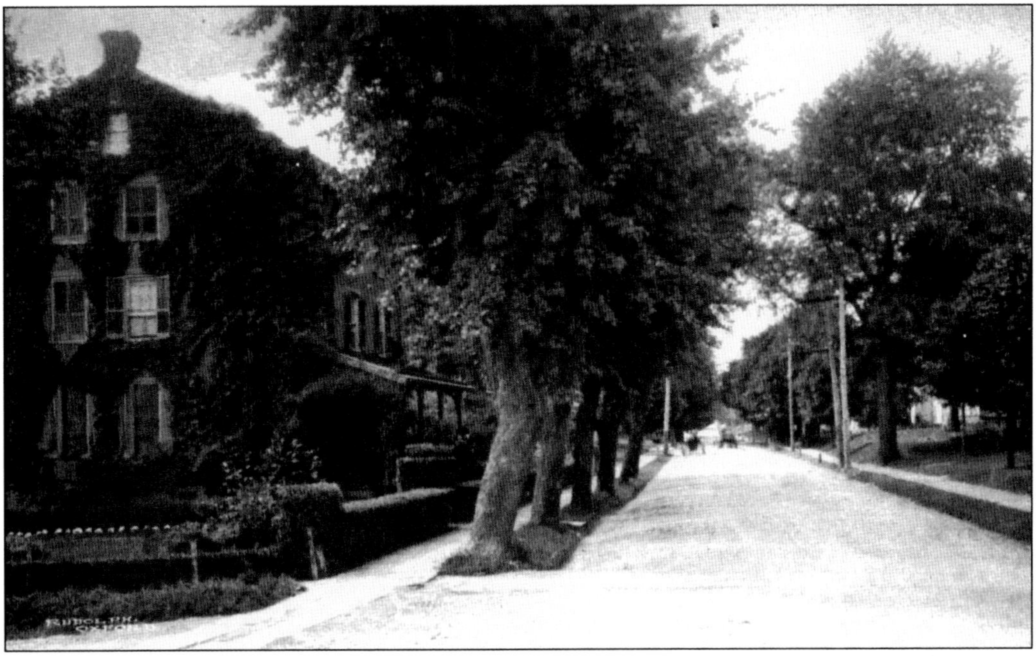

Pine Street is one of the beautiful residential streets in the borough near the center of town. In a 1907 tour of Oxford, it was stated that it was an "aristocratic street" and that the "difference between Pine Street society and other kinds is that up there they have parties and serve cream peppermints, vanilla wafers and intellectual discussions and in other society they have something fit to eat and gossip!" For many years, the lovely home on the left was the residence of candy manufacturer N. P. Alexander. This view looks north from the intersection of Lancaster Avenue. The postcard below shows the houses at 132, 126, 120, and 114 Pine Street, looking south from Mount Vernon Street.

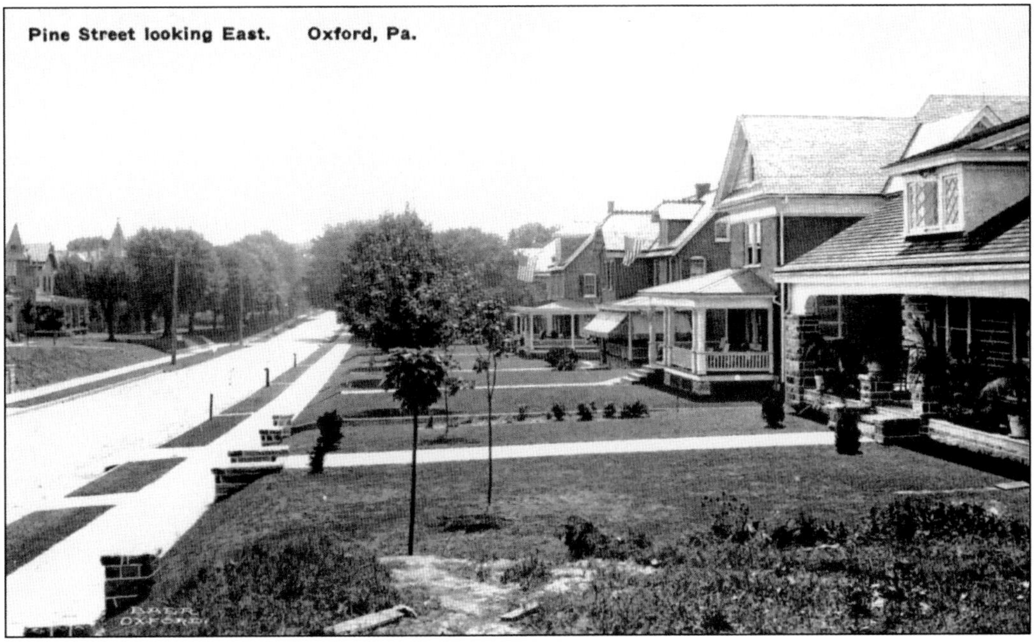

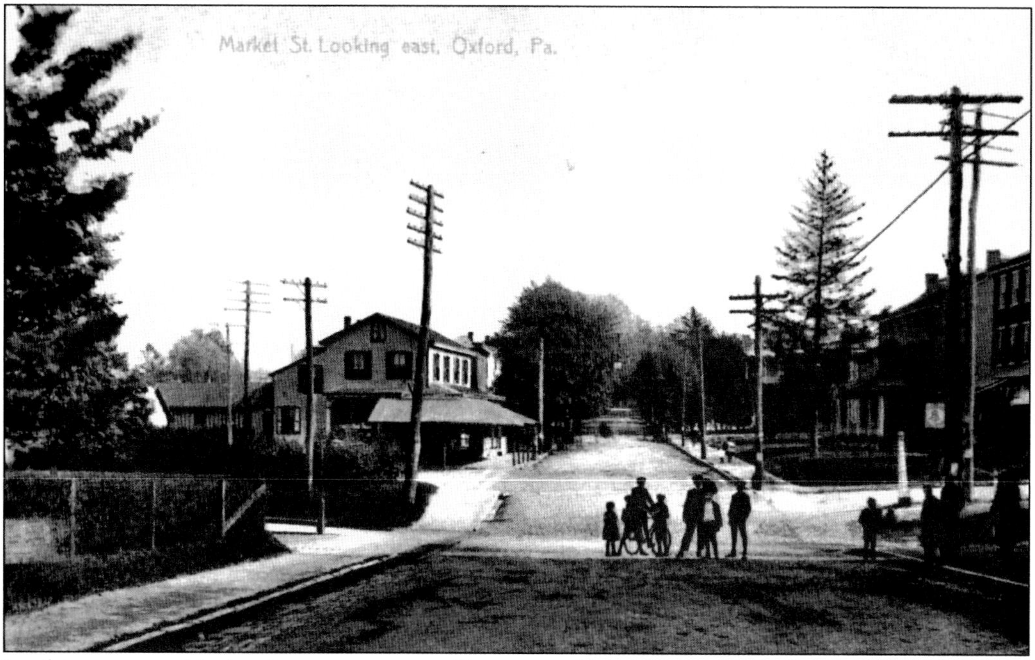

Looking east on Market Street are a row of houses at 401–409 Market Street; a series of grocery stores operated there from the 1890s into the early 1900s. The sign above the awning reads, "Jos. [Bere]tta, Candies." Beretta and Garrett A. Johnson were in the candy-making business at the time of this 1908 postcard, published by Carrie Johnson.

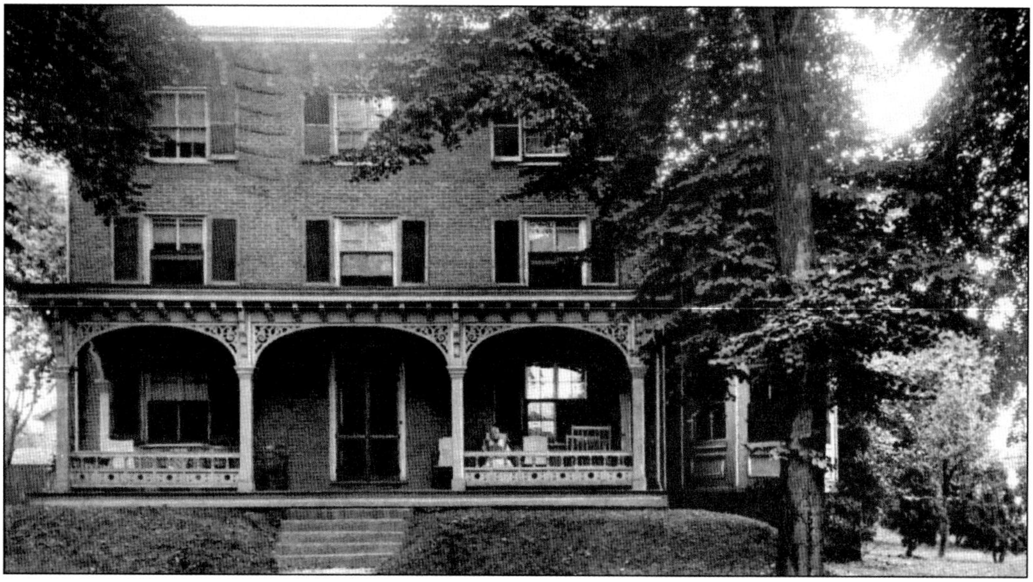

The Italianate-style mansion of Samuel R. Dickey IV was located at 309 Market Street (now the site of the Union Fire Company). When Samuel died in 1884, Jennie Rutherford Dickey, Samuel's second wife, took over his business interests. In 1887, she built a small brick building that became the post office, and in 1895, she tore down the 1869 farmers' market and constructed a three-story commercial building known as the Masonic building. She moved to her son's farm in the early 1920s and died in 1926.

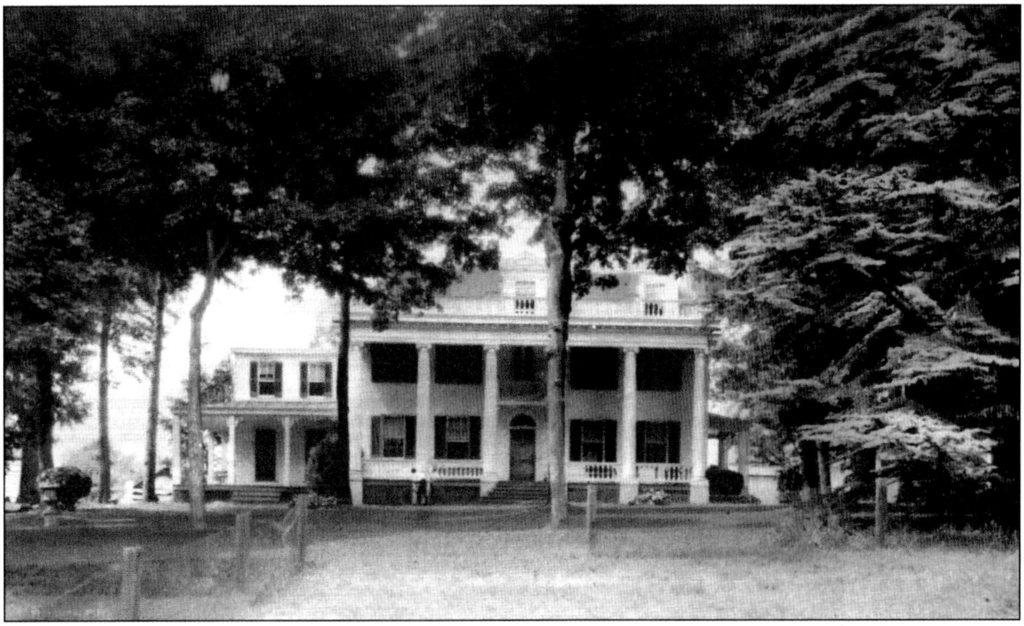

The Dickey family has been an important part of the area's history since Samuel and Jane Dickey arrived in the early 1730s. Members of the family became leaders in agriculture (farming, dairying, and patents), manufacturing (mills, cotton-weaving, and brick-making), education (Oxford Female Seminary and Ashmun Institute), religion (ministers and missionaries), transportation (railroading), and community affairs (Continental Congress, town library, state representatives, banking, and doctors). The home shown in these two postcards was built by John Miller Dickey in 1834 and was owned by his second son, John Miller Cresson Dickey, who died in 1908 and was remembered as "Oxford's most prominent citizen." This home was on the grounds of what became Ware Presbyterian Village but was demolished in 1975.

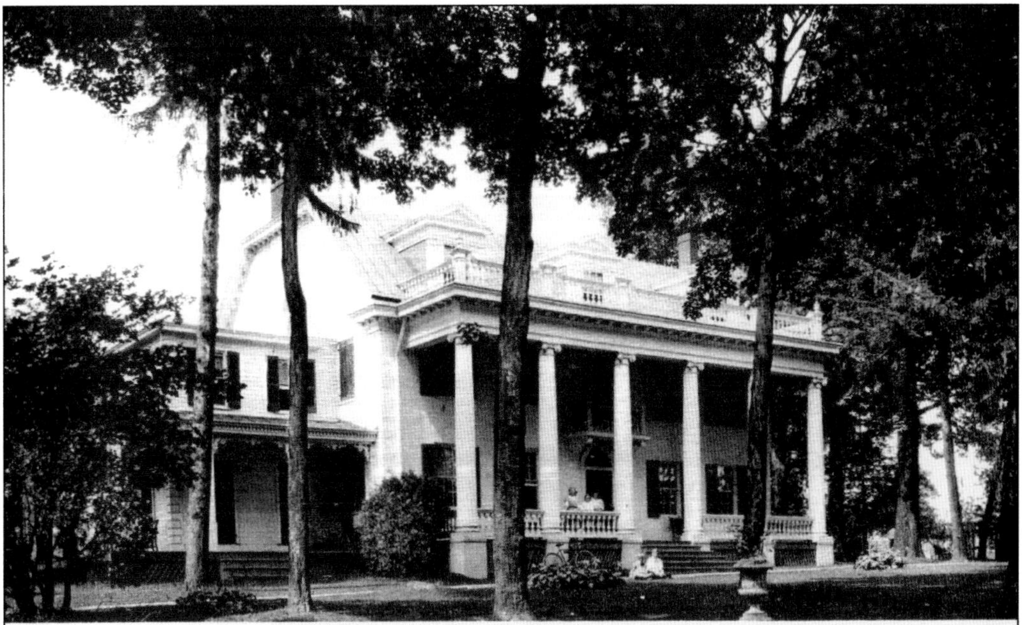

RESIDENCE MRS. ANNIE A. DICKEY. OXFORD, PA.

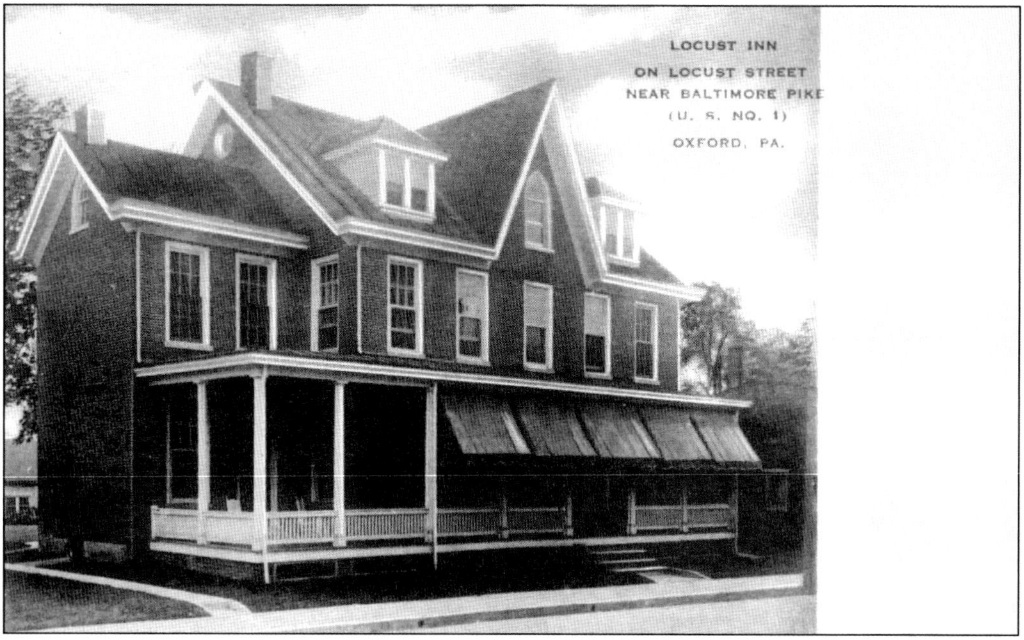

For almost 25 years, Mrs. S. Annetta Brown maintained the Locust Inn at 204 Locust Street (previously No. 120) as an inn and boardinghouse. On January 1, 1946, the property passed to photographer Robert Adams, who opened his new photographic studio in December 1946. Adams and Adams produced many distinctive postcards of Oxford. In 1946, Adams and Adams offered a free print with any order of other prints and reminded its customers that "Photographs are always in good taste as gifts."

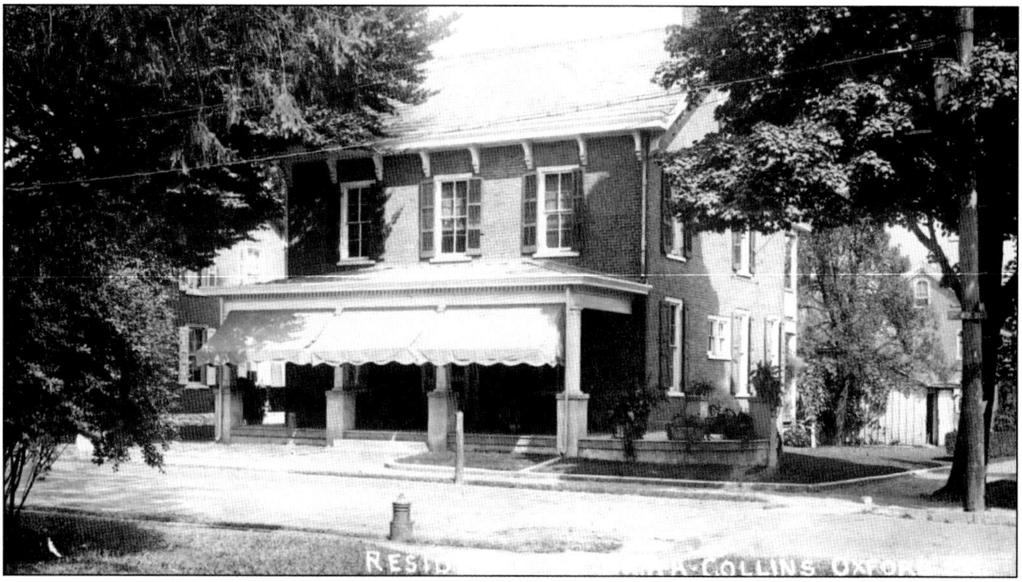

Thomas Sloan built this house in 1870. Dr. Arthur A. Collins opened an office in Oxford in 1913 after graduating from the University of Pennsylvania and serving his residency at the Methodist Episcopal Hospital in Philadelphia. He purchased this home at 51 South Fourth Street in 1922. The house then passed into the possession of Dr. Samuel C. Wilson, who practiced in Oxford from 1924 until his death in 1944.

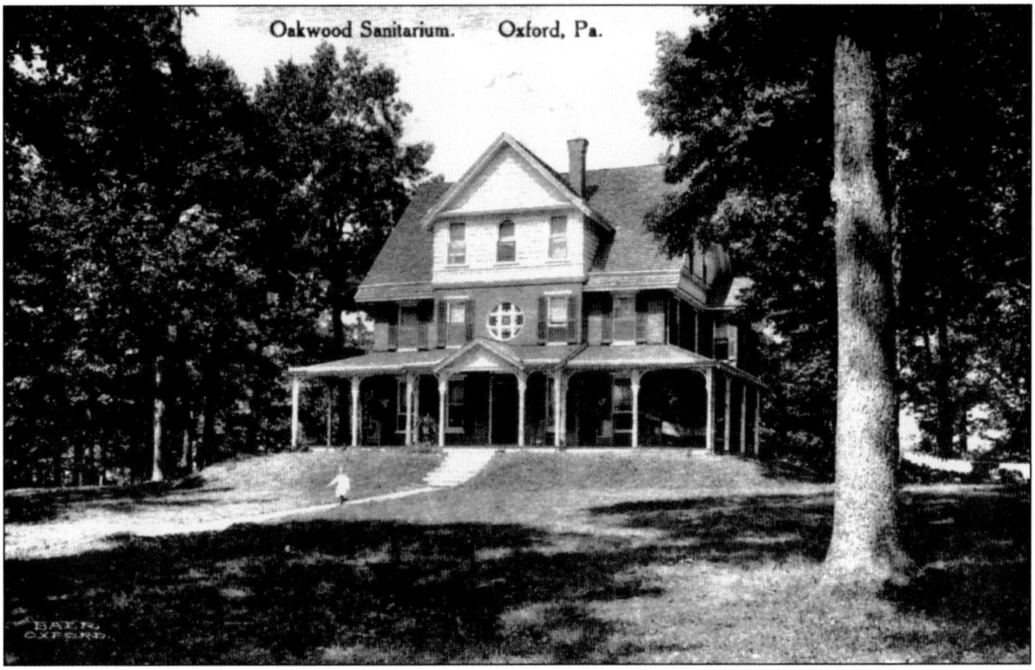

Located on Mount Vernon Street, Oakwood Sanitarium was established in 1915 by Dr. Willard G. Lent. With Lent as hospital administrator, it served as Oxford's only hospital. Unfortunately, the young Dr. Lent died in 1918, a victim of the influenza pandemic. John H. Ware Jr. purchased the property and, later, in the autumn of 1931, moved the house across Lancaster Avenue to a space between Lancaster Avenue and Locust Street. In the 1980s and 1990s, the sanitarium served as apartments for the elderly.

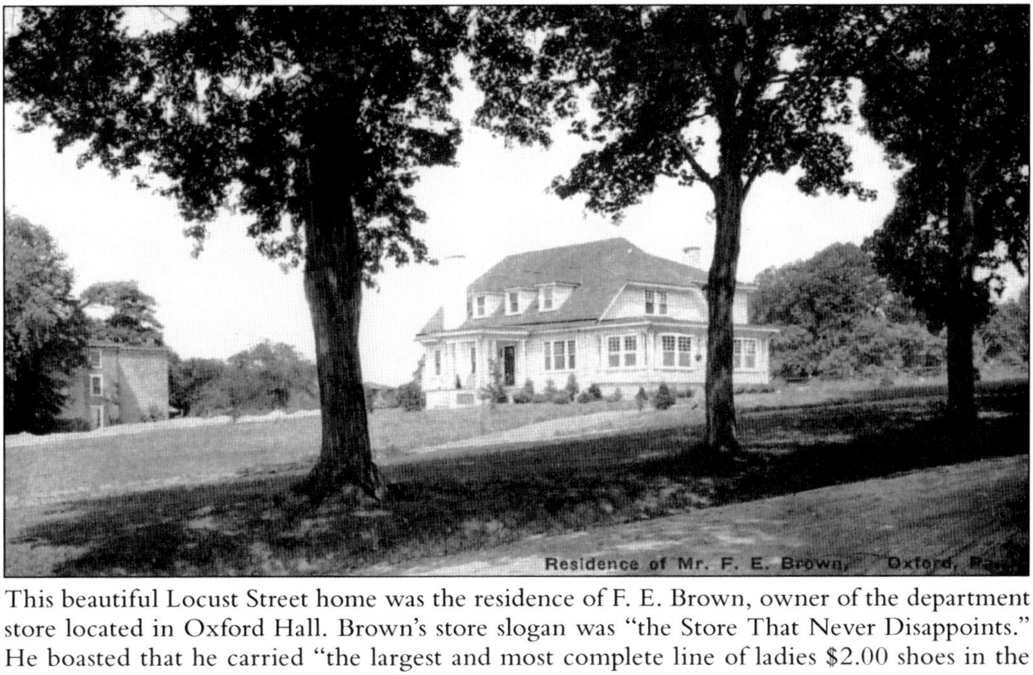

This beautiful Locust Street home was the residence of F. E. Brown, owner of the department store located in Oxford Hall. Brown's store slogan was "the Store That Never Disappoints." He boasted that he carried "the largest and most complete line of ladies $2.00 shoes in the country—our specialty."

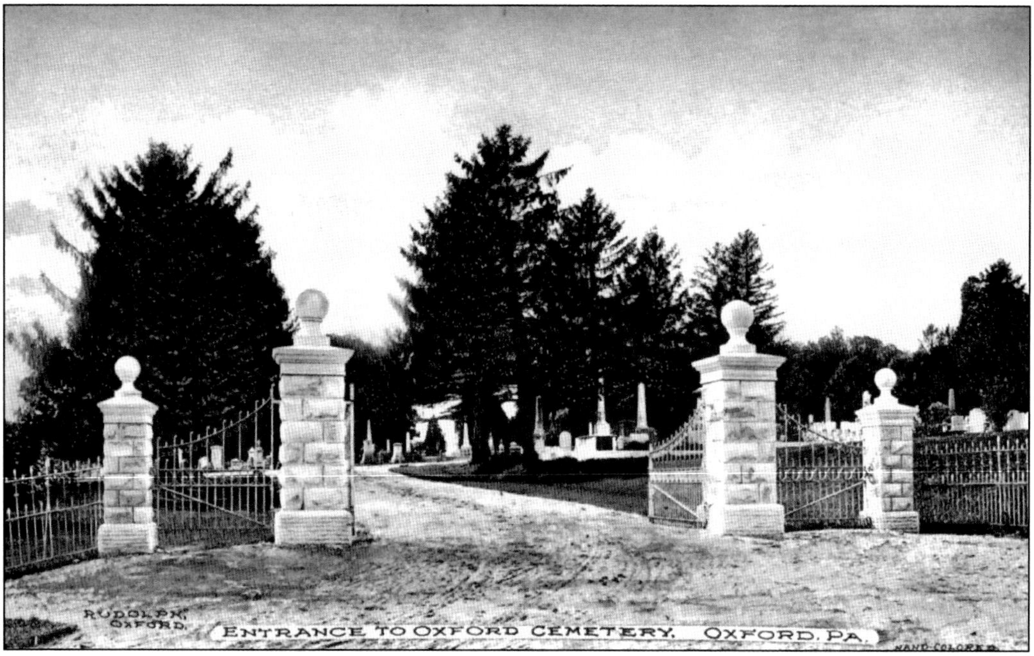

In 1856, the Oxford Cemetery moved to a parcel of land donated by Thomas Hood. It was felt that having a cemetery located in churchyards was not as aesthetic as "amidst the verdure of the field under the broad and cheerful light of heaven," so many cemeteries were moved to the edge of towns. The first interment in the Oxford Cemetery was Margaret Smith, wife of Samuel Smith, on January 3, 1856. The first male was David D. Dickey, one of the charter members of the Oxford Cemetery Association.

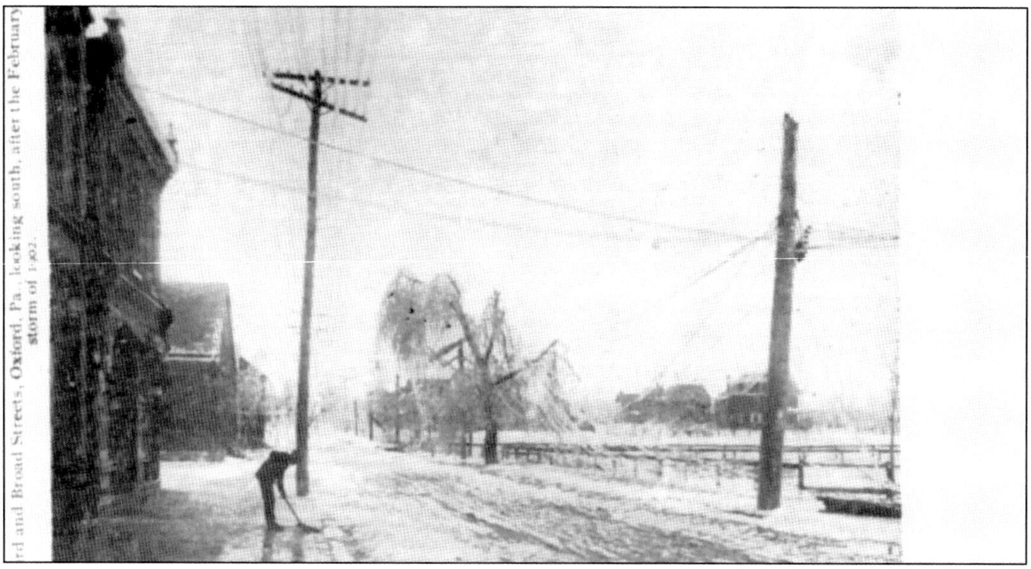

This pre-1907 postcard shows South Third Street looking south toward Hodgson Street after the winter blizzard of February 1902. At the far left is the Walker building, with the finials on top, then located at No. 113 (now No. 117), and the Oxford Electric Light and Power Company building to the right. Several hardware stores were located at this address, including William Burling's, T. D. Alexander's, and J. Morton Ivison's.

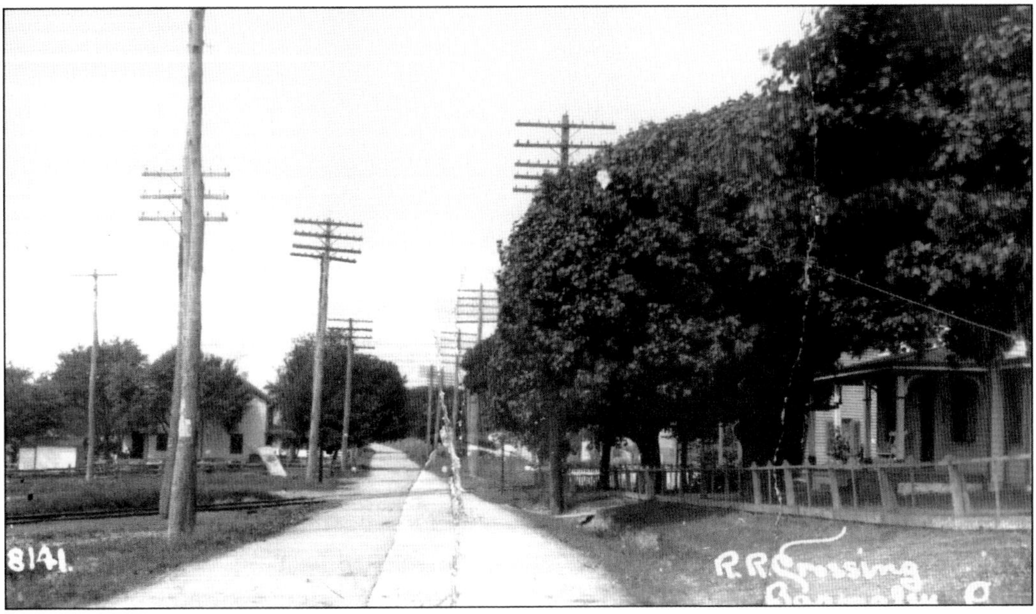

Barnsley, two miles south of Oxford, was known under various names, including Beantown, New Prospect, and Bea Town (after the Bea family). When the Philadelphia, Baltimore and Central Railroad established a station there, the first freight cars carried stone for a new barn on the farm of Elmer Reynolds. From then on, it was known as Barnsley. The area became well known with the establishment of the Barnsley-Tattersall sales. It started as an auction in 1934 and existed until 1965. They sold livestock, produce, household goods, and whatever the stall-holders would bring. One night, it was reported that 10,000 people showed up for a sale.

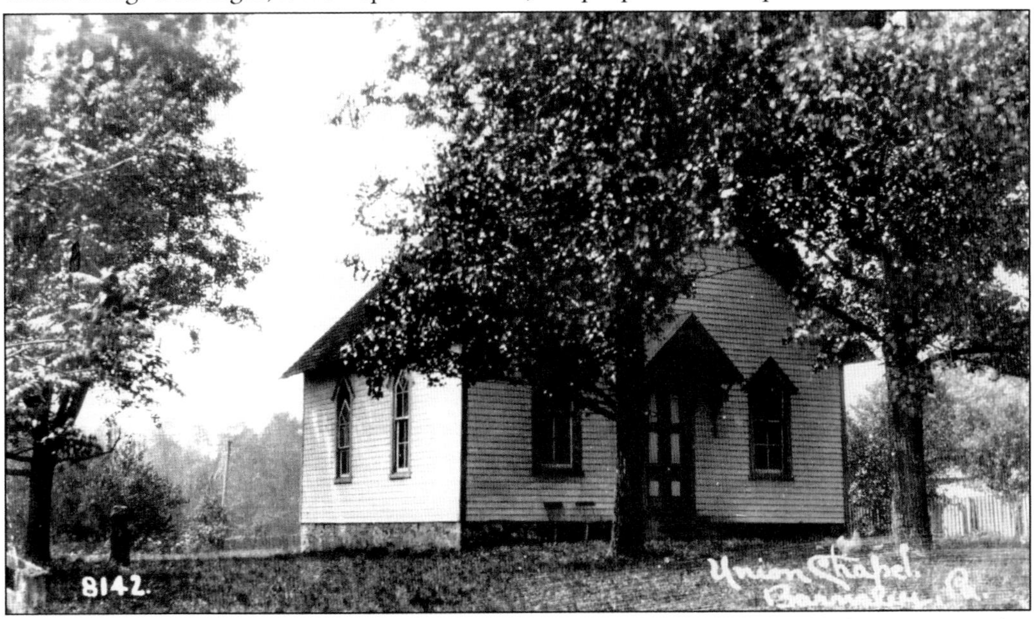

This real-photo postcard shows the old Union Chapel at Barnsley (located at 185 Barnsley Road). J. M. C. Dickey built the chapel in 1885. Over the door in Greek letters were the words "House of Prayer." In the 1930s, it was a Nazarene Church. Now enlarged, it is presently the Faith Tabernacle Church. (Courtesy of Howard Steinberg.)

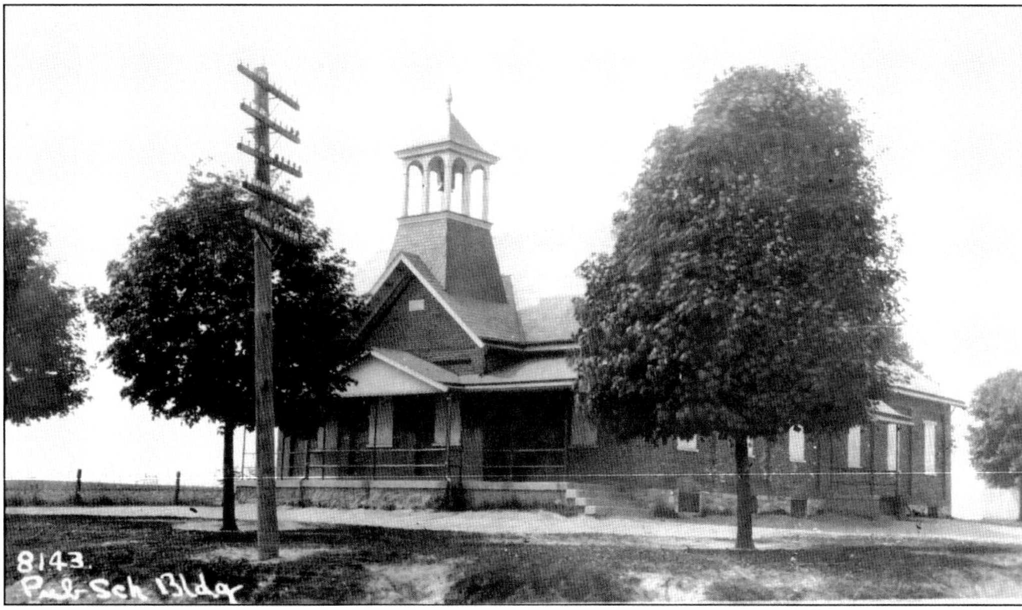

The 1895 public school building at Barnsley is seen in this real-photo postcard. The class of seven that graduated on Thursday, May 5, 1904, included Horace R. Stubbs (president), Florence J. P. Miller (secretary), Annie L. Crowl (treasurer), Lauretta A. Williams (class prophecy), Mabel R. Moore, Fred P. Connor, and Ephraim L. Anderson. The school flower was the white carnation, and the school colors were purple and gold. Located on Barnsley Road, the building is now being used by the Erin Dudley Forbes Charter School. The cupola is no longer in place. (Courtesy of Howard Steinberg.)

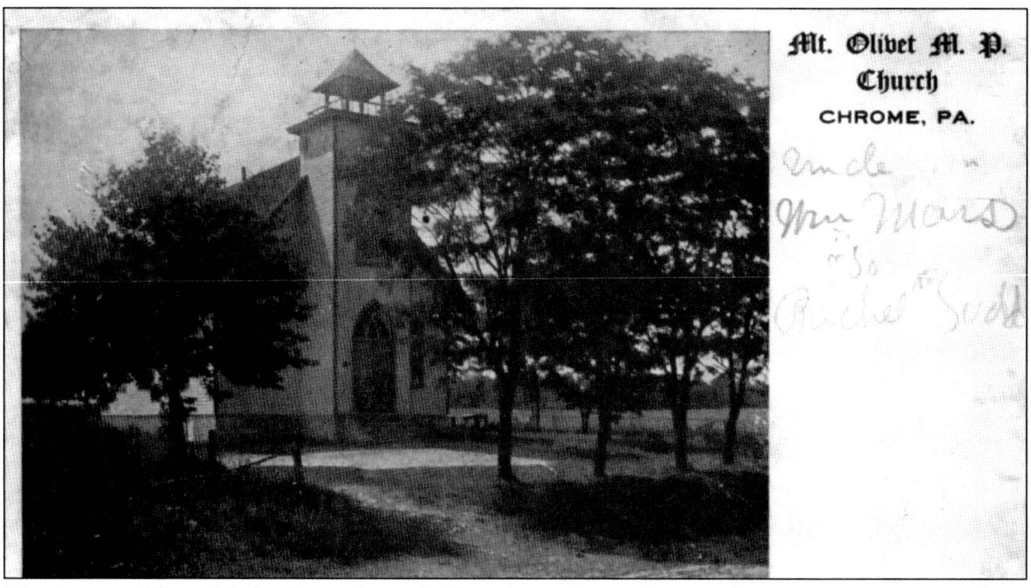

The Mount Olivet Methodist Episcopal Church was located near Chrome in East Nottingham Township. In 1906, around the time of this postcard, the church was remodeled, and in 1932, the steeple was rebuilt. By 1940, the building was being used by the Nazarene Church. The church was demolished in the mid-1970s, and only a small cemetery remains. Chrome was named for the extensive mining that took place in the surrounding area.

Five

Lincoln University

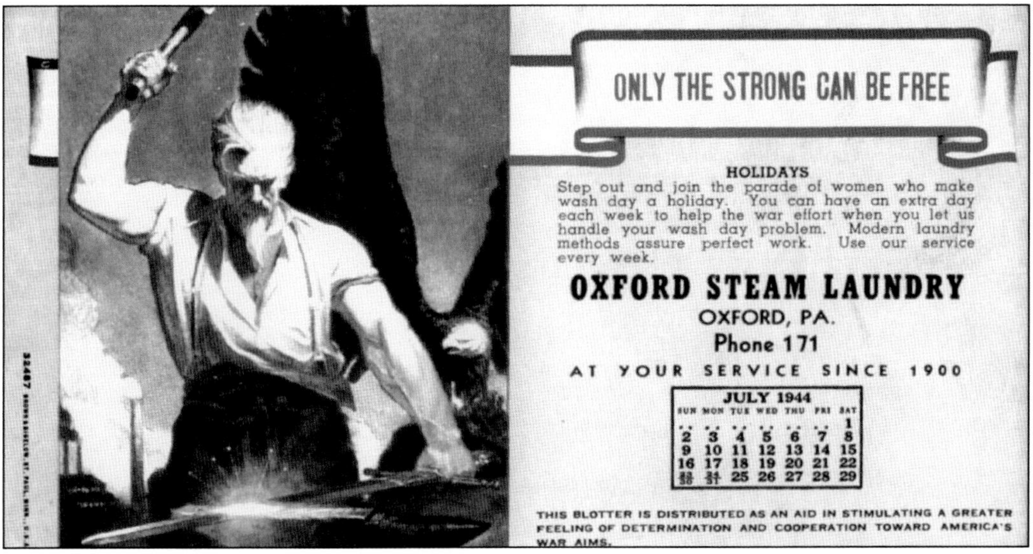

R. Hayes McFadien, proprietor of the Oxford Steam Laundry, distributed this patriotic-oriented blotter in 1944. Originally located at Lincoln University, he later moved his operation to Oxford in 1901. After the Oxford Steam Laundry fire of 1942, the laundry business was moved to a site nearby.

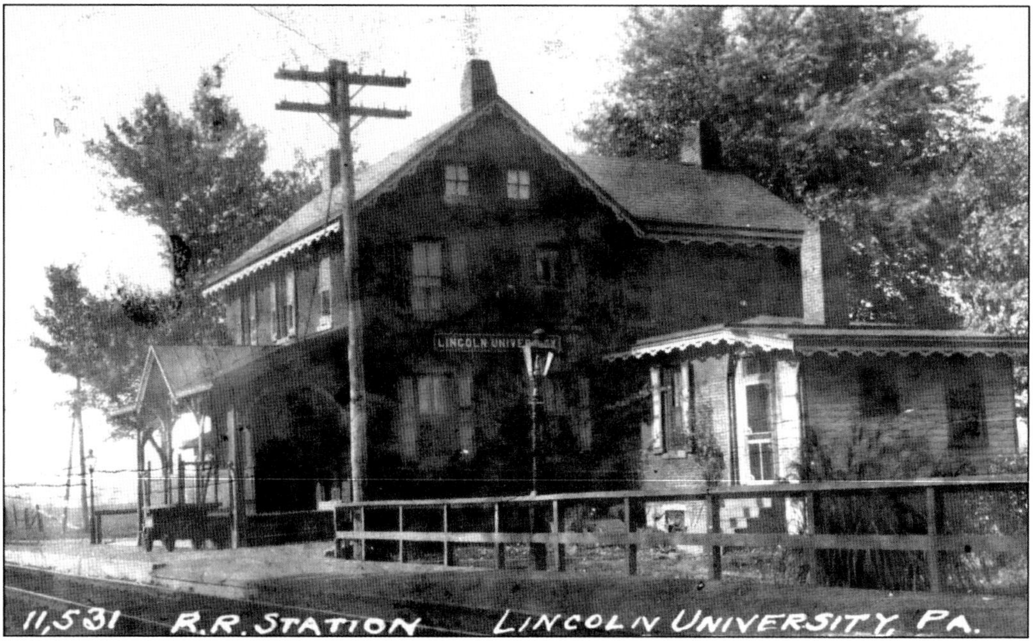

Lincoln University was originally a settlement called Hinsonville after one of its earliest settlers, Emory Hinson. It was a settlement of free black landowners. The station shown here was originally called Buttonwood because in 1775, Revolutionary War captain James McDowell drilled his recruits under the buttonwood tree at his nearby home. The Philadelphia and Baltimore Central Railroad arrived here in 1860, and when the post office opened to serve the college the station became known as Lincoln University. This rare real-photo postcard dates from 1914.

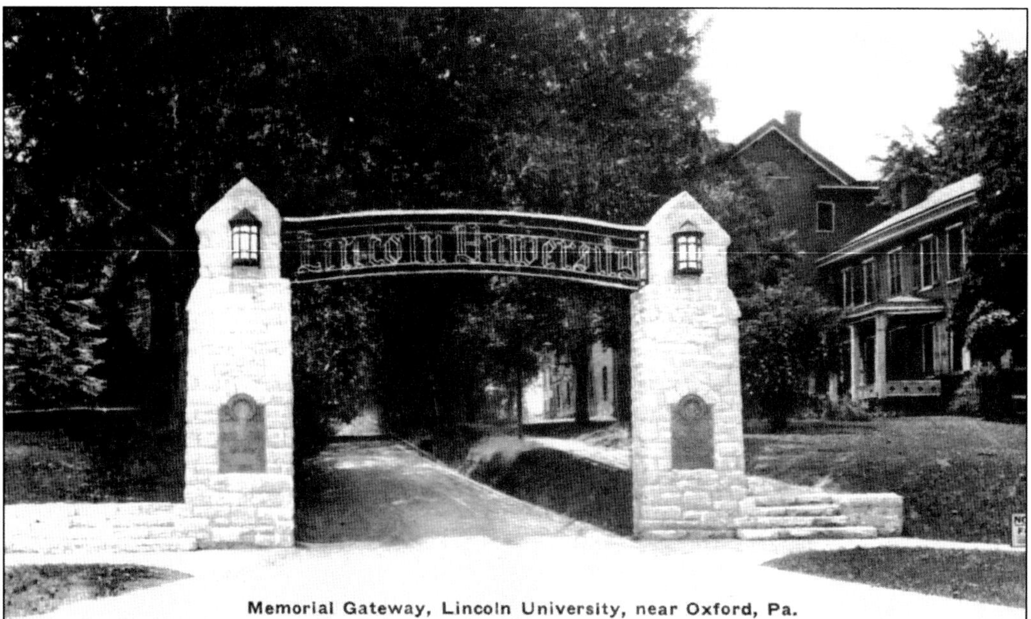

This postcard shows the Memorial Gateway at Lincoln University that was erected in 1921 by the school's alumni in honor of those who lost their lives in World War I.

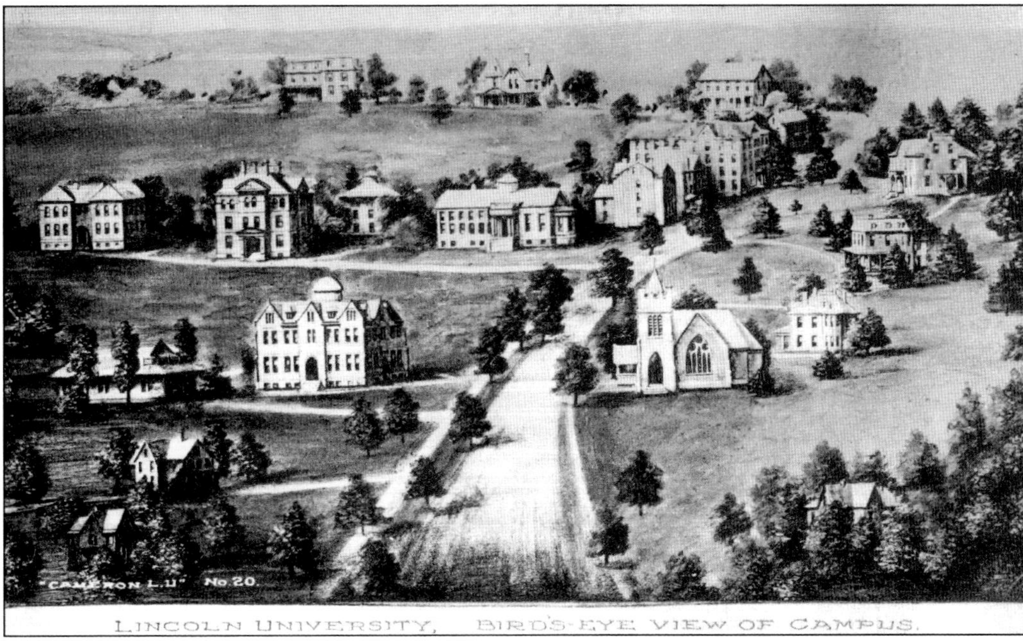

This interesting view of Lincoln University looks west on Maple Avenue toward Old Baltimore Pike. Lincoln University was chartered in 1854 as the Ashmun Institute after Jehudi Ashmun, a white missionary sometimes called the founder of Liberia. Its purpose was to give a "liberal, scientific, classical and theological education to colored males." Rev. John Miller Dickey, who was instrumental in the formation of the institute, wanted to train the "colored youth" to be missionaries in Africa. On April 4, 1866, the name of the institute was changed to Lincoln University. It is the oldest degree-granting black college in the United States. The top postcard dates from 1910–1912, and the bottom postcard from September 18, 1905. It is the earliest Lincoln postcard in the authors' collection and shows several campus buildings.

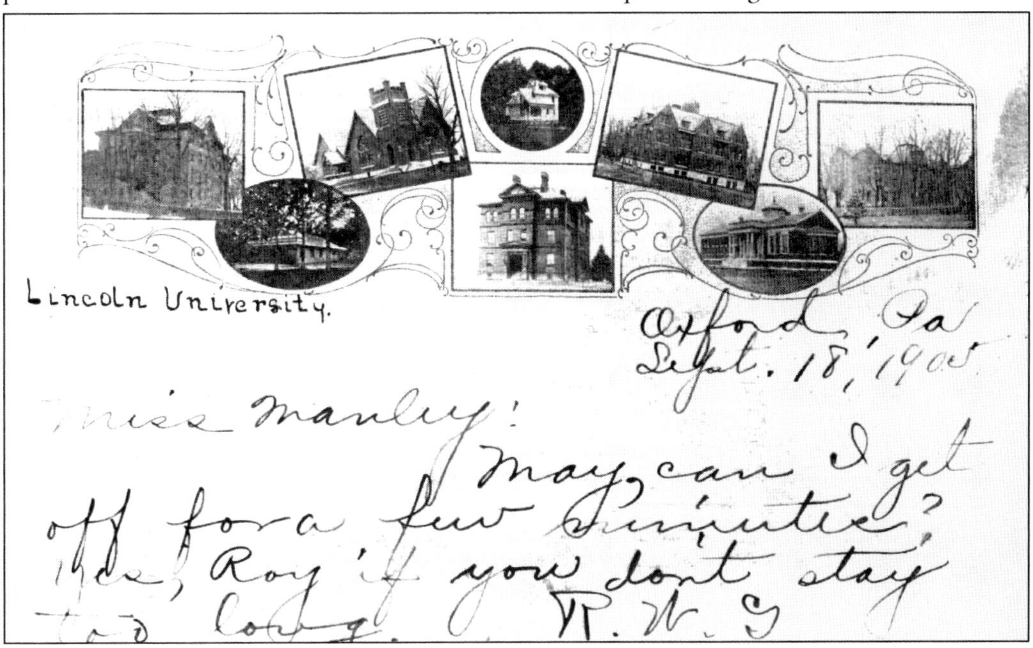

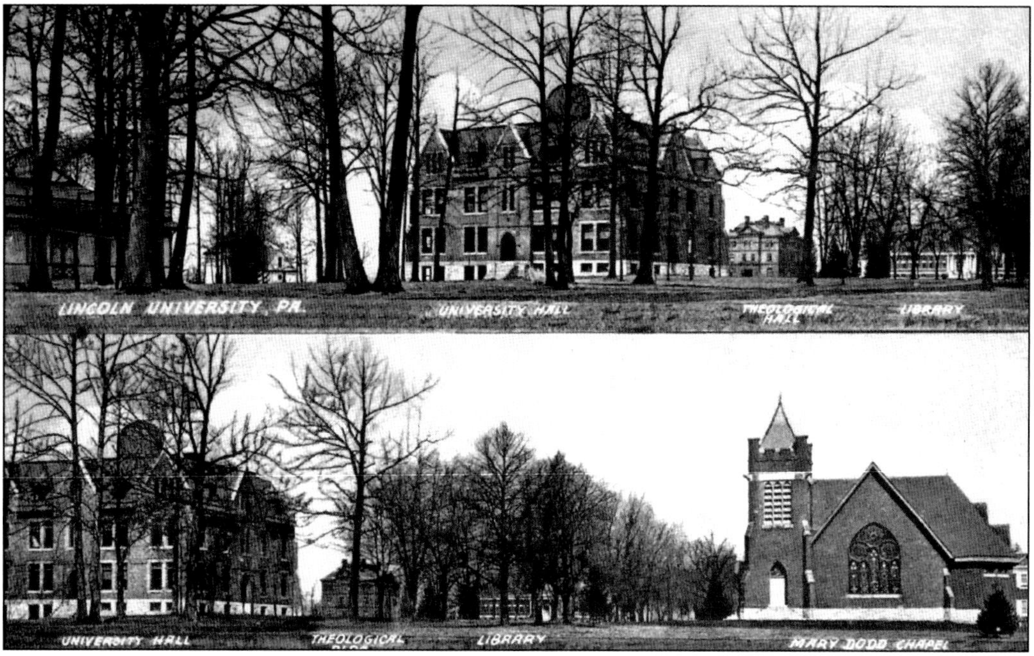

W. H. Tegeler of West Grove produced these two postcards around 1910–1912. The top postcard shows part of Livingstone Hall at the far top left, University Hall, the Theological Hall, library, and the Mary Dodd Chapel. The bottom postcard shows the Dining Hall, Theological Building (Houston Hall), library, a dormitory, University Hall, the hospital, and the heat and light plant. University Hall was heated by steam; the chemical and physical science rooms were located in the basement. Charles P. B. Jefferys, Esq., donated the revolving observatory that sits atop the building. At the beginning of the 20th century, the college also had nine residences for college professors.

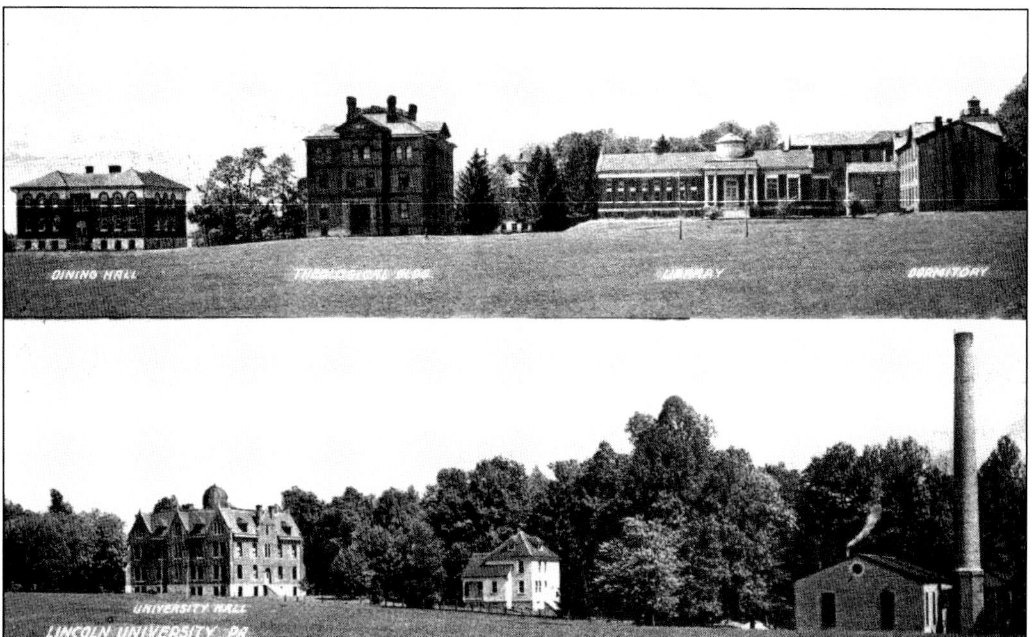

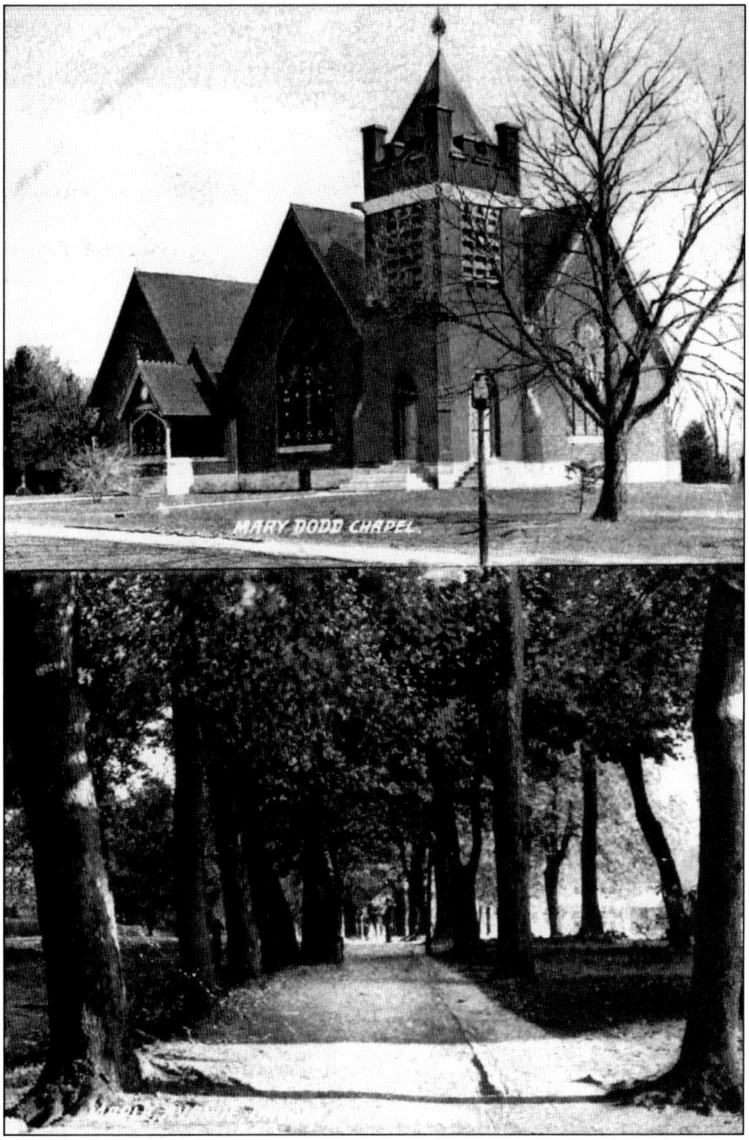

The Mary Dodd *[sic]* Chapel and Maple Avenue are shown in this postcard produced by W. H. Tegeler of West Grove. As Lincoln University bought up most of the land of the original Hinsonville residents, it closed a portion of the Russellville-Elkdale Road and incorporated a quarter mile of it into the campus; today it is called Maple Drive. The university grounds surrounded Hosanna Church and what was left of Hinsonville. In 1871, Lincoln University bought Elias P. Draper's store, later the site of this chapel. Lincoln University was the alma mater of some well-known names in American history. Langston Hughes, acclaimed poet, was educated here, as was musician Cab Calloway. Thurgood Marshall, Supreme Court justice, also graduated from Lincoln. Before becoming a justice, Marshall argued the case of *Brown v. the Board of Education* that overturned the "separate but equal" education of blacks and whites. The father of Paul Robeson, William Robeson was an alumnus who met his wife, Louisa Bustill (a Hinsonville resident), while at the school. Paul Robeson was a renowned baritone, social activist, athlete, actor, writer, and recipient of both the Spingarn Medal and Stalin Peace Prize. Future leaders of African nations also attended Lincoln, including Kwame Nkrumah of Ghana.

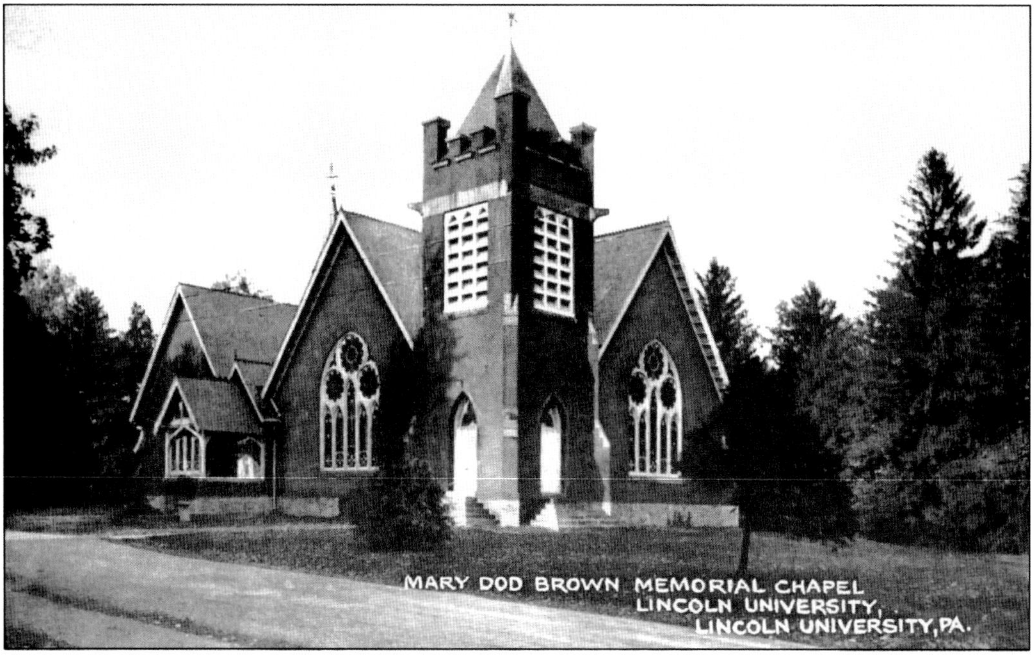

The Mary Dod Brown Chapel was constructed in 1890–1991, with a gift of $20,000 from Susan Dod Brown of Princeton, New Jersey. The building, named in honor of Susan's daughter, is 115 by 67 feet and built in the neo-Gothic style with a seating capacity for 400 persons. The church was dedicated on April 19, 1891, and is divided into four parts—the church proper, a prayer hall, and two classrooms. The postcard below shows the interior of the chapel in 1920. The organ was received from the Presbyterian Church of York. At the time, it was one of the largest instruments of its kind in Chester County.

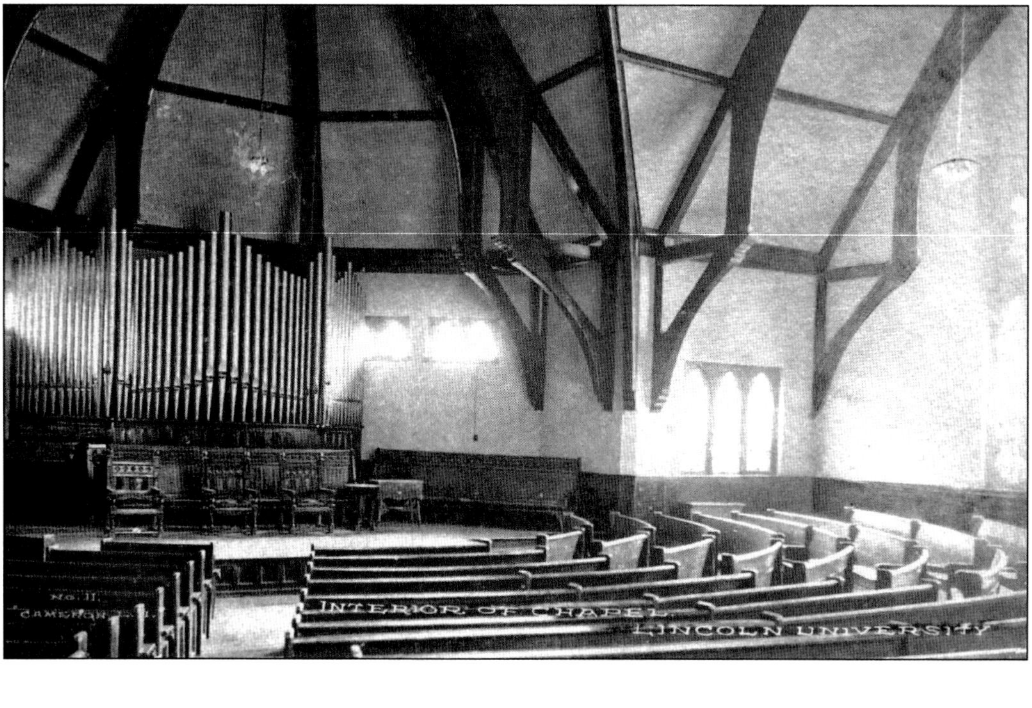

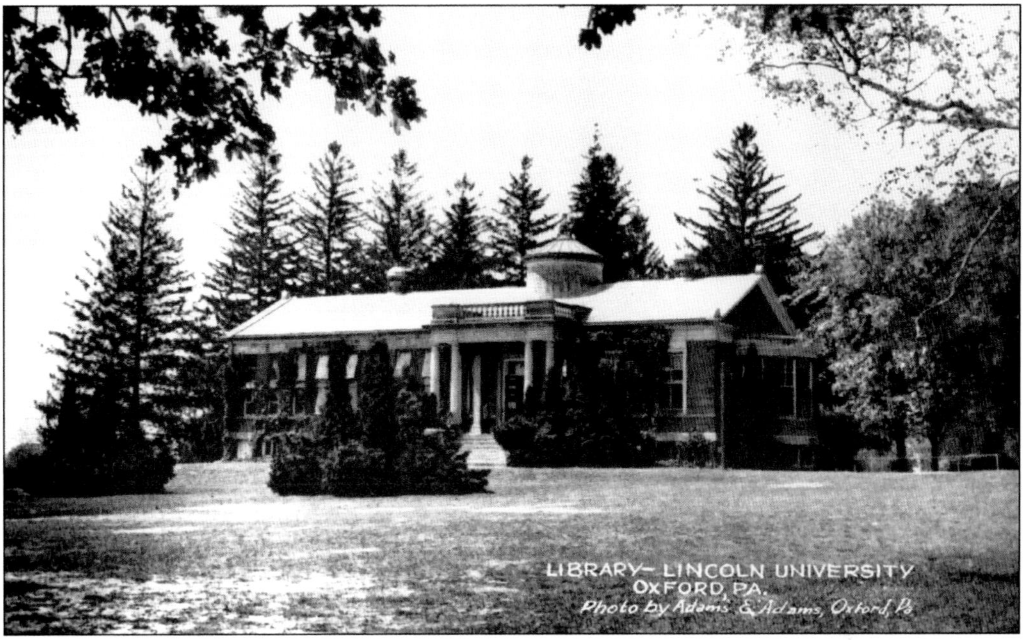

The cornerstone of the Vail Library was laid on Wednesday, June 28, 1893, with president I. N. Rendall making the opening remarks. The fireproof library was designed by architect Addison Hutton and constructed of iron and Media brick, and finished in 1898. The building measured 33 by 90 feet, cost $28,000, and used hot water for heating. Dr. William H. Vail of Blairstown, New Jersey, erected the library as a family memorial. It served as a library until 1972 and is now used as administrative offices.

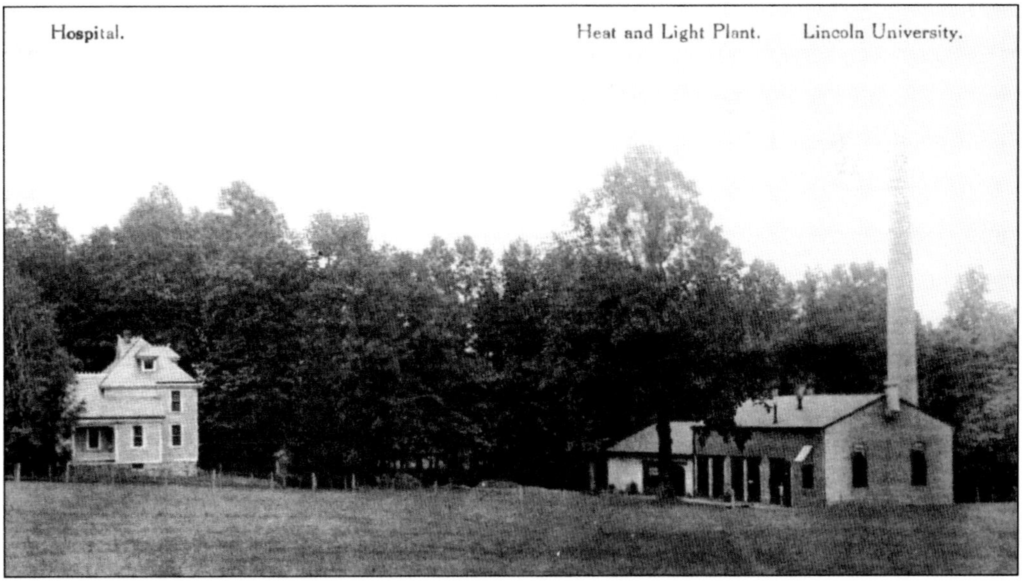

On the left side of this postcard is the Harriet Watson Jones Cottage Hospital, a three-story, 26-by-31-foot frame building constructed by Milton Walker in 1895–1896. It was named in memory of president Rendall's deceased sister and erected with a donation by J. M. C. Dickey. On the right side is the old heat and light plant. The postcard is No. 13 in a series published by local druggist Arthur T. Cameron in the early 1920s.

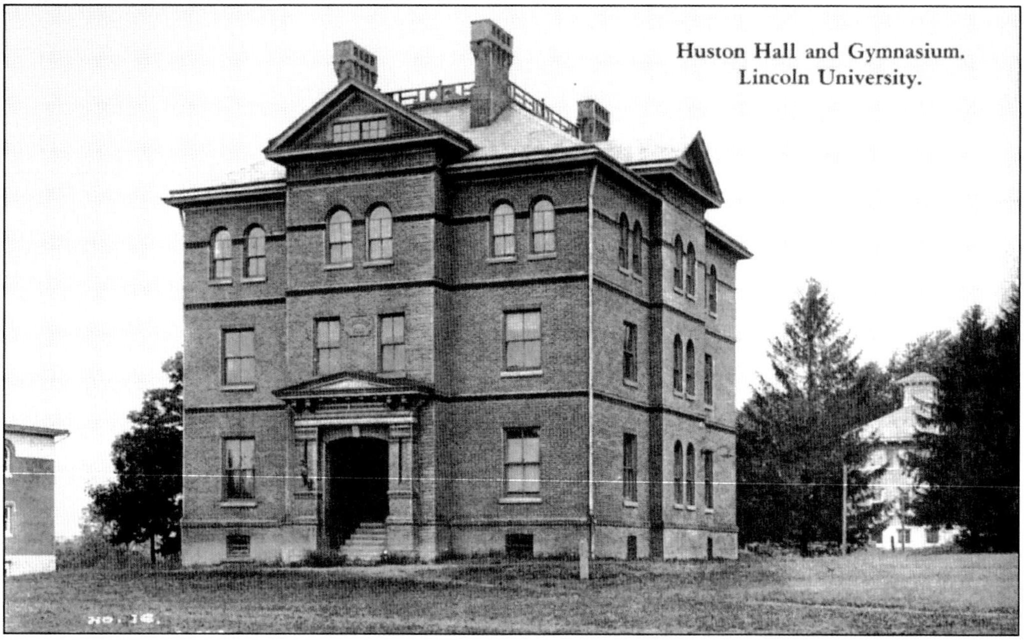

Milton Walker, an Oxford builder and carpenter, built 14 new buildings at Lincoln University and was involved in the repair and remodeling of three others. In 1881–1882, Houston Hall became his first project at Lincoln University. This 48-by-68-foot three-story brick structure cost $10,000, which was donated by Henry Howard Houston, a wealthy philanthropist from Germantown. It served as a dormitory for students studying to be ministers and was also the headquarters of the theological and missionary societies until 1959. The building was nicknamed "Mount Sinai" by the theology students. The bottom postcard shows Cresson Hall, a dormitory.

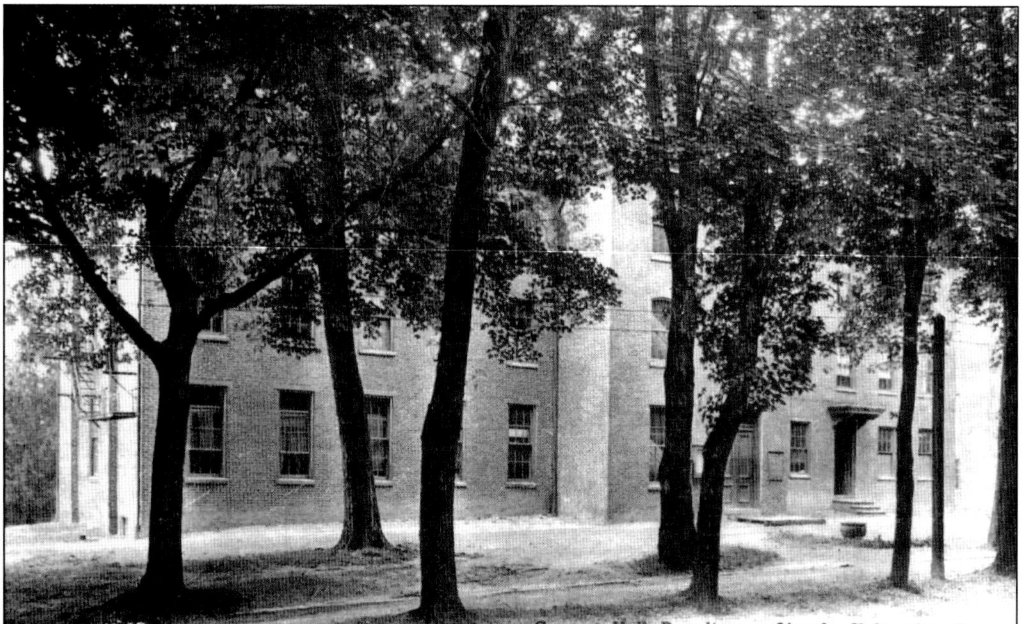

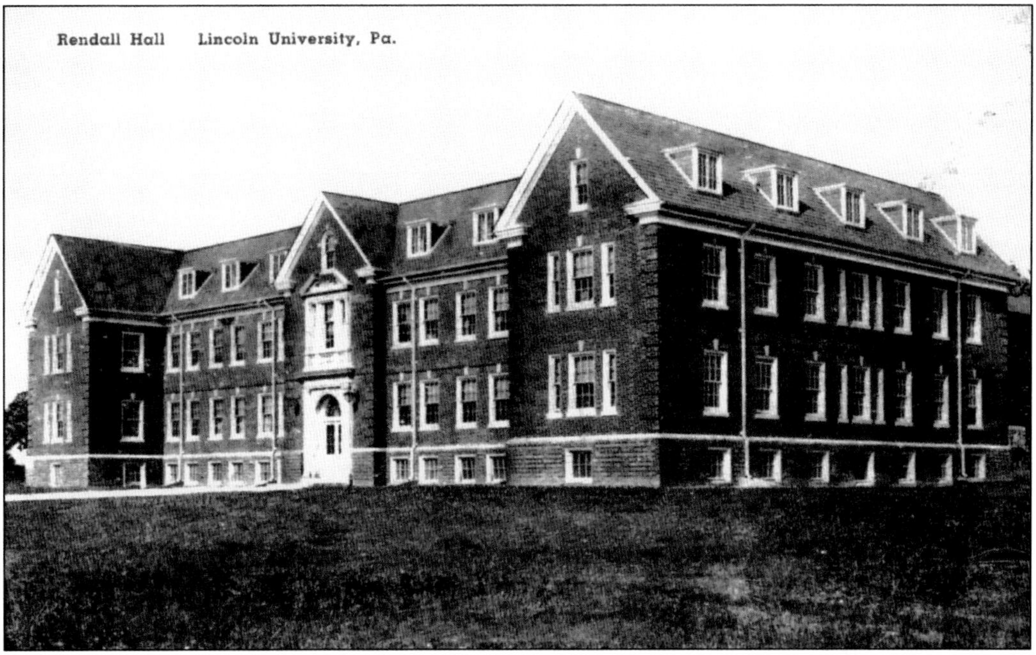

Isaac N. Rendall was the third president of Ashmun Institute and led the institution's transformation to Lincoln University. He resigned in 1906 and was succeeded by his nephew John Ballard Rendall, who served as president from 1906 until his death in 1924. In June 1891, ground was broken for the construction of Rendall Hall, a 62.5-by-78.5-foot two-and-one-half-story brick building that cost $25,000 to build. The postcard below shows the interior airy reception room of Rendall Hall.

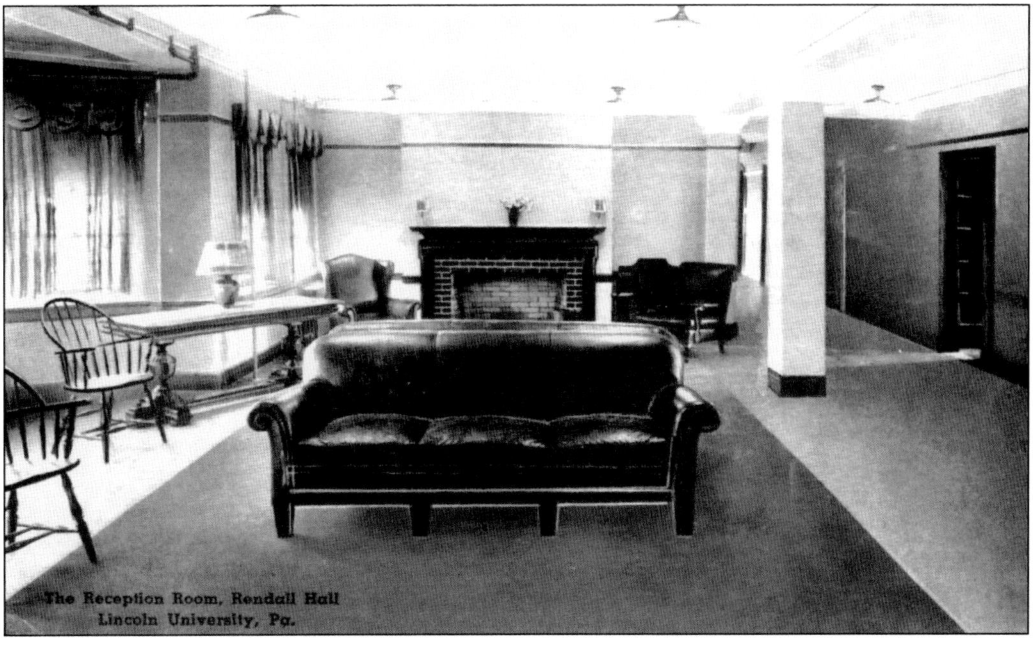

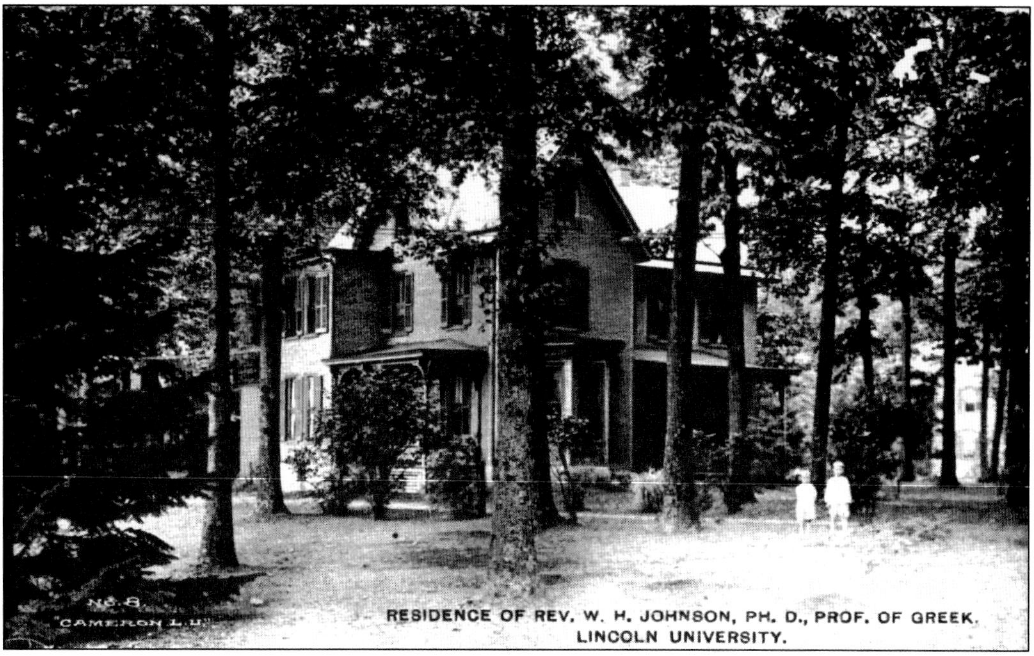

The university supplied homes for some of its professors. Above is the home of W. H. Johnson, professor of Greek in 1903. He was also president of Lincoln University from 1926 to 1936. The house below was the home of Walter Livingston Wright, professor of mathematics. He succeeded Johnson as president, serving until 1945. Both postcards date from 1910 to 1912 and were published as part of a series of postcards by Arthur T. Cameron, a Lincoln University druggist.

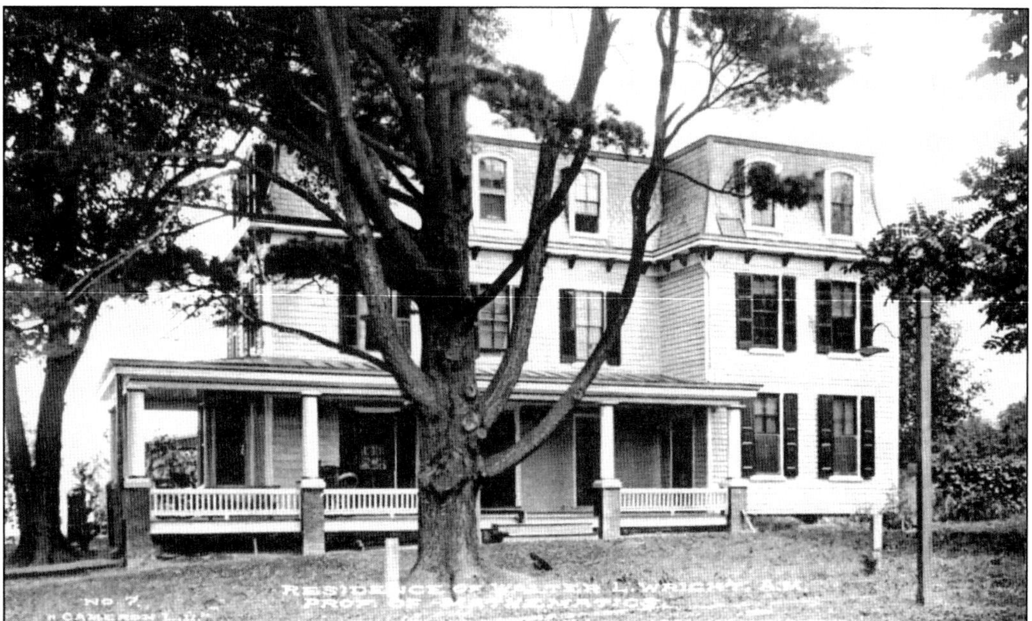

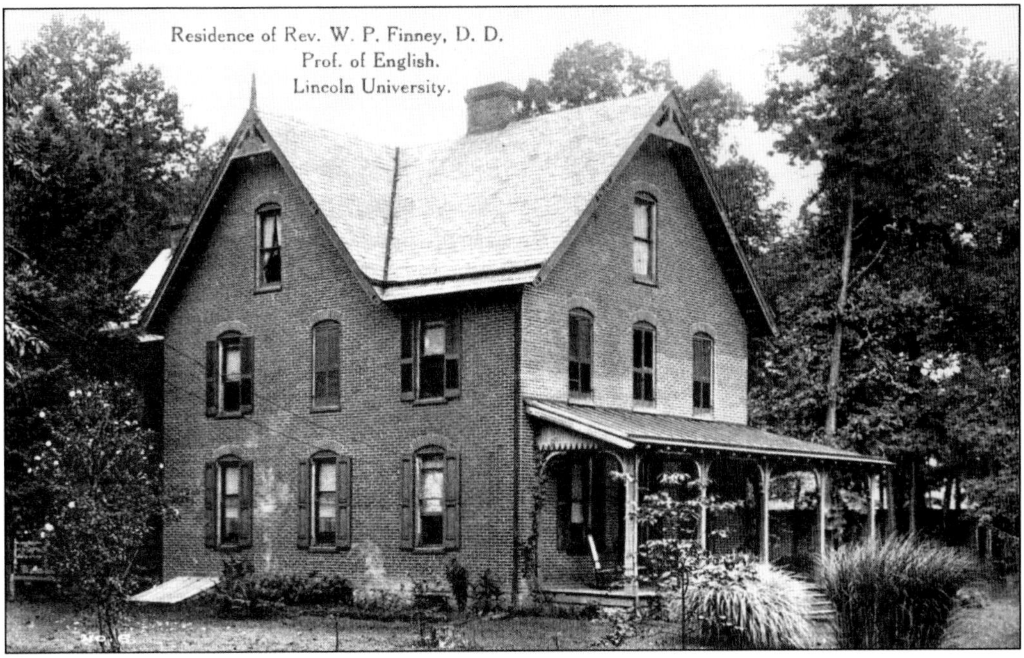

The top postcard shows the residence of Rev. W. P. Finney, professor of English. The bottom postcard shows the residence of Rev. R. L. Stewart, professor of apologetics, who was most likely replaced by W. J. L. Kieffer at the time this postcard was mailed in 1920. Arthur T. Cameron published the top postcard as No. 6 and the bottom postcard as No. 1 in his Lincoln University series.

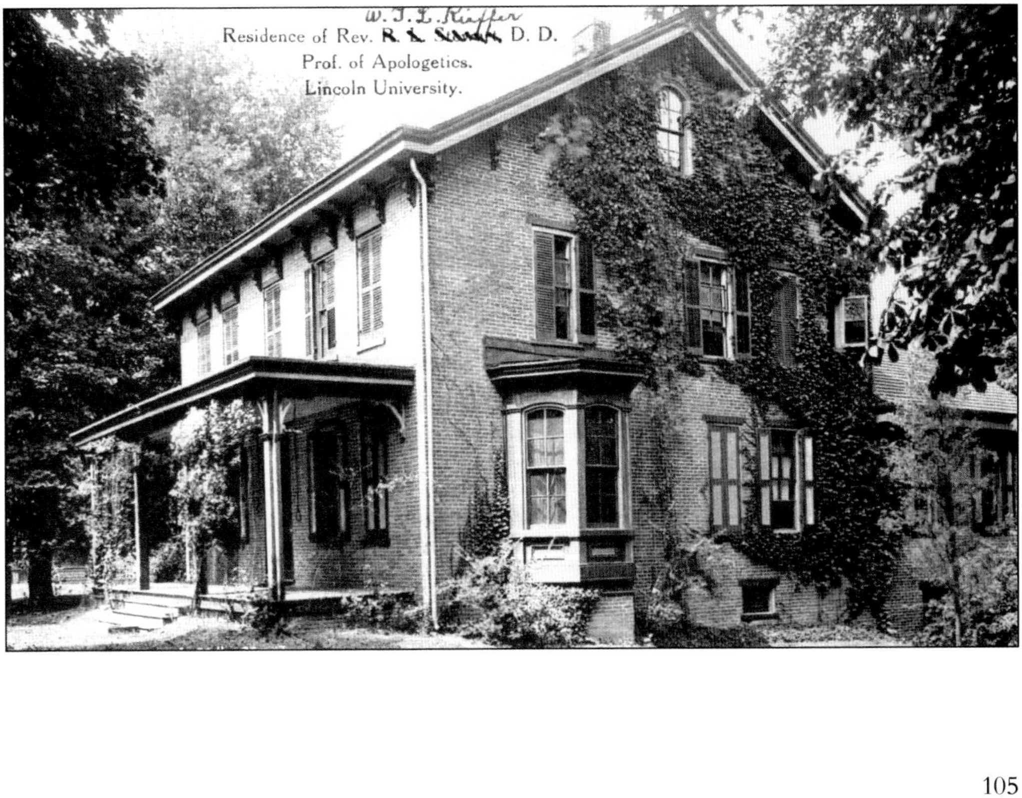

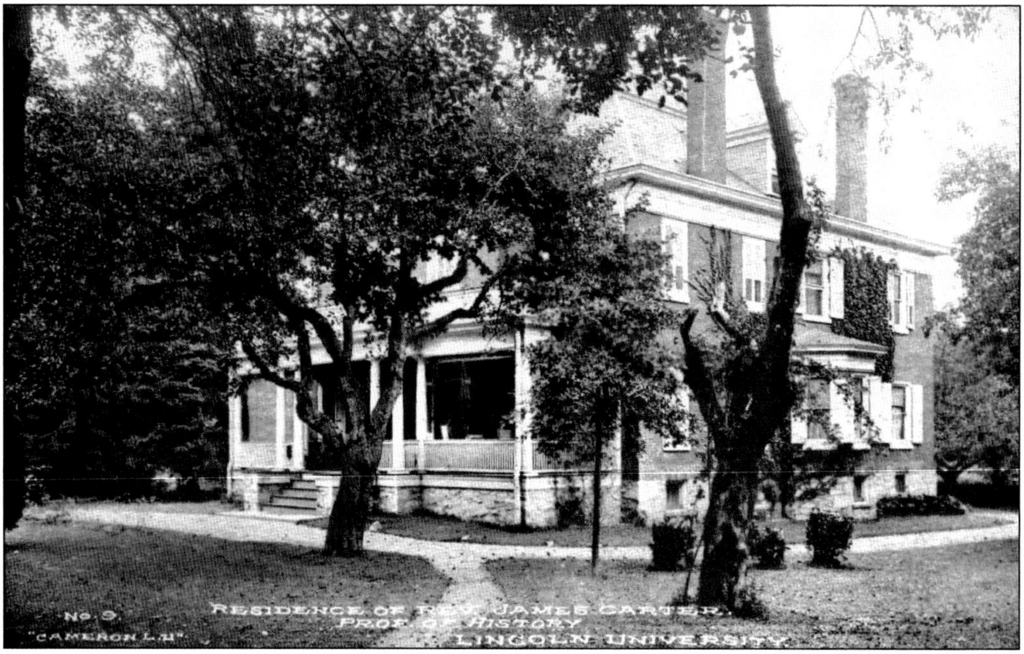

These two postcards, No. 9 and No. 10 in the Cameron series of Lincoln University postcards, show, at top, the residence of James Carter, professor of history, and on the bottom, the residence of ex-president Rev. Isaac Norton Rendall, D.D. (1825–1912), and Pres. John B. Rendall, D.D. Isaac graduated from Princeton Theological Seminary in 1855 and was ordained a Presbyterian minister in 1860. He came to Lincoln University in 1865 after a pastorship in Oneida Valley, New York (1860–1864) and Emporium (1864–1865). Isaac, a bachelor, retired as president of Lincoln University in 1906 and was succeeded by his nephew John.

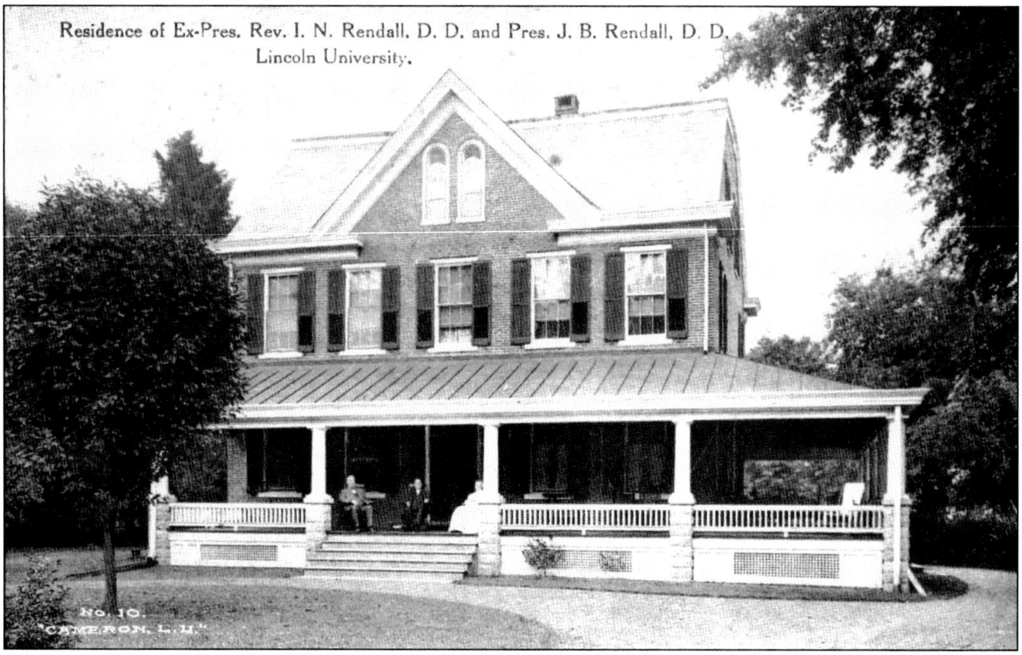

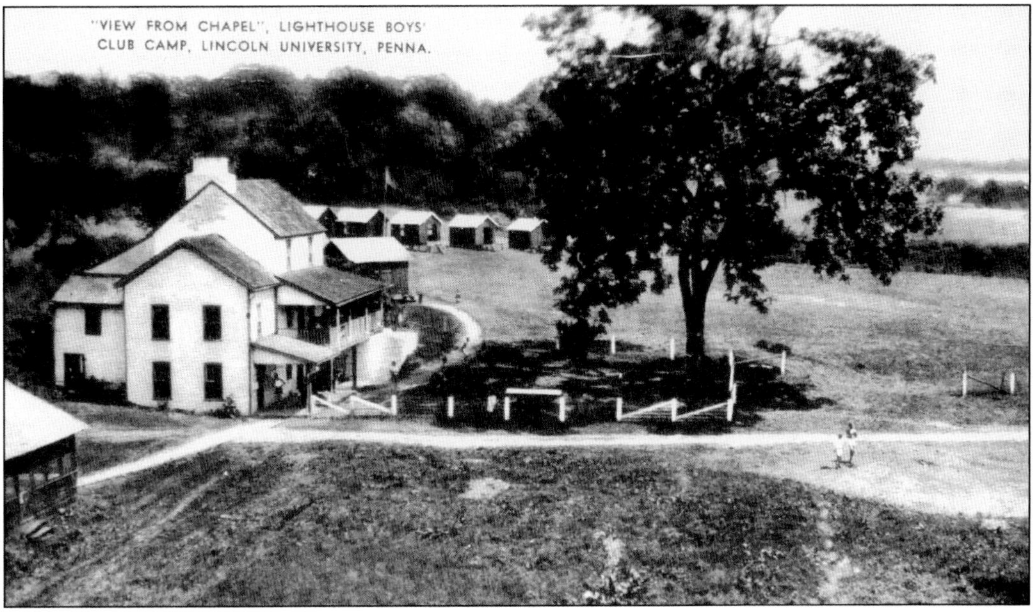

The Lighthouse Boys' Club was established in 1897 as a part of the Lighthouse, a social organization founded by Esther W. Kelly Bradford in 1893. Its primary focus was to provide needed social services to residents of the Kensington section of Philadelphia. Summer camps were held near Lincoln University at a site rented from the Brotherhood of St. Andrew until 1928, when the boys' camp moved to a farm at Chester Springs.

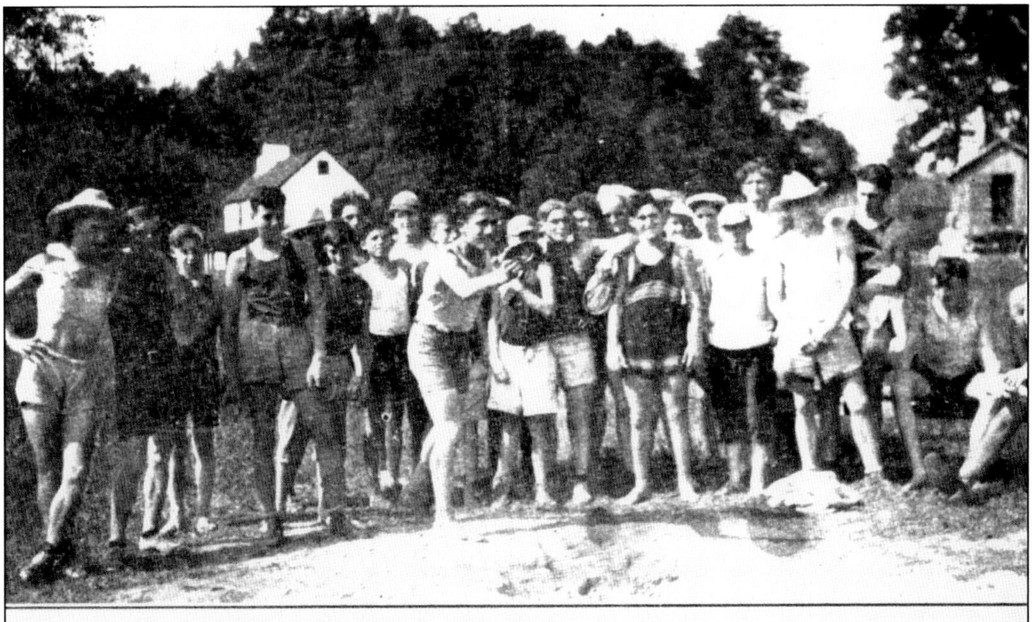

QUOIT TOURNAMENT AT CAMP — Lincoln University, Pa.

This postcard shows a quoit tournament at the Lighthouse Boys' Club camp at Lincoln University sometime before 1928. Oxford also had a quoit club. A September 1911 newspaper article proudly tells that Oxford beat the Chadds Ford team 397-235. Evidently, the Chadds Ford team was the team to beat at the time.

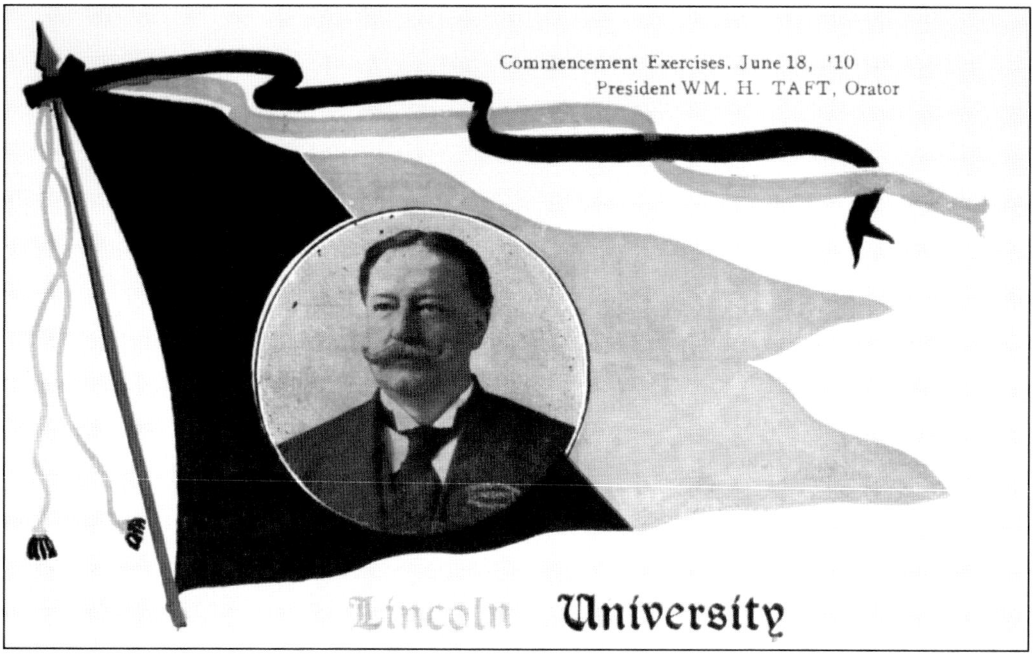

Pres. William Taft gave the commencement address at Lincoln University on June 18, 1910. Introduced by president J. B. Rendall as a "man of calmness," Taft paid tribute to Tuskegee and Hampton Institutes and Booker T. Washington as "one of the greatest men of the century." After the commencement, Taft made a whistle stop in Oxford, where he made a five-minute speech from his train on his way back to Washington.

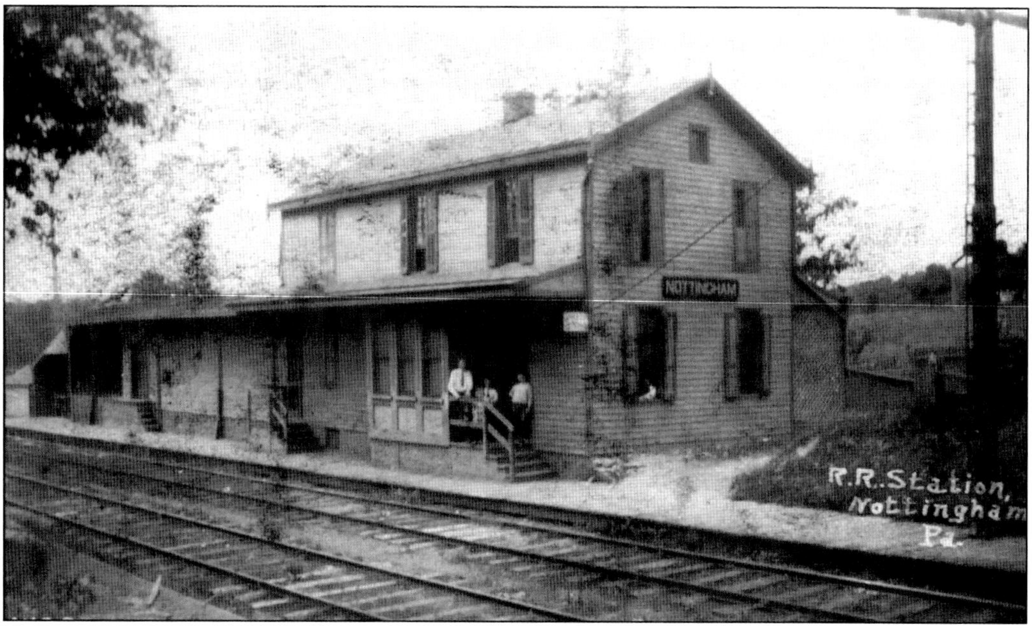

Nottingham station was on the Philadelphia and Baltimore Central Railroad's Octoraro line between Barnsley and Sylmar, Maryland. In November 1892, a train wreck occurred near here but, luckily, the only injury was an engineman with a broken wrist. The Nottingham station is seen in this rare real-photo postcard dating from 1914.

Six

Nottingham and the Octoraro Valley

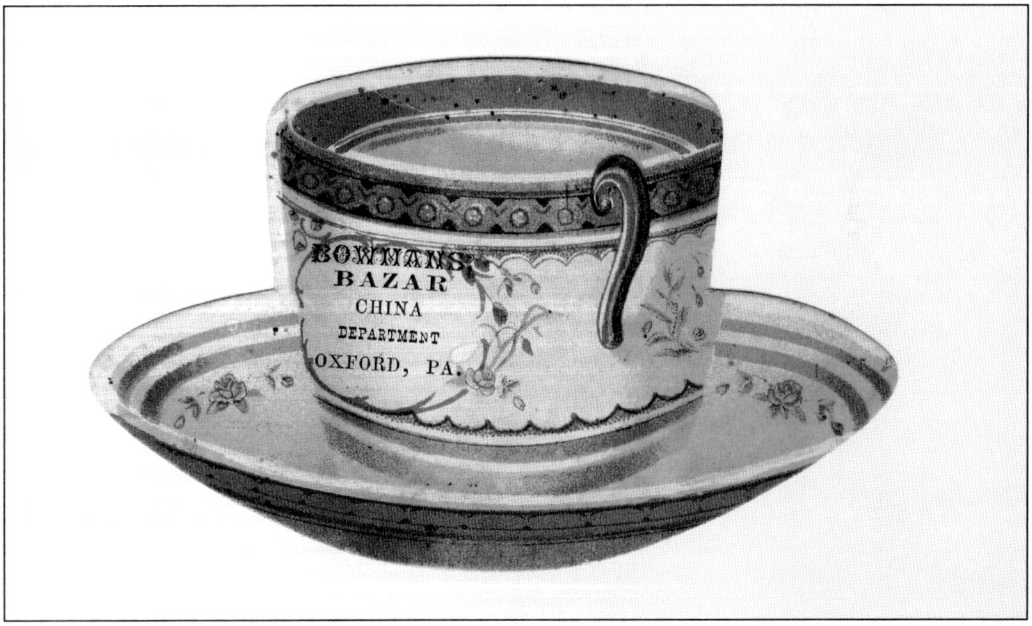

In 1886, J. Warren Bowman constructed a new store around the old one. After it was roofed, the old building was dismantled piece by piece while the store was still open for business. When completed, there was an opening in the second floor that allowed, from the first floor, a view of the ceiling that was painted with cloud effects. The unusual trade card pictured above dates from the mid-1880s.

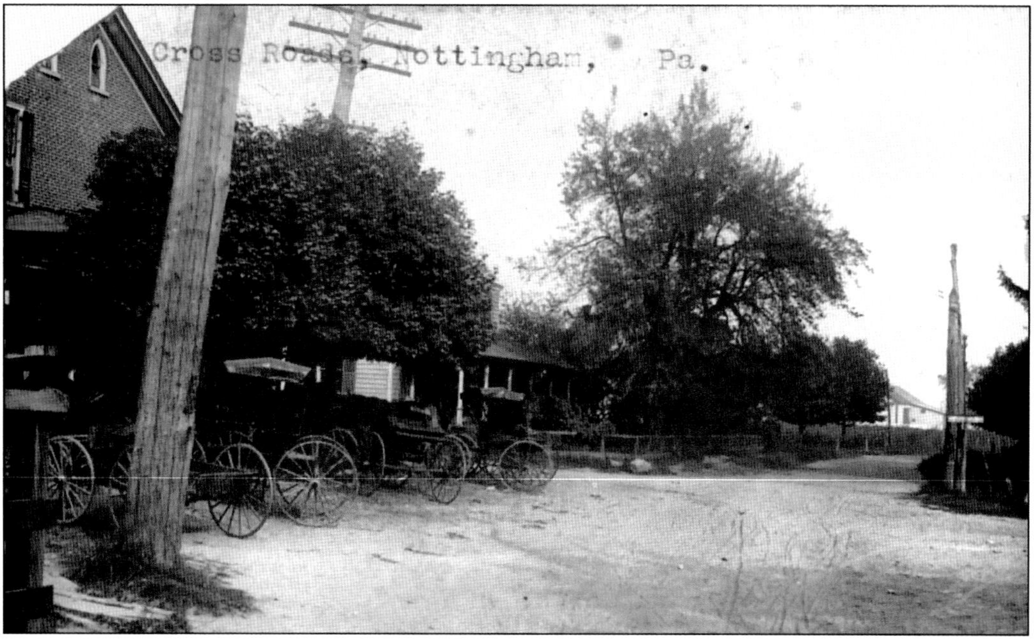

Nottingham was first called Christine after the Swedish queen. The town was later called Fountain Mills before being changed in 1853 to Nottingham after Nottingham, England. The crossroads in Nottingham is seen in this real-photo postcard from 1909. The small directional sign on the right directs travelers to Barnsley and Oxford.

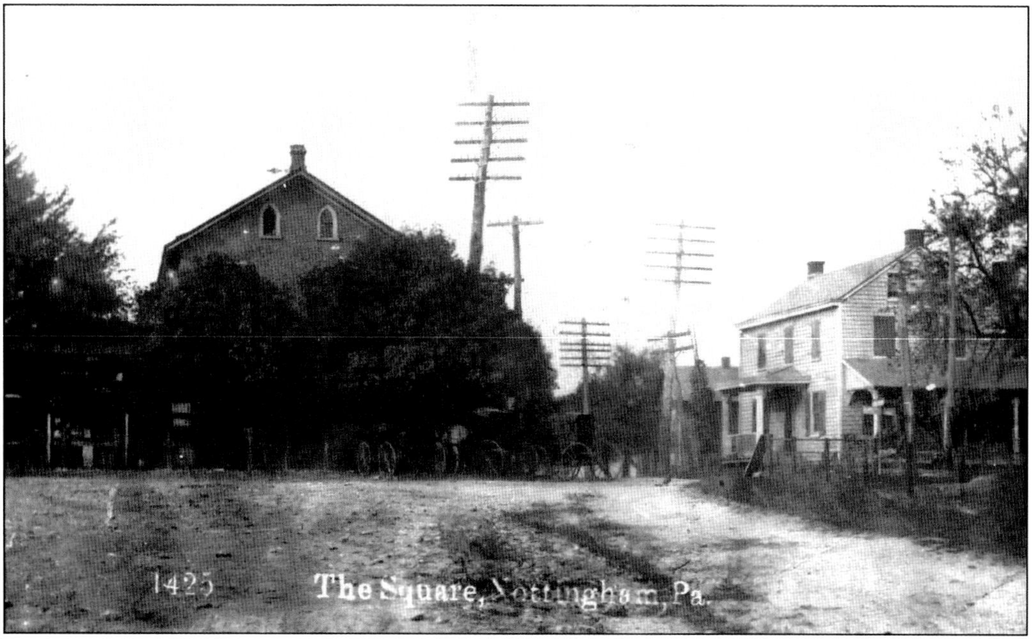

The area was divided into East and West Nottingham Townships sometime between 1715 and 1718. The village of Nottingham lies in the west section. The home on the left is located at 525 Christine Road at Old Forge Road and is now an office for a real estate agent and attorneys. The house on the right has since been demolished and replaced by a building for Union Fire Company No. 1.

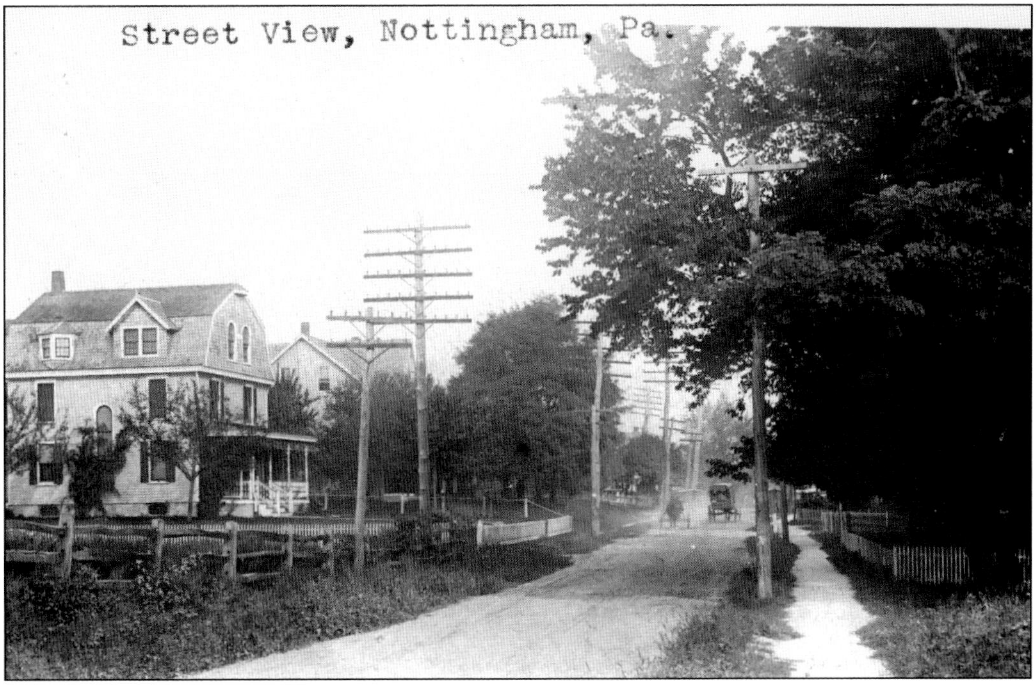

Ed Herbener of Newark, Delaware, published this *c.* 1907 real-photo postcard. It shows a street scene in Nottingham looking south, with the three-story house on the left still standing at 505 Christine Road.

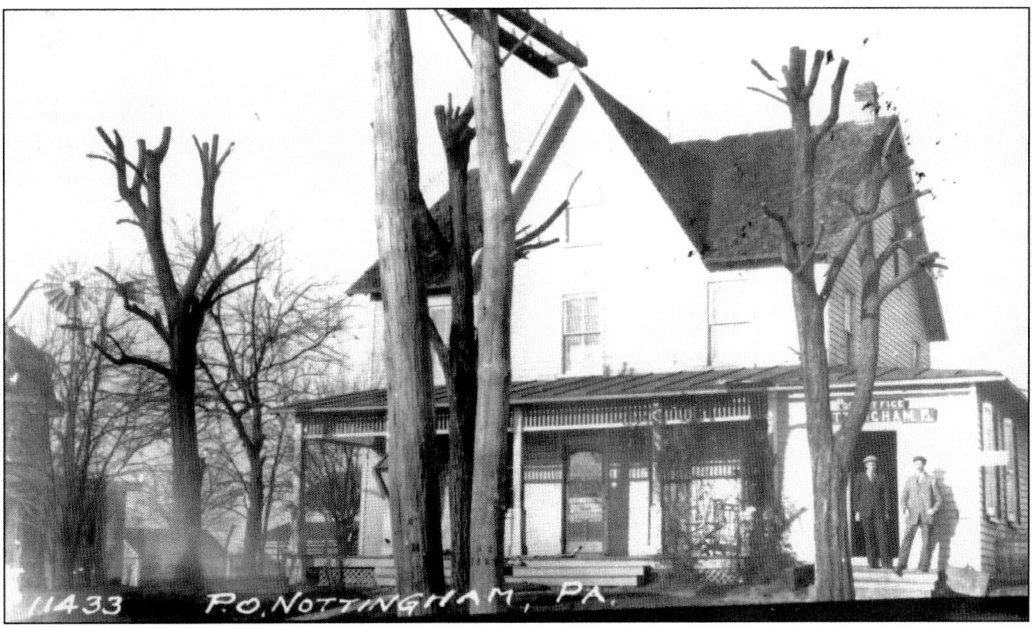

Daniel Stubbs and his son had a blacksmith shop, gristmill, dairy farm, lumber and coal yard, and store in Nottingham. In 1851, a post office was established in the store with Stubbs as postmaster. It was later moved to a location near the railroad station. The building pictured here is located at 519 Christine Road and is now apartments. Ed Herbener of Newark, Delaware, produced this 1909 real-photo postcard.

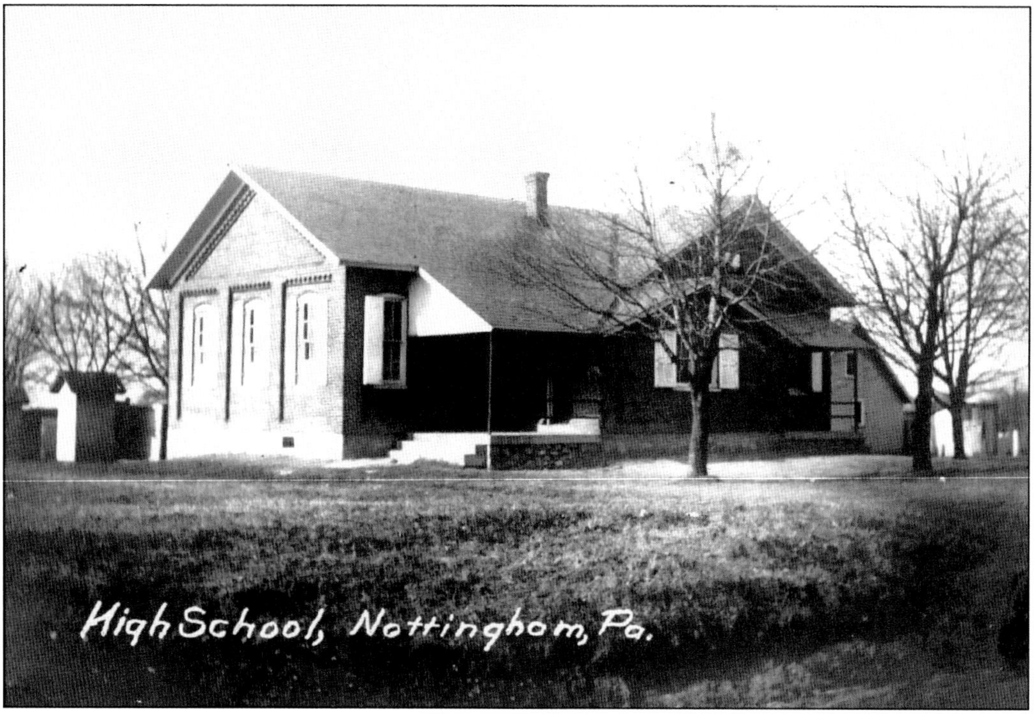

The Nottingham High School building dates from 1887 and is located at 598 Christine Road (PA Route 272). Two young ladies made up the first graduating class in May 1907. By the time of the eighth commencement in May 1914, there were seven graduates. The old school building is now the home of Euphoria Spa and Salon.

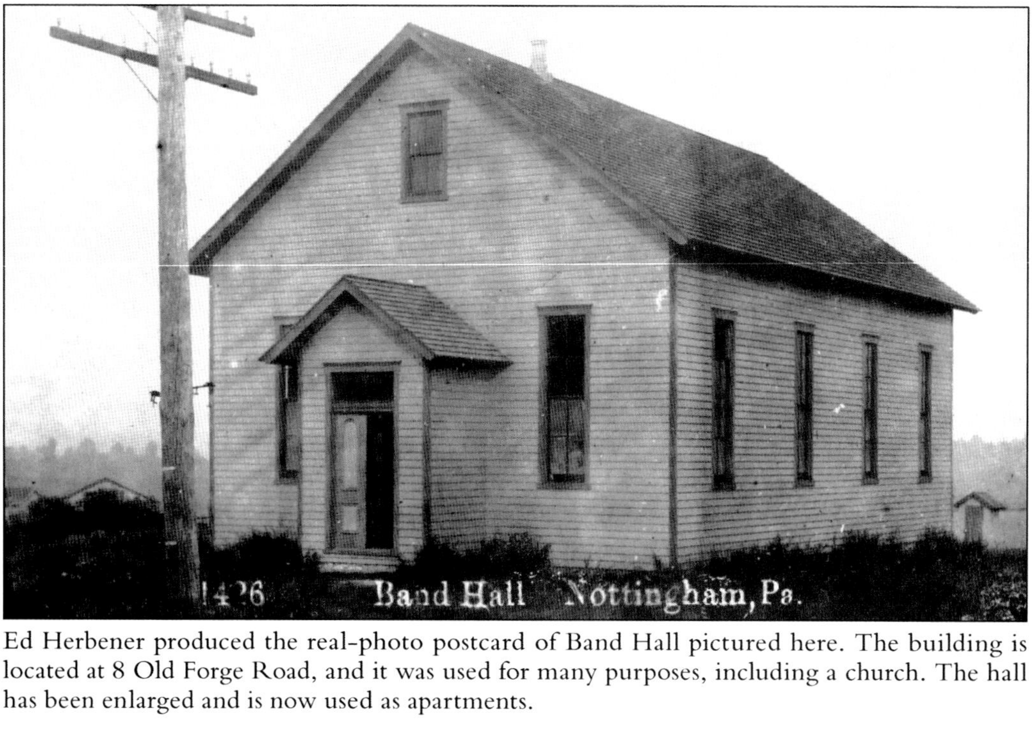

Ed Herbener produced the real-photo postcard of Band Hall pictured here. The building is located at 8 Old Forge Road, and it was used for many purposes, including a church. The hall has been enlarged and is now used as apartments.

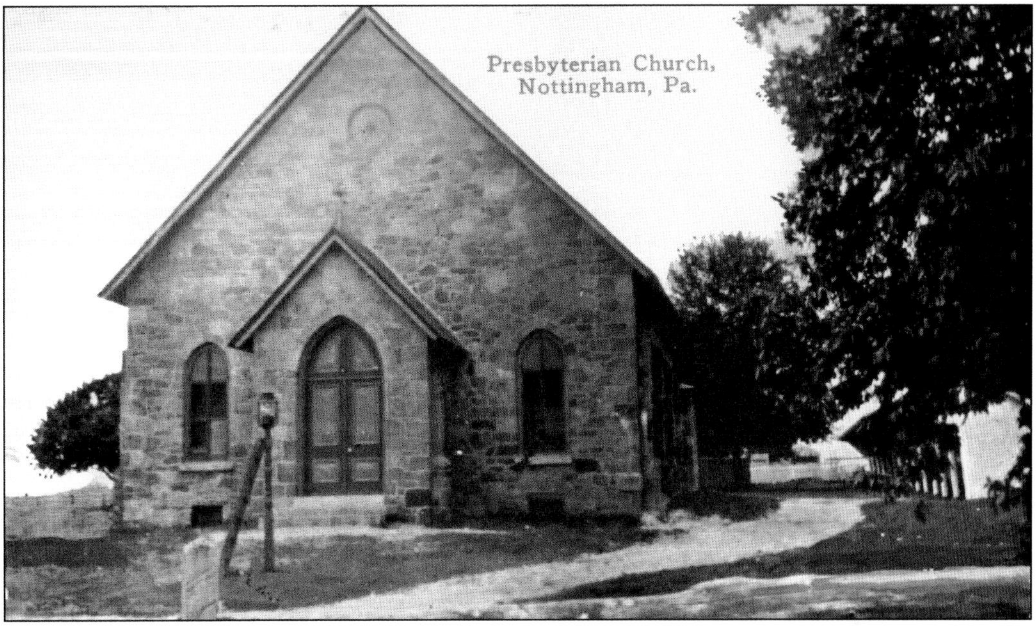

In 1800, a group of Methodists and Presbyterians built a log church in Fremont, but the collaboration lasted only a year or two and the Methodists took over the building. The Presbyterians then built a church in 1802 on ground donated by Samuel McMaster (now Nottingham Cemetery). The history of Nottingham Presbyterian Church dates from the beginning of the 19th century when the charter of incorporation was granted in 1811 to the organized church then known as Upper West Nottingham Presbyterian Church. The cornerstone for the new serpentine stone church above was laid in August 1878, during the pastorate of Rev. L. C. Rutter. The church name was changed at that time.

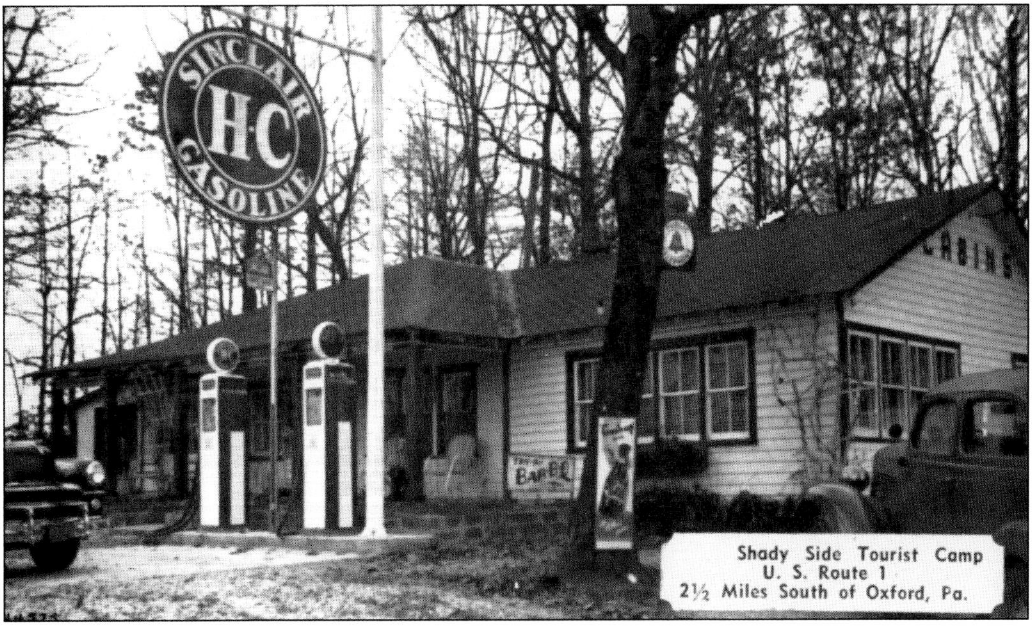

The Shady Side Tourist Camp was located at Old Baltimore Pike and Forge Road. The site is now a mobile home park. Locals called it "Featherman's" after the owner.

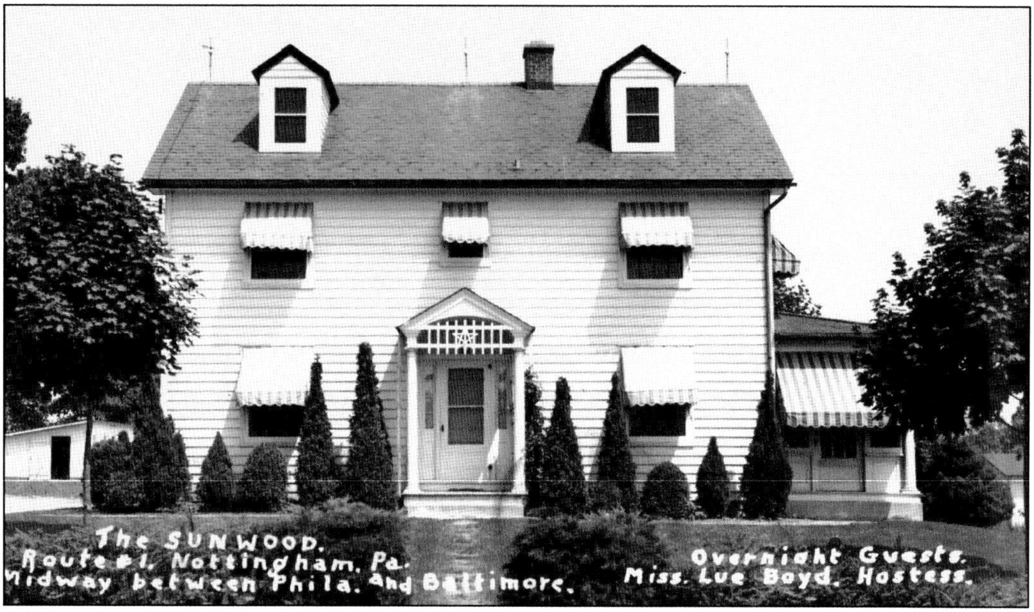

Located at 289 Old Baltimore Pike (off Herr Drive), the Sunwood tourist home was operated by Lue Boyd in the late 1930s. She provided overnight guests with meals and sold fresh eggs and poultry. The back of a similar postcard of the home reads, "here one has the opportunity of enjoying all of the comforts of home amid the loveliest rural setting." The house is located just south of the Herr's visitor's center.

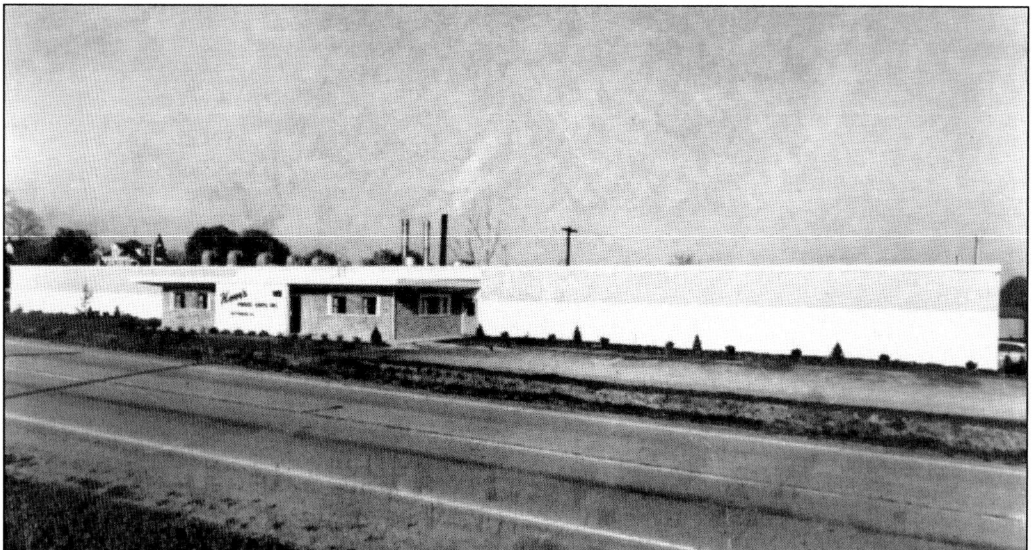

Herr's Potato Chips, Inc., has been a part of the Nottingham landscape since 1951, when James Herr purchased 30 acres in Nottingham and moved his factory from Lancaster County. This card dates from 1964, when the company issued an invitation to visit its new plant in operation on May 23, 1964. Today the plant has over 100,000 visitors per year touring its totally modern facility.

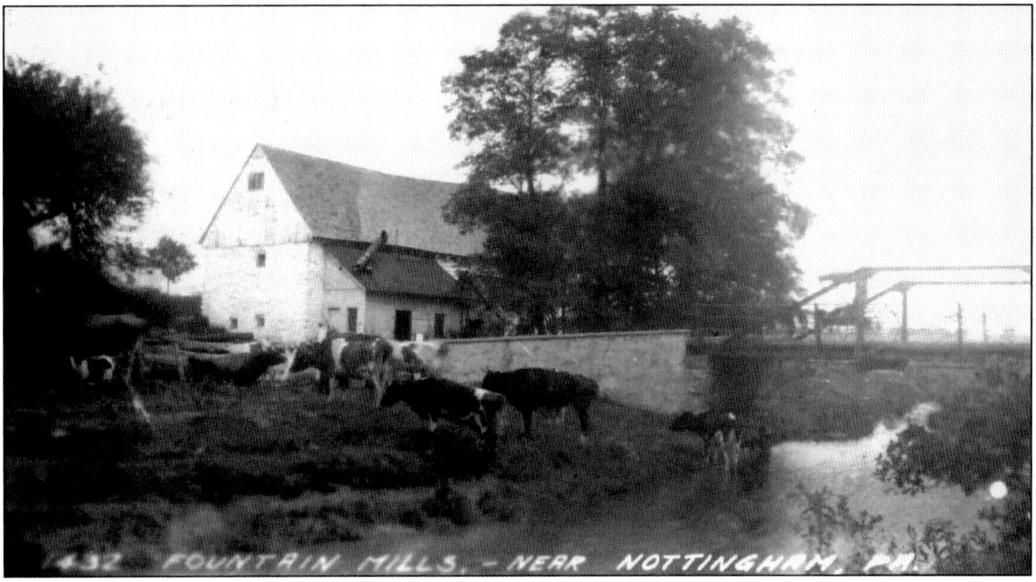

John M. Herr was miller and proprietor of Fountain Mills, located on the Northeast Creek near Chrome. Herr purchased the property about 1886 and made several improvements to the property. One of these improvements was to the head of the race in order to improve waterpower, which was then said to be hard to surpass.

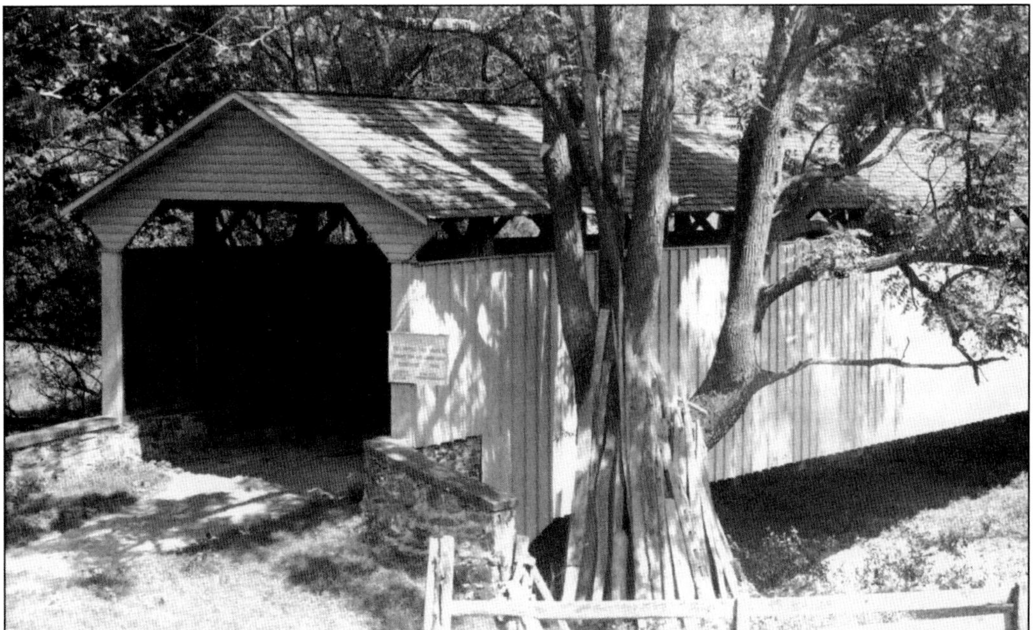
McCreary's Bridge, also known as Black Run Bridge, was built in 1860 and named for Hiram McCreary, known locally as "High Jack" because of his height. He was owner of gristmills and sawmills nearby. The bridge was located on Fremont-Kirk's Mill Road and crossed the Black Run Creek. It was rebuilt and painted yellow in 1889 by George E. Jones at a cost of $2,116. It was 80 feet long with a 16-foot roadbed. On May 27, 1967, it was destroyed by fire and, because of its remote location, never replaced.

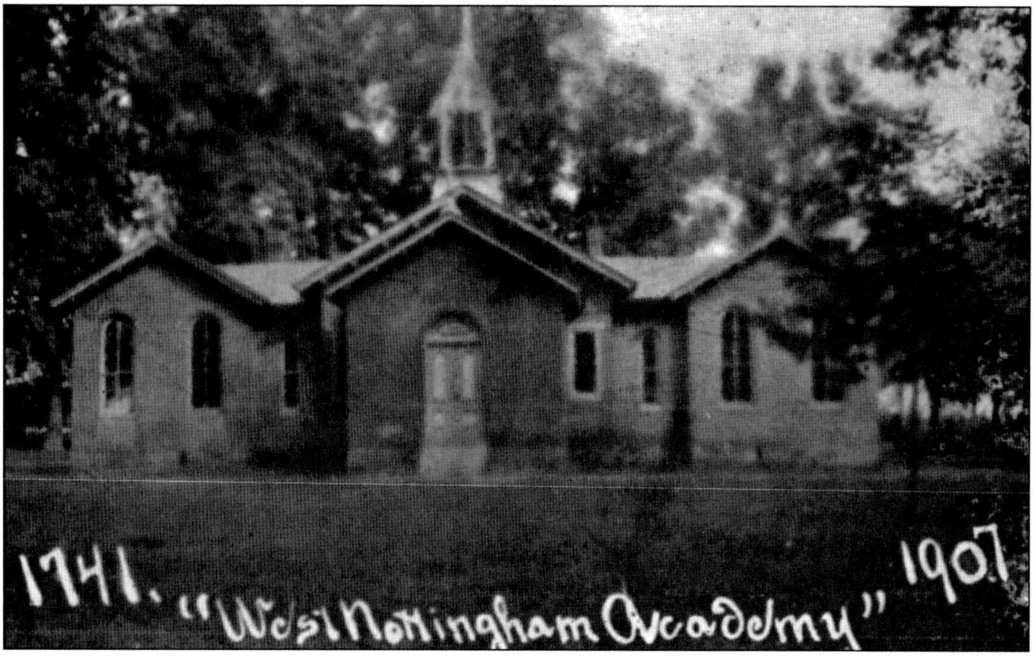

West Nottingham Academy was established in 1744 by Irish Presbyterian pastor Samuel Finley. He started a school for males in a log cabin (near the present Rising Sun Middle School). He was known as a strict disciplinarian, thus the school motto *Nihil Sine Labore*, "nothing without labor." In 1761, Finley left the academy and became the president of the College of New Jersey, now Princeton. When the Mason-Dixon Line was established in 1767, the academy did not move, but the state it was located in did! Now in Maryland, the academy moved to a new site in the village of Colora in 1811.

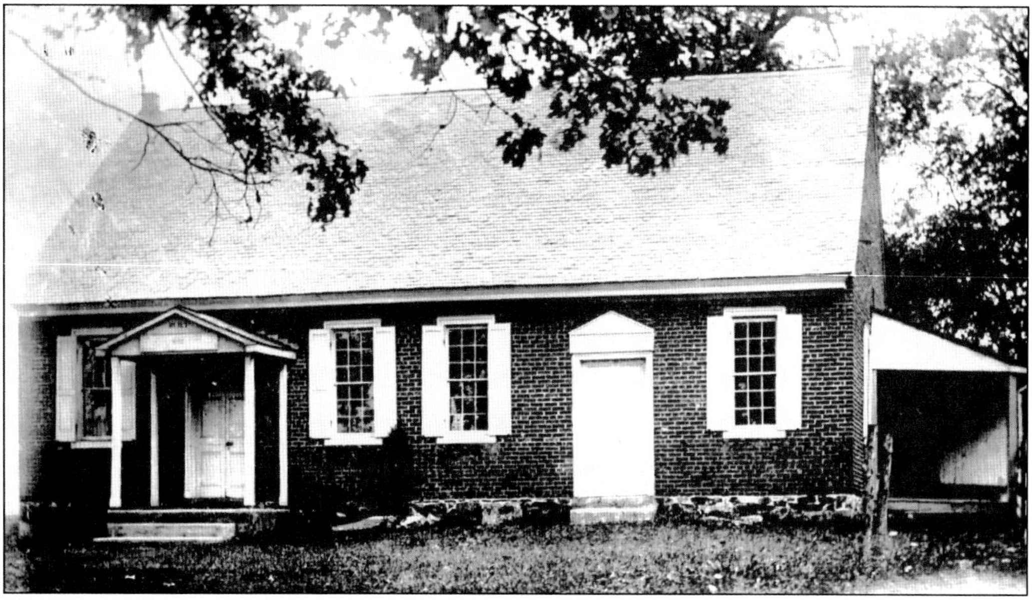

The Nottingham Friends Meeting House was established about 1710 and was known as the "Little Brick House" to distinguish it from the Brick House Meeting in Calvert, Maryland. The meetinghouse shown above was built in 1811 and is located on Harrisville Road near Nesbitt Road in Rising Sun, Maryland.

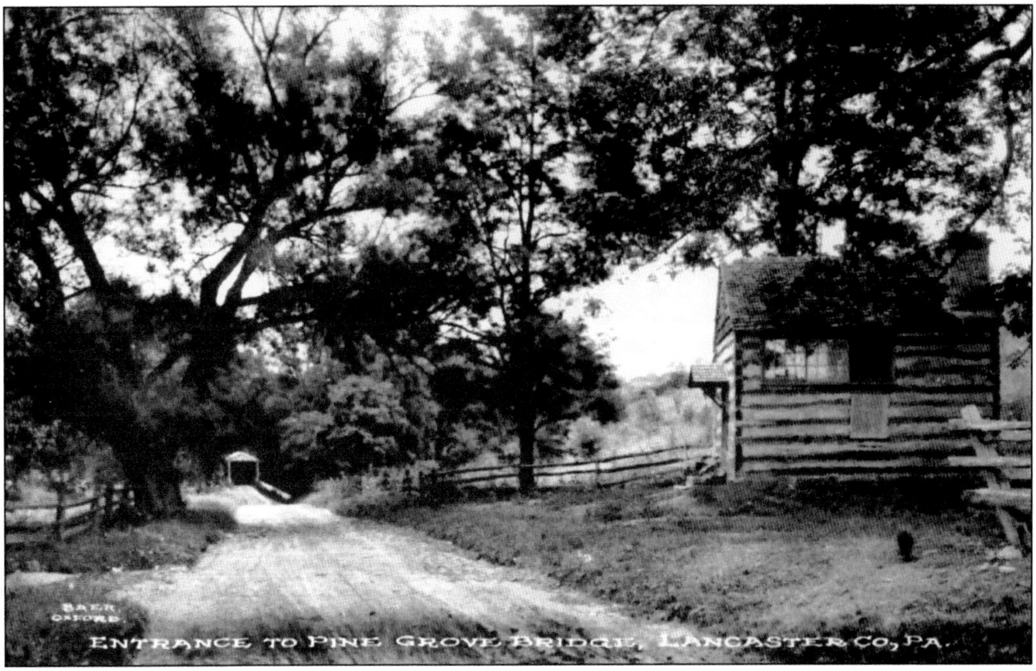

The area around Pine Grove was a popular destination. An 1895 newspaper article states that the "Romantic Octoraro" was a wonderful area for picnicking, camping, and fishing. The creek was said to be stocked with many types of aquatic life, including bass, pike, trout, catfish, sunnies, eels, snappers, and suckers. Below the bridge is a deep hole known as the pool. This postcard shows the road leading to the covered bridge at Pine Grove.

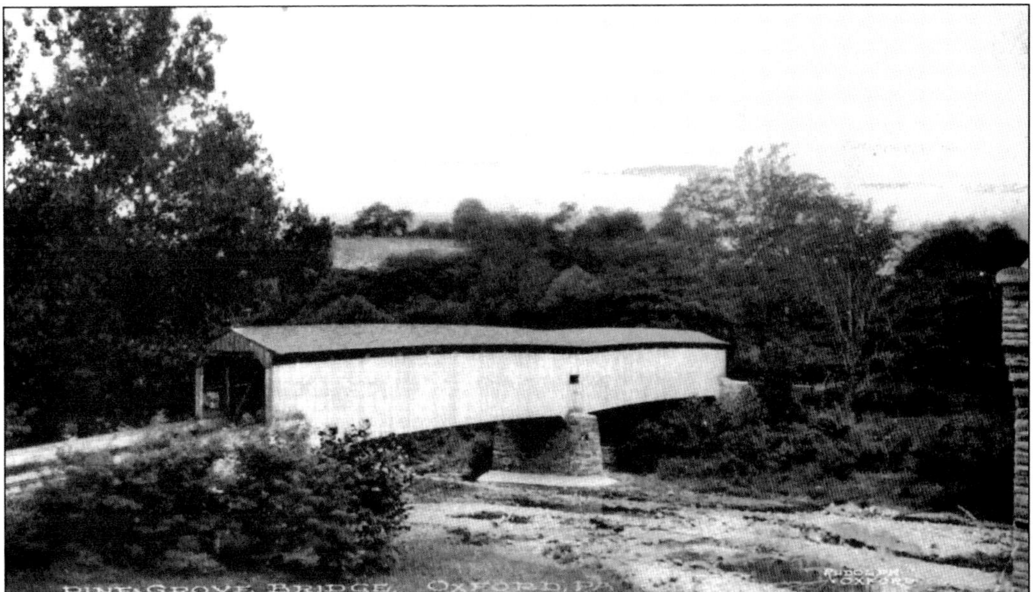

In 1800, Ellis Passmore and Jonathan Webb named their iron forge (on the Lancaster side of the Octoraro Creek) Pine Grove after a stand of pines nearby. In 1816, a bridge was constructed, the first bridge connecting Chester and Lancaster Counties. In 1844, William Pennock moved the forge to the Chester County side and also built a mill.

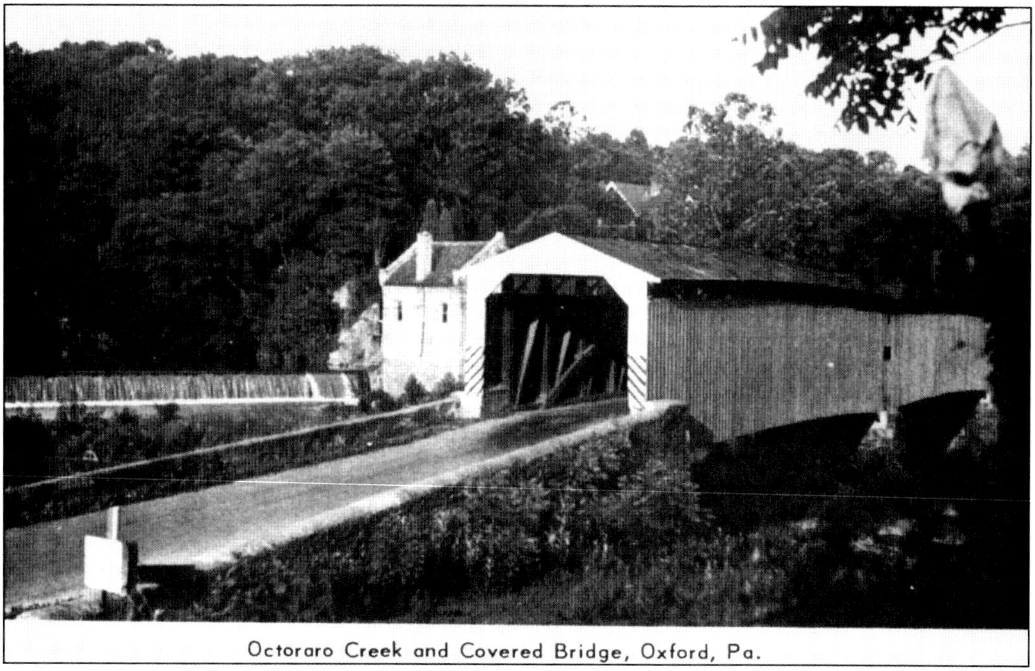

In 1846, the 1816 bridge was destroyed in a storm. Robert Russell and Joseph Elliott were hired to construct a new bridge for $3,450. The bridge was 175 feet long with a span of 15 feet. During the great flood of June 1884, the 1846 bridge was destroyed. After the 1884 flood, Capt. Elias McMellen of Lancaster County built the new 204-foot two-span bridge shown above at a cost of $4,450.

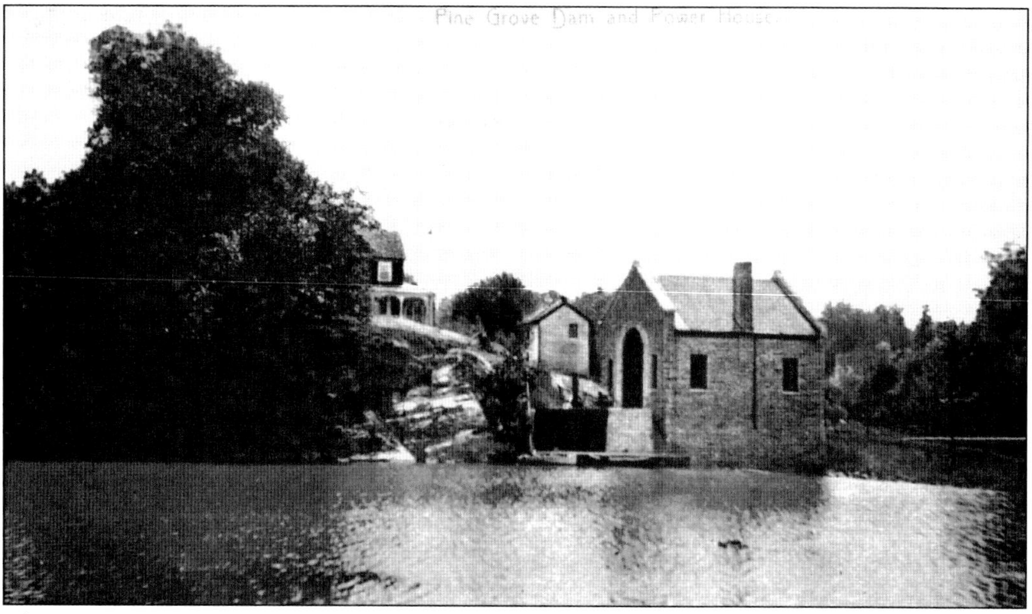

The pumping station shown above was built in the early 1900s by the Pennsylvania Railroad to supply water for its steam engines. Once diesel engines became common, this use was no longer needed. About 1950, the Chester Municipal Authority acquired the water rights and equipment to pump water 40 miles to the city of Chester.

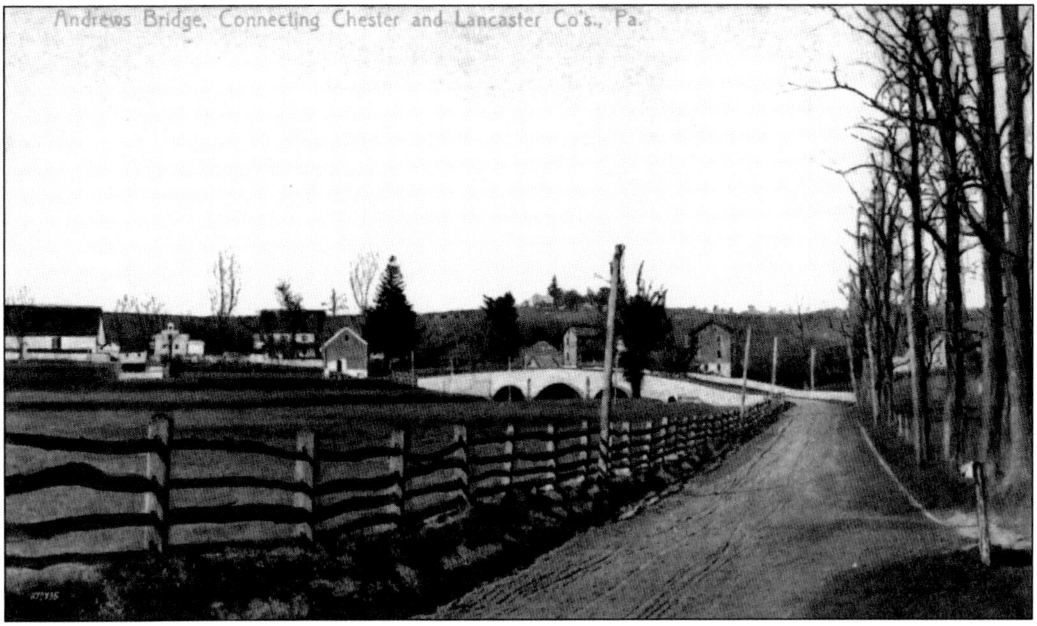

Built in 1814, the beautiful stone arched Andrews Bridge crosses the Octoraro Creek in Upper Oxford Township as PA Route 896. Another span may have been constructed in 1874. The area around Andrews Bridge was well known for its harness track, owned by Walter Jackson. He later sold his property to Walter Jeffords, a Gradyville sportsman. The track continued in operation until the World War I era. Andrews Bridge was the scene of many famous fox hunts. On August 9, 1942, the bridge was washed out and, in 1946 a new span was constructed with funds from the department of highways. The contract of $85,271.17 was given to J. D. Eckman of Atglen. In the postcard below, a lone swimmer poses for a photograph at the Octoraro Creek "swimming hole."

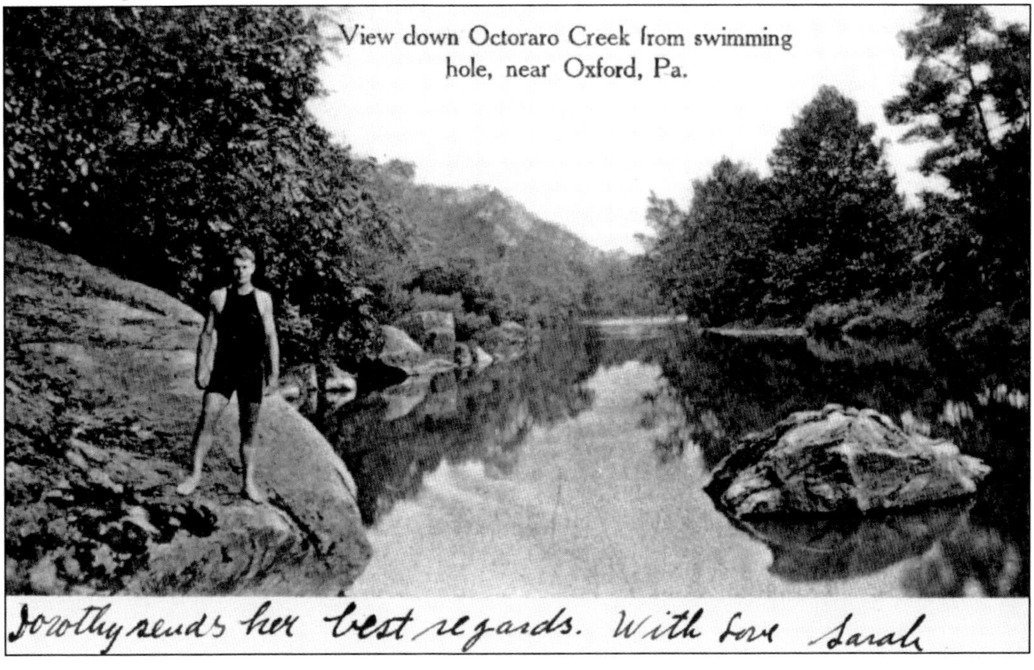

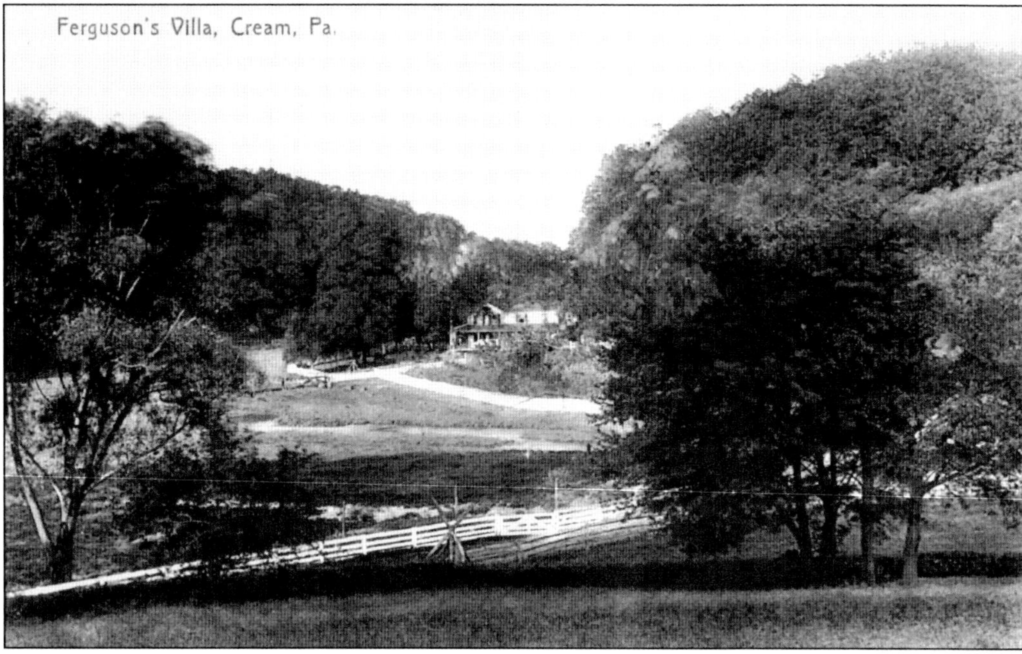

James and Mary J. Ferguson owned 177 acres of land near the Muddy Run in Lower Oxford Township. In 1893, James's mill at Valley Mills on the Muddy Run was destroyed by fire; subsequently, he built a large three-story flour mill of stone that was 38 by 70 feet with a 26-foot wing. It, too, was destroyed by fire on March 12, 1910. All the components of the mill were destroyed, including the roller flour mill, a creamery store, and an electric light plant. Insurance of $4,500 covered the building but not the contents. Coincidently, at the same time as the burning of the mill in Cream, a similar mill was destroyed in Wilmington, also owned by a different James Ferguson.

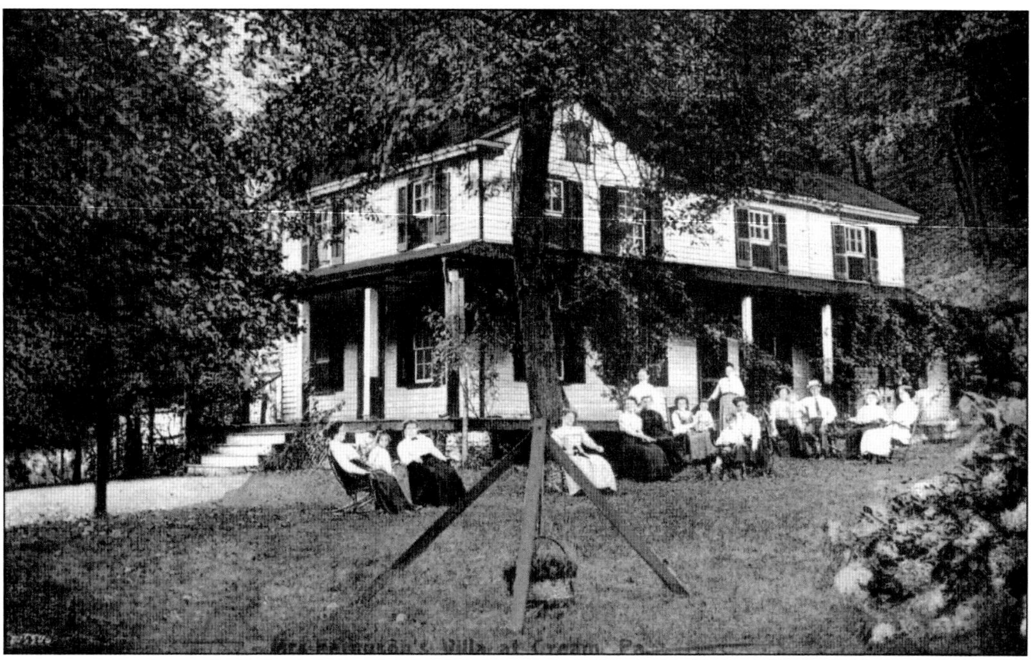

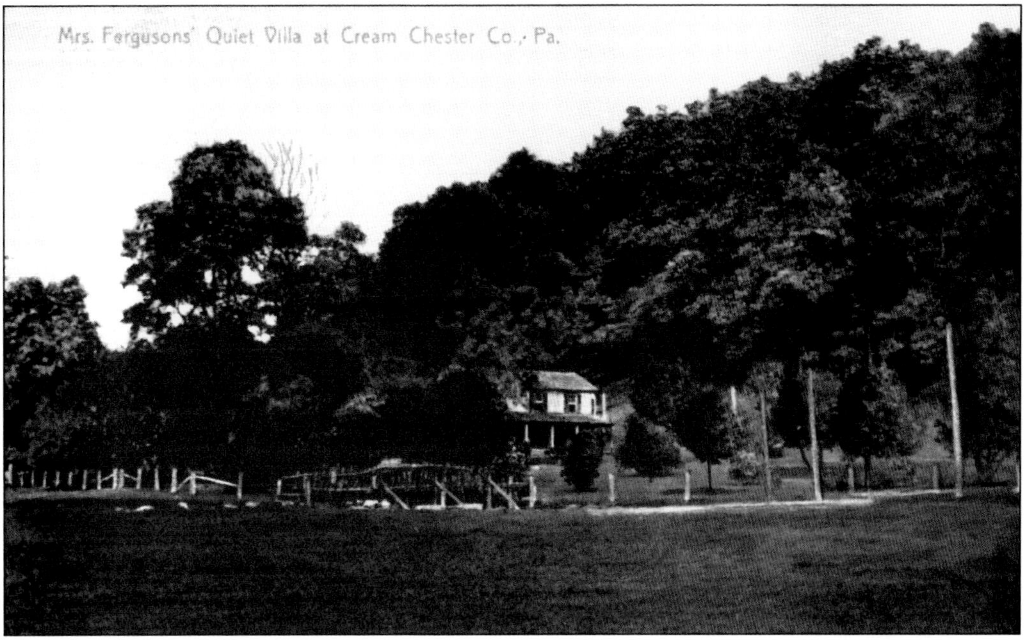

The Fergusons operated a resort during the summer months at their home (seen in these two postcards, and the two on the previous page). They had accommodations for several guests who could stay in any one of the 16 bedrooms. In 1902, James Ferguson installed a 60-light water turbine dynamo in his mill to generate electricity for his resort. At the same time, he added a second story to his boardinghouse. Guests came from as far away as Philadelphia and Baltimore. Ferguson made cheeses, one of which was a soft spreadable cheese. He sold this recipe to Sharples of West Chester, and it is believed to be the forerunner of Philadelphia Cream Cheese. The villa closed in 1910.

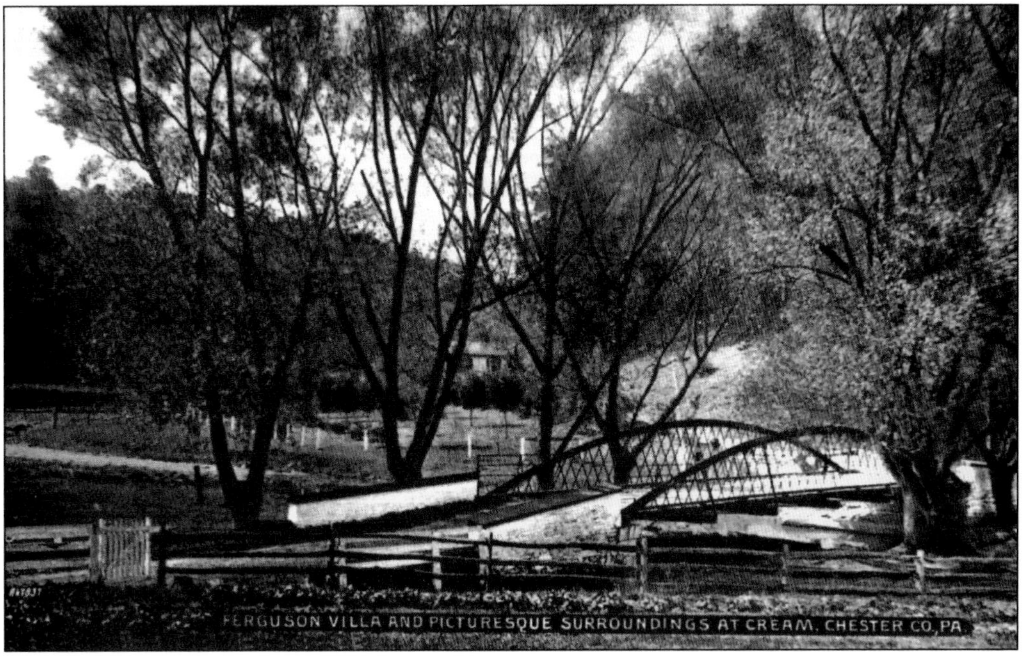

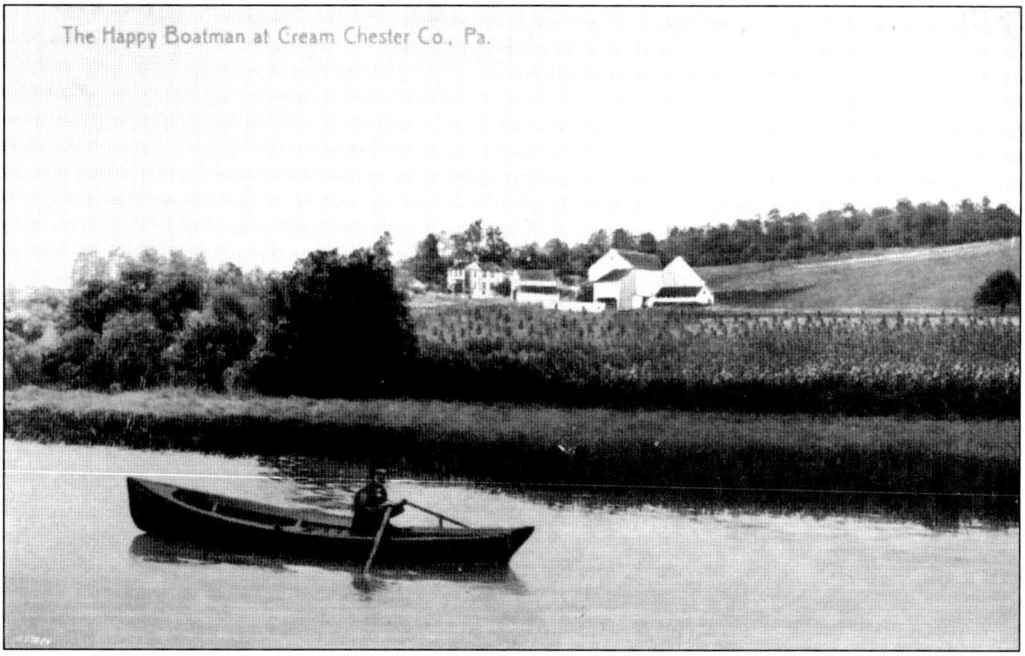

James Ferguson also conducted a country store at Cream and, in 1895, he felt that putting a post office in his store would help business. He proposed giving the name of the post office Arbutus. Since there was a milk receiving station at the site, someone else suggested Cream. Ferguson became the first postmaster, but the office closed in 1904 because of a lack of business. The name Cream still remains for the name of the area. The Enterprise Farm at 5522 Homeville Road is now located on the site of Ferguson's villa.

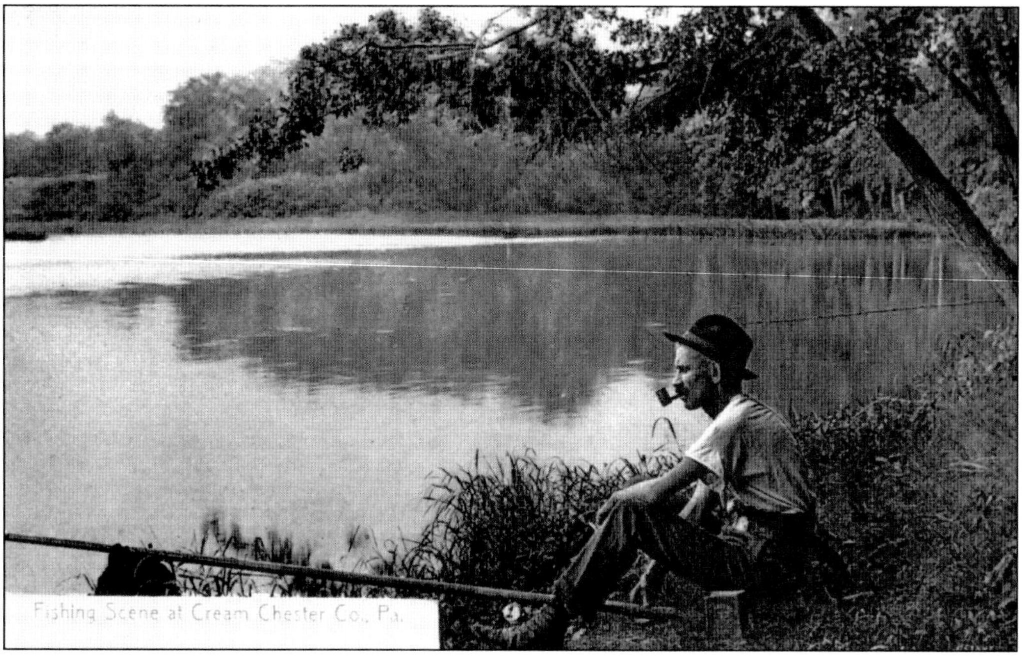

Frank Burton, barber at R. E. Long's in West Grove, is shown here fishing along the Muddy Run in Cream.

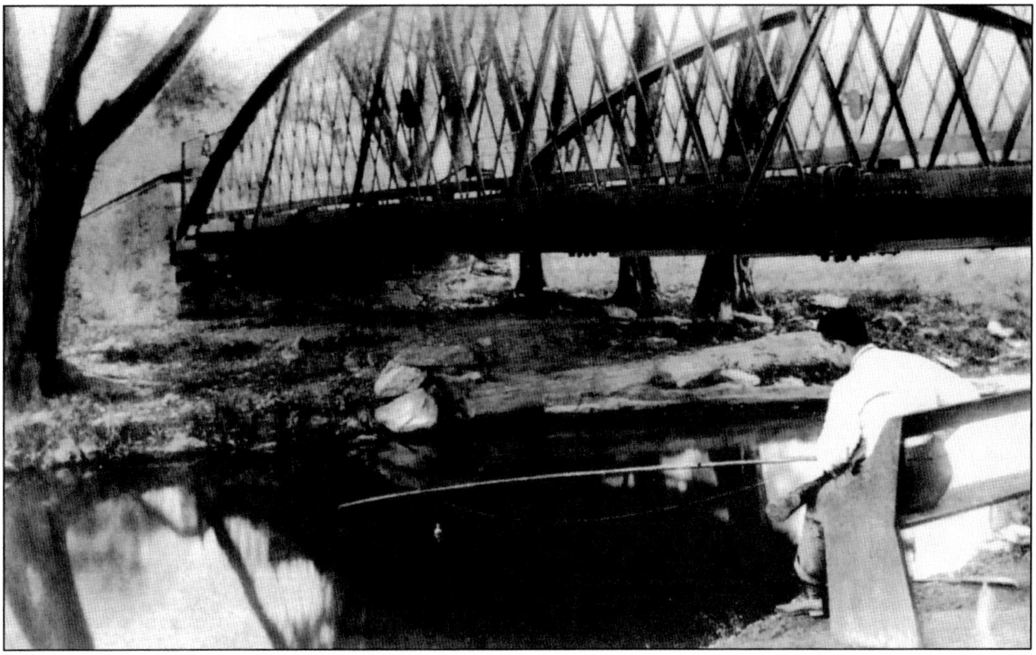

The rustic iron bridge over the Muddy Run was a favorite spot for fishermen. The bridge was later replaced with a concrete span.

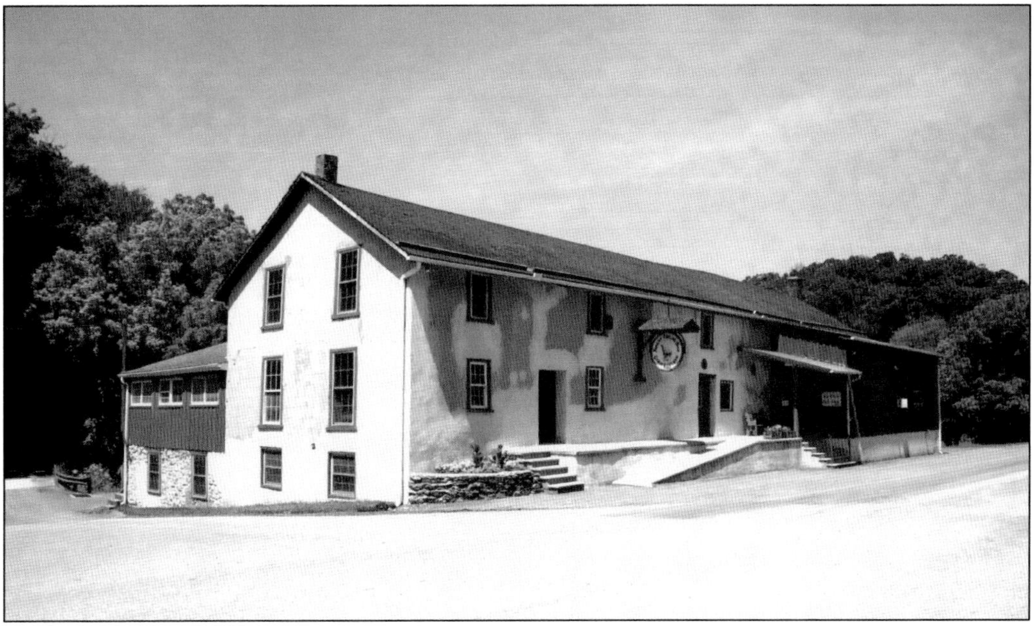

By 1928, cabinetmaker and woodcarver Robert Treate Hogg Jr. (1905–1971) converted the old mill at Cream into his workshop. He used the same basic tools and methods as those of Colonial furniture makers and worked on copies of Francis Trumbull's Windsor chairs and settees, as well as reproducing some of the furniture used in Independence Hall. Hogg also made candlesticks, bowls, trays, and clocks. In 1973, E. Stevenson Morris acquired the mill at 5650 Homeville Road for $49,000. It was subsequently purchased by William and Gail Dillon and, later, Michael Hoffmeier.

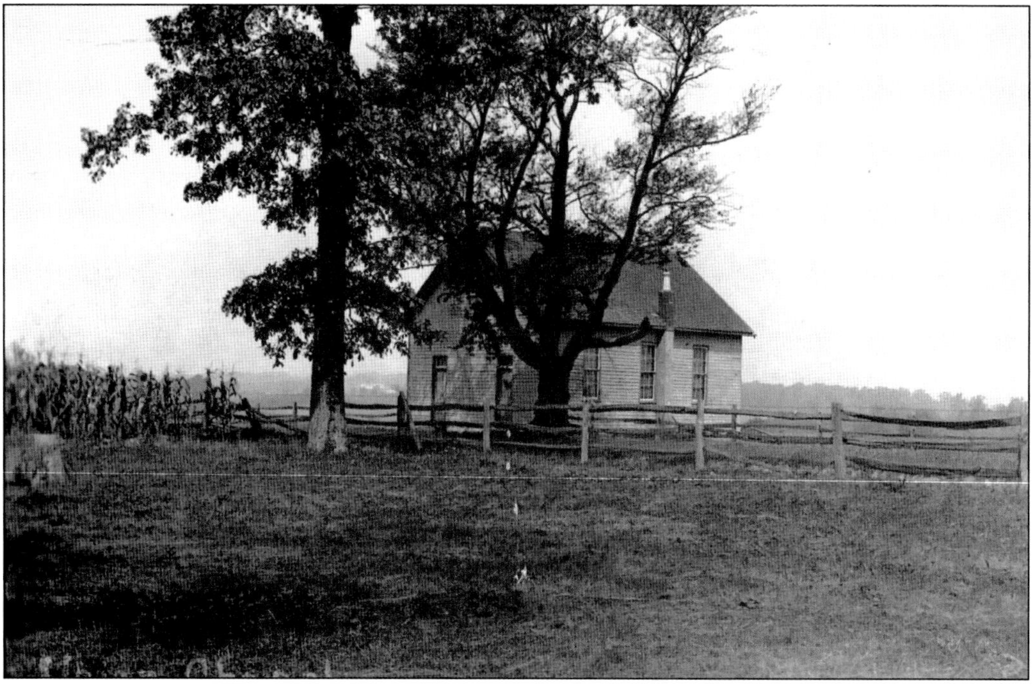

Because Hickory Hill was too small to support a church, it had a union chapel. The chapel was dedicated on February 4, 1875, and was a 36-by-26-foot frame structure. Various activities were held in the chapel, including Sunday school classes, revivals, temperance lectures, and prayer meetings. The chapel was active into the early 20th century.

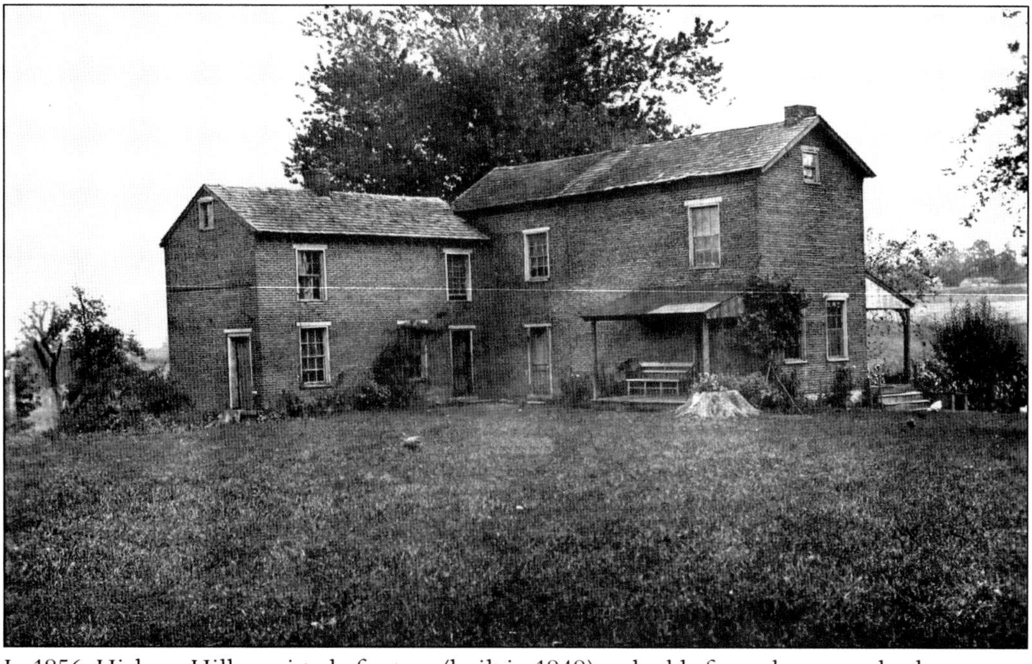

In 1856, Hickory Hill consisted of a store (built in 1848), a double frame house, and a three-story brick dwelling. By 1870, there was a school, a singing teacher, a doctor, and a dentist. The 1927 real-photo postcard seen here shows the Hickory Hill home of David Ross.

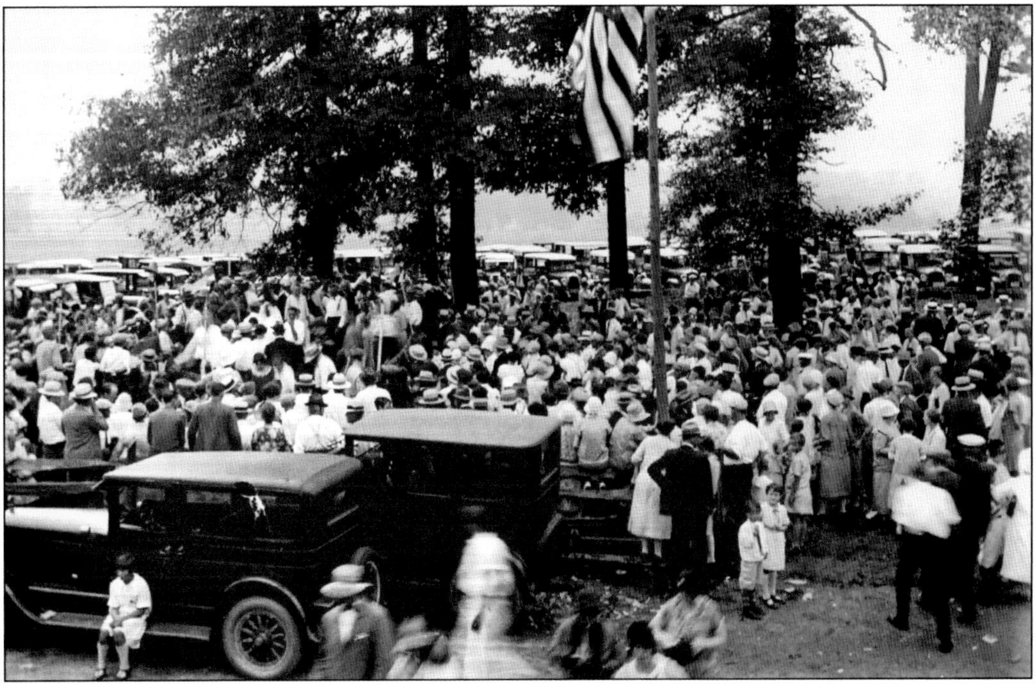

Charley McComsey was one of the organizers of the Old Timers of Elk and East Nottingham Township. The first reunion was held on September 3, 1927. The invitation to the event stated, "Bring plenty of chicken. Bake a pie, and bring some cheese. Pie without cheese is like a kiss without a squeeze. Don't forget the cake. There will be plenty of ice cream to balance it." The real-photo postcard shows the second annual reunion of the Old Timers at Hickory Hill on August 18, 1928.

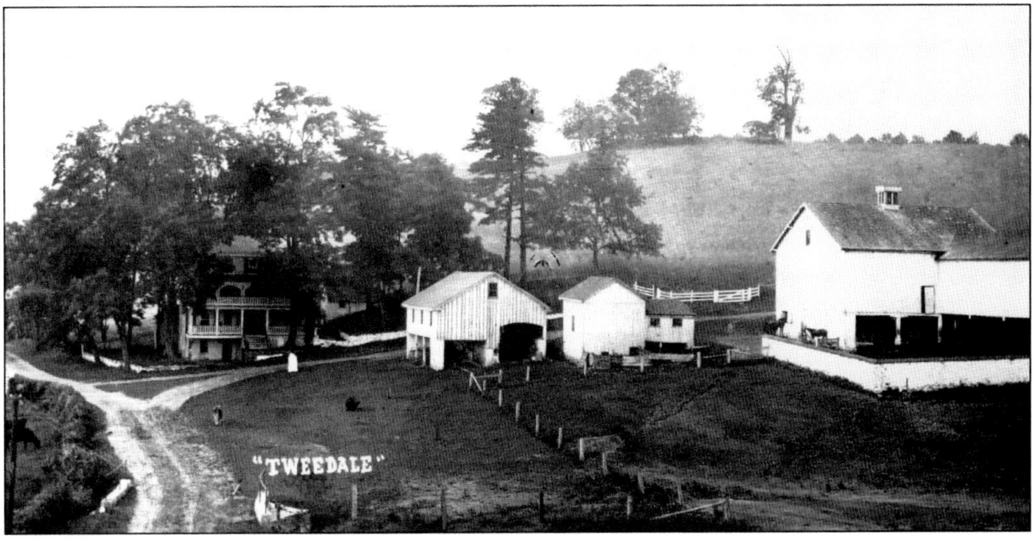

Tweedale is located at the intersection of Bethel and State Roads. The house in this real-photo postcard is known as the Lemon Tree Inn. It was once the home and tavern of Dr. David Thomas (1820s and 1830s) and, later, John Twaddell (1840s and 1850s). Camp Tweedale, home of the Girls Scouts of Freedom Valley summer camp, is located along Octoraro Creek, just west of this beautiful home. (Courtesy of Howard Steinberg.)

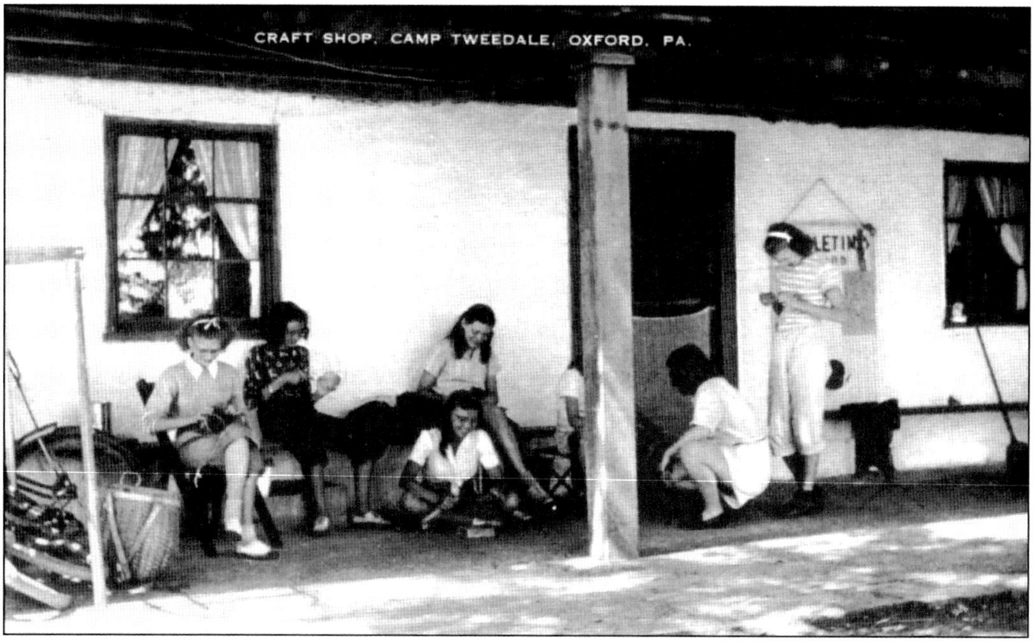

Camp Tweedale still offers many activities, including crafts (shown here), boating, wildlife adventures, archery, sports, cooking, swimming, hiking, and group activities. The swimming pool was dedicated in August 1936 with a "beautiful water pageant" presented under the direction of Margaret Montgomery, director of the camp.

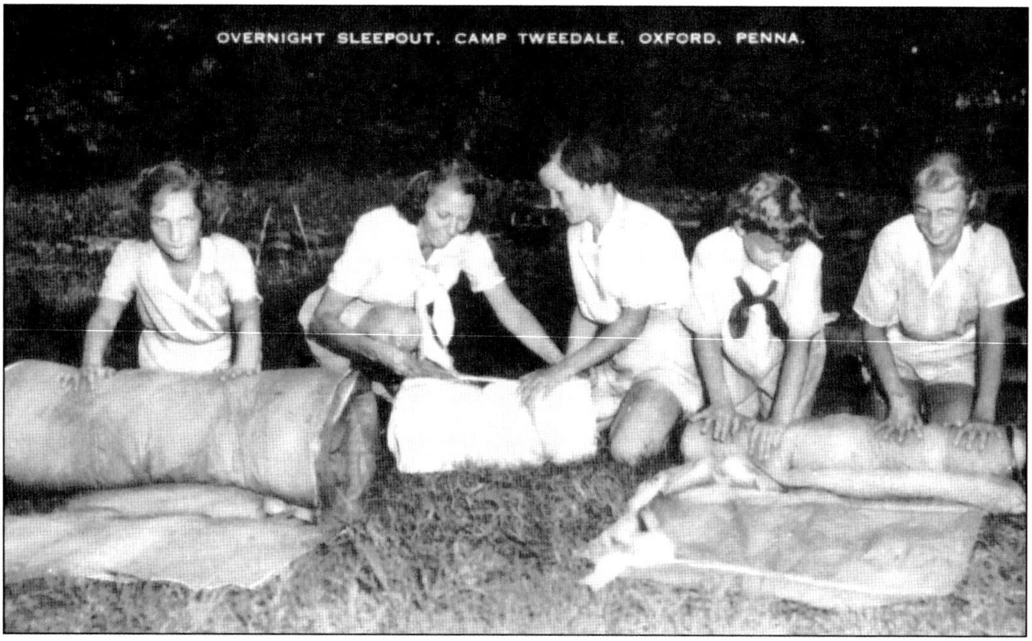

Overnight accommodations varied and included sleeping bags (shown here), cabins, platform tents, A-frames, and even Conestoga wagons. The "units" (Brownies, intermediates, and seniors) each sent members to the camp's council; this gave the girls the "daily practice of democratic self-government." Units also presented different activities for the entire camp such as a progressive all-camp party, water pageants, and other adventures.

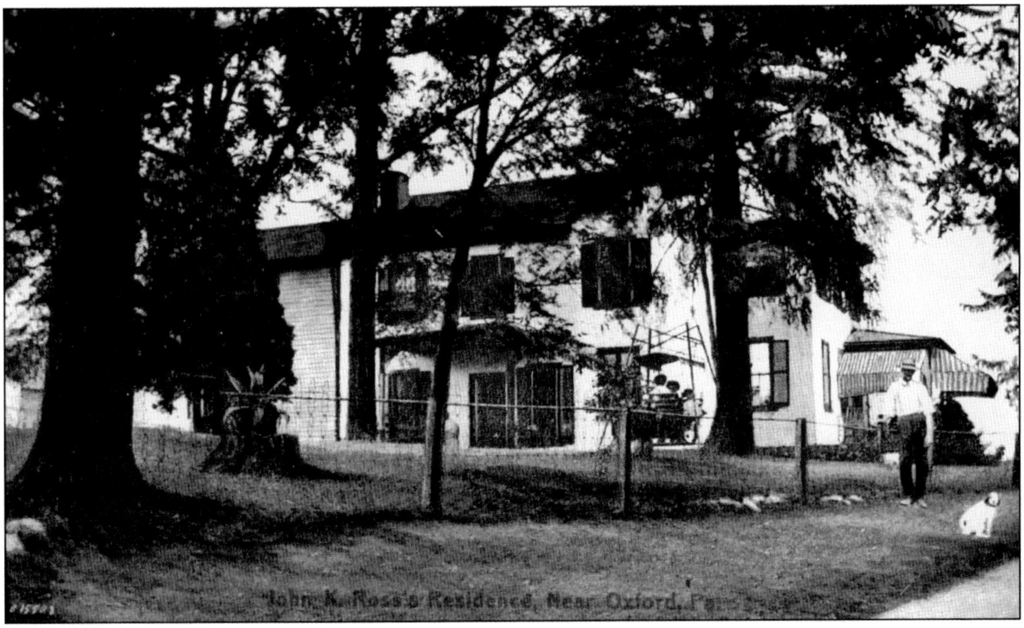

According to the 1910 census of the United States, John K. Ross was a resident farmer in Upper Oxford Township. He and his wife Mary, both listed as being 45 years of age, also lived with John's brother David and his wife. John and David were two of three sons (and one daughter) of Samuel R. and Ella Kennedy Ross. Samuel was a prosperous township farmer who died on May 20, 1906, at the age of 75. W. H. Tegeler of West Grove published this postcard around 1910–1912.

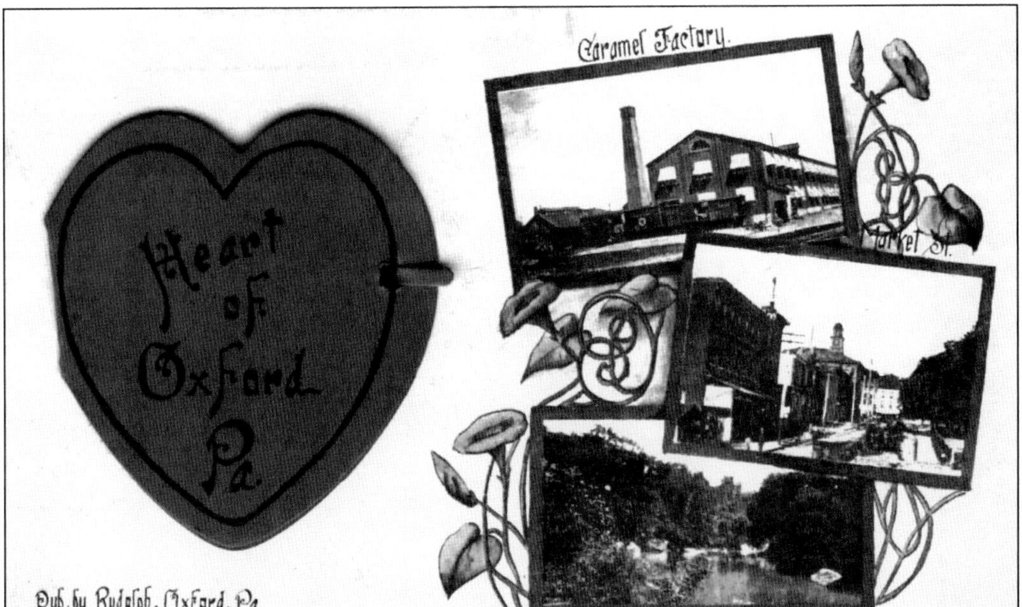

This tour of Oxford and vicinity ends with the "Heart of Oxford," a postcard published by George Rudolph around 1907. When the metal tab is folded back a series of small local scenes unfold. The three scenes on the front show the caramel factory, Market Street, and the Octoraro Creek. Many towns in America produced similar "heart" postcards.